PELICAN BOOKS

Pelican Library of Business and Management

THE MANAGEMENT OF GOVERNMENT

John Garrett was educated at a grammar school and
University College, Oxford, where he obtained a first
class honours degree and a B.Litt. for research into
industrial location. From 1956 to 1957 he was a
George VI Fellow at the University of California,
and after managerial experience in the chemical and
motor industries he joined Inbucon/AIC Ltd in
1963 where he is now a management consultant.
Mr Garrett has led major assignments in the agricultural supply, plantation, engineering, confectionery,
paper and oil industries and in government departments. In 1966–8 he was a member of the management consultancy group employed by the committee
on the Civil Service (the Fulton Committee). He is
the author of a number of articles and papers on
management, public administration and economics.

JOHN GARRETT

THE MANAGEMENT OF GOVERNMENT

PENGUIN BOOKS

Penguin Books Ltd, Harmondsworth. Middlesex, England
Penguin Books Inc., 7110 Ambassador Road, Baltimore, Maryland 21207, U.S.A
Penguin Books Australia Ltd, Ringwood, Victoria. Australia

—

First published 1972

—

Copyright © John Garrett, 1972

—

Made and printed in Great Britain by
Hazell Watson & Viney Ltd,
Aylesbury, Bucks
Set in Monotype Times

Contents

1. The Managers and their Environment 7
2. Fulton: The Establishment, The System and The Amateur 30
3. Organization 58
4. Planning 97
5. Control 150
6. Accountable Management 185
7. Management Services and Efficiency Audit 213
8. Personnel Management 234
   Conclusion 275
   References 277
   Index 297

CHAPTER 1

The Managers and their Environment

FOR the past five years there has been much public discussion of the way in which government departments are managed. Conventions of public administration which have grown up over a hundred years or more have been challenged as no longer appropriate to departments which have acquired executive responsibilities on the scale of the largest businesses. Criticism of these conventions led to the inquiry carried out by the Fulton Committee in 1966–8, which proposed a number of major reforms in the management and organization of the Civil Service, some of the most important of which appeared to be accepted by the government of the day. More recently, administrative reform has come garnished with slogans: 'a new style of government', 'a quiet revolution', 'open government', 'accountability'. The Service has been exhorted, mostly by young politicians and elderly industrialists, to make itself more 'business-like' and teams of business men have been hired to range through departments in search of areas in which to apply business methods.

This book examines the results of all this apparent turmoil and considers recent developments in organization and in systems of decision-making, planning, control and manpower utilization in the non-industrial Civil Service. It also considers the likely course of future developments in a number of important areas of management in the light of comparable experience outside the Service. Its purpose is to promote discussion and experiment among managers in government and to provide an explanatory background for those who are interested in the modernization of our great public institutions.

This chapter sets out the general background to the book. It first briefly discusses the environment within which managers in government departments operate. Secondly, it describes the origin and form of the system of Civil Service career classes to which the discussions in later chapters frequently have to refer.

THE CHANGING TASK

At the time of writing the British government employs nearly 500,000 non-industrial civil servants and about 200,000 industrial workers (in, for example, the ordnance factories and dockyards). Government departments account to Parliament for the collection of around £14,000m. per annum in revenue and for an expenditure of around £9,000m. The largest departments are comparable in employment and 'spend' to the largest public companies. They also plan, supervise and, to varying degrees, control a further £13,000m. of public expenditure by such bodies as local authorities and nationalized industries.

The growth in the Civil Service, from a non-industrial employment of around 40,000 one hundred years ago, is one result of what is usually characterized as the evolution from a 'regulatory' to a 'positive' or 'interventionist' State. The regulatory activities of government are exemplified by the enactment, inspection and enforcement of such protective legislation as the Poor Law, the Factory and the Public Health Acts in the nineteenth century. Modern government has greatly extended regulation in these fields and in such others as the protection of the consumer, the shareholder and the tenant, the protection of minority groups, the protection of the environment and the regulation of vehicles and transport. Governments have developed their regulatory activities to the point of intervention in the economics of industrial and agricultural investment, employment and wage-fixing, transport, housing and amenity. In addition, the 'positive' State has taken on the tasks of providing a very wide range of services to the community, beginning with old-age pensions and labour exchanges in the early years of the century and now encompassing all the social provisions of the welfare state. Some manufacturing and construction projects are so costly or so essential to economic development or to national standing that only government can fund or manage them; in the aerospace, atomic energy, computer, ship building, civil engineering and transport industries, for example. Above all this, positive government has come to involve the formulation of policy and objectives for the economy as a whole, the management of demand and of the markets for capital and labour, the redistribution of wealth and promoting social change. The result is that government has acquired an array of policy-making, legislative, judicial, service, supervisory, inspectorial, representational, transaction-processing and production functions which together present a managerial task of a range and complexity rarely encountered in any other form of organization.

The distinctive features of management in government are not confined to greater complexity in function and responsibility but also arise from the political dimension within which managers in the Civil Service have to operate.

MANAGEMENT IN A POLITICAL DIMENSION

The Management Consultancy Group which reported to the Fulton Committee defined the total management task of the Civil Service as:

(a) formulation of policy under political direction,
(b) creating the 'machinery' for implementation of policy,
(c) operation of the administrative machine,
(d) accountability to Parliament and the public.[1]

Political direction makes itself felt in frequent and sometimes radical changes in the content or emphasis of policy. Civil servants are expected to be able to adapt to rapid change, at the time of a change of government, for example, and to implement entirely new policies without any break in continuity. Prime Ministers frequently reshuffle not only their Cabinet colleagues but also whole departments and agencies, so that the Civil Service has to cope almost overnight with the creation and dissolution of substantial organizations (the Land Commission, the Ministry of Aviation, the Department of Economic Affairs, the Civil Service Department, the National Agricultural Advisory Service, the Prices and Incomes Board) which in large-scale industry would usually be undertaken after the most lengthy and careful analysis of their potential effects.

Parliamentary and public accountability makes itself felt at all levels in departments. The Consultancy Group observed that 'whether he be a clerical officer helping a pensioner to fill in a claim form or an engineer concerned with the line and design of a motorway, a civil servant has to make even small decisions in the light of their effect on the lives of his fellow citizens. His fellow citizens have come to expect of him the utmost impartiality and scrupulous care for their rights, concern for their views, the most careful stewardship of public money and property and, at the same time, have little toleration for delay or vacillation.'[2] Public accountability requires meticulous attention to the maintenance of equity in implementing decisions and in dealing with specific cases. It requires elaborate arrangements to insure consistency in the application of policy within, and between, departments. The greatest care has to be taken in accounting for public assets and for the regularity and proper authorization of expenditure. Elaborate recruitment and promotion procedures have to be operated to insure the equitable treatment of applicants and staff. All these activities are open to challenge by 'a number of watchdogs of the community, both official and self-appointed, who frequently call him [the civil servant] or his superiors to account on matters large and small'[3]: the Ombudsman, the Public Accounts Committee, Select Committees of the House of Commons, Royal Commissions and Committees of Inquiry, Members of Parliament, private citizens and the media all require the civil servant to be prepared to justify, or to enable his Minister to justify, any action he takes.

The tasks of civil servants are defined, to varying degrees of clarity by the legislation which they have to operate. Once the legislation is in existence, they have to deal with whatever case or problem arises within its field of operation. In addition, over large tracts of legislation, the responsibility for implementation lies not in the originating department but with such external bodies as police forces, hospital boards or local authorities. In this situation, the department tends to be expected, in the eyes of its 'publics', to carry the responsibility for action over which it has no executive authority: to make and adjust policy in the light of results on which it has inadequate information; to supervise the implementation of policy at a level far removed from where implementation takes place.

The question of measuring the efficiency and effectiveness of the Civil Service is discussed elsewhere in this book. Here we need only note that many of the activities of governments have results which are either virtually unquantifiable (defence, law and order) or which may take a very long time to become apparent (health, education). This situation greatly complicates attempts to measure the efficiency, and more particularly the effectiveness, of managerial action. We shall see that the irregularity and unreliability of feedback from the environment has marked effects on the development of systems of planning, control and accountability. The success criteria of the industrialist – growth, profit, volume of sales, market share, the values of the shareholders' equity – can usually be displayed as quantifiable managerial objectives and sub-objectives, and for each level of management a flow of information can be arranged to enable results to be compared with these objectives. When we consider the success criteria of the manager in government – carrying out the requirements of the Minister, defending and rescuing him from potentially embarrassing situations, securing value for money both within the department and in external agencies, limiting growth (particularly in the numbers employed) in the face of an increasing workload and providing a very wide range of benefits and services to the community efficiently, effectively and equitably – we are generally in much less tangible fields of planning, objective-setting and control.

There has been a tendency, particularly in the higher reaches of the Civil Service, to over-emphasize these constraints of political direction, public accountability and intangibility of output and to understate the scope for systematic management. There are, however, very large executive and professional activities in government which have a stability and continuity comparable to much of industry: the research establishments, the technical inspectorates, the purchasing and accounting divisions, the design and construction directorates, the divisions processing cases under long-established legislation. Most of these, and many others, operate in a largely unchanging environment, are not greatly affected by political turbulence and produce measurable outputs. They often require management processes similar to those which have been developed in industry for handling transactions and information and for planning, estimating, budgeting and accounting, for managing internal communications and personnel, for controlling inventories, for managing design, research and construction projects. Many managers, scientists and technologists in industry and commerce would recognize these managerial tasks as closely similar to their own.

CAREER CLASSES

We shall see that many critics of the Civil Service have called for the reform of its system of career classes as a first step towards the modernization of its management processes. Since the discussion of management in the Civil Service frequently touches on the arrangements by which civil servants are classified it is appropriate at the outset briefly to describe their origin and present form.

In 1853, Sir Stafford Northcote and Sir Charles Trevelyan reported on the organization of the permanent Civil Service.[4] They found that admission to the Civil Service had been sought after by the unambitious, the indolent and the incapable, with the result that the public service suffered both in internal efficiency and in public estimation. The Northcote–Trevelyan report proposed four main reforms as required to create an efficient body of permanent officers: entry into the Civil Service by competitive examination; promotion on merit, as assessed by the reports of superiors; the placing of first appointments on a common footing throughout the Service; and the establishment of a proper distinction between 'intellectual' and 'mechanical' labour. For the superior situations involving intellectual work 'endeavours should be made to secure the services of the most promising young men of the day, by a competing examination on a level with the highest description of education in this country'. The distinction between this work and the mechanical work of the lower class of clerks (copying, posting accounts, keeping diaries) was left to the discretion of the chiefs of offices.

In 1874, the Playfair Committee allocated routine work to a 'Lower Division' of clerks with a tested knowledge of reading, writing and arithmetic, and intellectual work to a 'Higher Division' (called the First Division after 1890) mostly of graduates. As departments grew, the lower division was further divided into senior and junior clerical classes. The growth of the inspectorial and supervisory functions associated with regulatory legislation also created a demand for numbers of professionally qualified men (solicitors, engineers, doctors) recruited at a mature age.

In 1920 a joint staff and management committee on the Organization of the Civil Service[5] considered career arrangements in the Service and proposed a division of 'administrative and clerical' work into three categories. The lowest category of work, 'the application of well-defined regulations, decisions and practices to particular cases', was given to the Clerical Class, to which entry was regulated by a competitive examination approximating to the standard at the intermediate stage of a secondary-school course (today's O-level). This class was later sub-divided into a General Clerical Class (requiring five O-levels on entry) and a Clerical Assistant Class (two O-levels). The middle category of work was defined as 'the critical examination of particular cases of lesser importance not clearly covered by approved regulations or general decisions, initial investigations into matters of higher importance and the direction of small blocks of business'. In its upper ranges, it was concerned with matters of internal organization and control, 'with the settlement of broad questions arising out of business in hand or in contemplation and with the responsible conduct of important questions'. This category was given to the Executive Class, recruited from secondary-school leavers by an examination at the standard of today's A-level. The highest category of work was described as concerned with the formation of policy, the co-ordination and improvement of government machinery and with the general administration and control of the departments of the public service. This work was laid to the Administrative Class, whose members were usually recruited from university graduates with first-class or second-class degrees. After a report in 1931, Civil Service scientists were organized on a Service-wide basis in two main classes: graduate scientific officers and technically qualified scientific assistants; and in 1946 Service-wide classes of engineers, technicians and draughtsmen were set up.

By the time the Fulton Committee examined the class system in 1966 the arrangement was that the direction and control of departments, the formulation of policy and the direct support of Ministers was the responsibility of the Administrative Class (numbering 2,500); middle non-technical management and the conduct of day-to-day business fell to the Executive Class (48,000); and routine clerical work fell to the two Clerical Classes (170,000). These classes were combined in an Administration Group in 1971, as a result of Fulton's recommendations (see Appendix, p. 29).

In addition to this group, there are over forty general 'Treasury Classes' whose members work in a wide range of government departments. These are organized on the basis of specialist skills or qualifications. Examples of these classes are the General Service Class of Cleaners (population 13,500); the Cartographic and Recording Class of Draughtsmen and Surveyors (4,200); the Duplicator Operating Class (1,600); the Illustrator Class (500); the Machine Operator Class (9,300); the Office Keeper, Paper Keeper and the Messengerial Class (9,800); the Photoprinter Class (2,200); Stores Supervisors (2,500); the Typing Class (26,000). Some Treasury Classes have important managerial and technical responsibilities and include top posts equal in salary to some of the highest positions in the Administration Group: for example, the Legal Class (800); the Economist Class (100); the Medical Officer Class (600); the Scientific Officer Class (4,000); the Works Group of Engineers, Architects and Surveyors (11,500). Just as a distinction was made between the higher work of the Administrative Class, the middle work of the Executive Class and the lower work of the Clerical Classes, so there were hierarchies of scientific, technical and professional ('specialist') classes. Thus, the Scientific Officer Class, whose externally recruited members usually had first-class or second-class degrees, were supported by the Experimental Officer Class (7,500), whose recruits had to have at least two A-levels, and the Scientific Assistant Class (5,500), whose recruits were required to have at least four O-levels. The

Works Group were similarly supported by the Technical Works, Engineering and Allied Classes (21,500) and the Architectural and Engineering Draughtsmen Classes (10,000). At the time of writing, arrangements are being made to merge the Scientific Officer Class with its supporting classes and the Works Group with its supporting classes.

There are also over 1,400 'departmental classes', that is, classes whose members are confined to a single department. Some departmental classes are very large and have terms and conditions of service which are linked to the Treasury Classes. For example, at the time of the Fulton Committee's report the largest single class in the Civil Service was the Post Office 'minor and manipulative grades', with a population of 225,000. Other examples of departmental classes are the Outdoor Service (7,000) and the Waterguard (3,000) of the Customs and Excise Department; Tax Inspectors and Officers (24,000) and Valuation Clerks (3,000) of the Department of Inland Revenue; and hundreds of classes of such specialists as prison governors, air-traffic controllers, agricultural advisers, alkali inspectors, macers, gas-meter examiners, inspectors of horses, park keepers, custodian-firemen, servants, starter rangers, engravers, unassimilated district inspectors, booksellers, eye fitters, inseminators and custodians of blocks.

Some of these classes have only one rank or grade within them (a few have only one member), but most have a hierarchy of grades representing different levels of responsibility, age or length of service. Thus, the Administrative Class had six grades until the recent formation of the Administration Group: Permanent Secretary (with three sub grades), which is that of the official heads of departments, Deputy Secretary, Under Secretary, Assistant Secretary, Principal and Assistant Principal. These grades covered a salary range from around £1,000 per annum to £10,000 per annum. The Executive Class had seven grades (Head of Executive Establishment, Principal Executive Officer, Senior Chief Executive Officer, Chief Executive Officer, Senior Executive Officer, Higher Executive Officer, Executive Officer), covering a salary range of £600 to £6,000 per annum. The General Clerical Class had two grades (Higher Clerical Officer and Clerical Officer) covering £400 to £1,400 per annum, and the Clerical Assistant Class had one grade at £6 to £15 per week. Similarly, in the specialist classes the Scientific Officer Class had seven grades (£1,000–£12,000 per annum) and the Technical Works, Engineering and Allied Classes comprised seven overlapping grade levels running from around £1,000 to just over £3,000 per annum.

An officer's career is normally within his class, but it is possible for some to be promoted from a lower to an upper class. An Order in Council of 1876 which attempted to clarify the Northcote–Trevelyan distinction between first-division and lower-division work made promotion possible from one to the other, but only as an exceptional measure. Over the years, promotion from the Clerical grades to the Executive grades had become very common (the Clerical Classes provided about half of the entrants to the Executive Class) and promotion (either direct or by limited competition) from Executive to the Administrative grades has been fairly frequent. Similarly, a large number of members of the junior grades of the Works Group was recruited from its supporting technical grades and a few members of the Scientific Officer Class were recruited from the Experimental Officer grades. 'Horizontal' transfers between classes were, and still are, rare and are hindered by the many rules relating to qualifying ages, academic attainments and experience which govern recruitment to a class.

MANAGEMENT AND CAREER CLASSES

The Fulton Committee dwelt at length upon the weaknesses of the career class system (see Chapter 2). Here we need do no more than comment on its broad effects. The main problem lies in its assumption that an organization which faces a world of rapidly increasing technical complexity can still neatly package its activities into those which should be handled by managers with a specialist education and those which should be reserved for 'generalists'.

We can exemplify this assumption from the case of the Executive grades of the Administration Group (formerly the Executive

Class) which provides the junior and middle management of the non-technical areas of most departments. Most of its members either enter the Service direct from school, or are promoted from Clerical grades either by examination or selection. Officials of these grades manage the clerical and computer branches in departments and most local and regional offices; they manage accounting, contracts and purchasing, stores, personnel, management services and training branches. Large sub-departments engaged on manual or automatic transaction and data-processing activities are entirely managed by these grades. They also provide support for higher officials in branches concerned with 'policy work' and, prior to the merger with the Administrative Class, at the level of Chief Executive Officer and above were virtually interchangeable with administrators. Most of the work of these grades is concerned with planning, controlling and making decisions on a flow of activities or cases passing through an administrative machine. As the managerial task has grown in size and complexity, members of the Executive grades have adapted remarkably well to new demands They have borne the brunt of departmental re-organizations, the implementation of major changes in policy, the growth of new managerial sub-professions (for example, purchasing, management services and data processing) and the ebb and flow of interventionism. They are as adaptable and as 'professional' a group of management as exists in industry. Some top executives have enormous responsibilities – for thousands of staff and millions of pounds worth of computers for example – and have the style and self-confidence of industrial tycoons. Despite these strengths this middle management group suffers from the weaknesses inherent in the concept of the 'generalist' or 'all-rounder'. Because any executive is supposed to be able to do the job of any other executive in his grade, a large number are posted into jobs for which they are not suited. Because breadth of experience counts very heavily for promotion, they are posted from job to job at three to five year intervals and the more able a man is the more rapidly he is moved. It is said to be harmful to a man's career to see a long project all the way through even in fields where continuity is important – in data processing for instance – because such specialization limits his range of experience. Though the work undertaken by executives is becoming so technically complex as to require a technical or professional qualification (in accounting, statistics, purchasing, personnel work) they have never been encouraged to take further qualifications because this would have lessened their value as generalists and would have narrowed their career opportunities.

There are signs that the day of the generalist manager will have to come to an end in many fields hitherto dominated by the Executive grades. Most of the new management systems described in this book – in the areas of policy research and planning; accounting, budgetary control and the measurement of efficiency and effectiveness; organizational change; personnel work and the application of the social sciences – are developments in fields which have hitherto been the preserve of the all-round middle manager with no formal higher education or technical training. Fulton's Consultancy Group observed: 'We were much impressed by what we saw of the current and developing role of the management group currently represented by the Executive Class and by the ability of many of its members. It is at present within this group of civil servants that much modern management thinking is already taking root and where many new management skills are being adapted and applied to the public service. Nevertheless the growth of these skills has been inhibited by the exclusive nature of the group inherent in the class system and its suppositions. In particular, the exclusion of specialists from the group and the lack of emphasis on formal qualifications prevent the best use of the management resources available to the Service ... these management skills have become increasingly important and their significance will certainly increase as the tasks of the Service expand and change.'[6]

In addition, the signs are that the flow of the best school leavers into the Service is beginning to dry up. The opportunity of going to a university is now open to many who would otherwise have joined the Service straight from school. There are now more openings for bright school leavers – particularly in the computer world and in companies that offer commercial or technical apprenticeships to degree level. The Service has a dusty and old-fashioned image and the security it offers is no longer highly prized. The work of the Executive grades is more demanding, but the supply of talent which it has traditionally tapped is turning elsewhere.

There are many areas of the Civil Service in which members of the specialist classes are employed entirely on professional and technical work: in research establishments, for example, and in technical and scientific directorates and inspectorates. These are entirely specialist organizations, headed by senior scientists or engineers who may report to the head of that specialism in the department or to a top administrative official. There are, however, many other areas where the formulation and development of policy and the management of operations call for both specialist and administrative expertise and where laymen and specialists are engaged on different aspects of a common task. In these cases, the general practice has been that the responsibility for policy, for preparing submissions to Ministers, for financial control and ultimately for management rests with the administrator, while the specialist has had an advisory role. In general, the management and financial control of departments rests with the Administration Group: the specialist classes act as supporters, advisers, researchers and managers of purely technical activities.

The subordination of the professionally qualified man to the lay administrator is a matter to which the Fulton Committee and other critics of the higher Civil Service have devoted much attention. It is an arrangement which has been a marked feature of British industry, one might say of British culture generally, for the past hundred years. In evidence to the Fulton Committee, the staff association representing the Administrative Class observed that it 'reflects the generally accepted principle in this country that non-specialists should take the major policy decisions on behalf of the community as a whole'.[7]

The exclusion of staff with specialist qualifications from the command group is carried to greater lengths and is more formalized in the Civil Service than in most other British institutions and, as we shall see from Chapter 3, leads to some cumbersome organizational arrangements. The convention of the precedence of the lay administrator (who not only enjoys superior authority and status, but better career prospects) is an arrangement that has not been adopted in the central administration of other countries, where the top jobs tend to go to technically qualified managers.

The general effect of the assignment of particular posts to particular career classes has been greatly to reduce the interchange of ideas and expertise between generalists and specialists and between different groups of specialists. Thus, since scientific research is laid to the scientific officer class and its supporting classes it is very rare for a project team to include an accountant or to be led by an engineer. Since efficiency ('O & M') studies are laid to the Executive grades, statisticians, engineers and accountants are rarely employed on them. Since the management of prisons is a prerogative of the Prison Governor Class, psychologists and social scientists do not usually run prisons. Since personnel management is laid to the Administration Group, professional social scientists and economists are usually excluded. On the other hand, specialists have had no way of gaining experience of legislative processes, of day-to-day administrative casework, nor of the general conduct of departments, so that they are rarely aware of the political constraints under which the department operates or the practical limitations of the administrative machine. The class system has prevented the development of the professional hybrids which are nowadays required to handle political/technical issues: the engineer/accountants, administrator/social scientists, scientist/administrators and so on.

Within the group of specialist classes, there are status differences which are not entirely explained by the requirements of the work they do. The Scientific Officer Class, for example, contains a disproportionate number of highly graded jobs and has some particularly favourable promotion arrangements. The Economist Class, though small, occupies a number of key positions in the top management of departments. On the other hand, engineers, accountants and social scientists have very few opportunities for reaching posts of any great power and are usually confined to fairly narrow areas of specialization. Indeed accountants, so prominent in the top management of organizations outside the Civil Service, are usually excluded not only from policy and planning areas but from government accounting altogether and are mostly engaged on examining the accounts of outside firms. In the Professional Accountant Class of the Civil Service there are posts for fewer than 400 of the 25,000 professional accountants in the country.[8]

THE ADMINISTRATORS

The formation of policy, the co-ordination and improvement of government machinery and the higher administration and control of government departments is primarily laid to the top four grades of the Administration Group – Permanent, Deputy, Under and Assistant Secretary (formerly the upper levels of the Administrative Class). As we shall see from the next chapter, discussion of the management of the Civil Service has focused almost entirely upon the work of these few hundred administrators and has barely recognized the existence of the other half million civil servants, many thousands of whom are managers.

The Civil Service Commission has observed that their work ('developing, helping to decide and carrying out policy on national issues under the direction of Ministers') 'has no counterpart elsewhere'.[9] They have been described as a group of officials 'who, whatever the subject matter of their particular work, may be said to specialize in the awareness of Ministerial responsibility'.[10] The Fulton Committee said that one result of this specialization was that 'few members of the class actually see themselves as managers, that is as responsible for organization, directing staff, planning the progress of work, setting standards of attainment and measuring results, reviewing procedures and quantifying different courses of action ... much of their work is not managerial in this sense; so they tend to see themselves as advisers on policy to people above them, rather than as managers of the administrative machine below them.'[11]

Implicitly, the Committee was contrasting the orientation of top management in industry with that of the higher Civil Service, though in doing so it may have somewhat idealized the managerial model. It is true, however, that a competent executive director in a large company would describe his job in terms not only of formulating policy and making the most important decisions in his area of responsibility, but as being responsible for setting objectives for his subordinate managers, establishing budgets for their programmes of activity and reviewing their subsequent performance. He would see himself as being concerned with the oversight of a hierarchy of management systems each designed to enable managers to optimize the use of their resources and monitor performance. A Deputy Secretary with comparable responsibilities for expenditure and manpower might describe his most important responsibilities on these lines:

(a) To maintain a review of the working of policy in his divisions, to estimate the consequences of particular decisions in the light of government policy and Ministerial views and to advise Ministers on developments.

(b) To oversee the development of a policy line and decide upon the areas in which new policy initiatives may be required as a result of the developments on current cases, the activities of outside pressure groups or Ministerial interest; to formulate or approve policy proposals for consideration by Ministers.

(c) To oversee the handling of specific cases and to insure their consistent treatment. To decide upon the method of handling major cases and decide when they should be referred to the Minister.

(d) To take responsibility for politically sensitive or unprecedented cases and to apply to them his judgement of Ministerial views. To initiate and prepare proposals for the Minister on the handling of such cases.

(e) To call on specialist advice and to consider it in a political context and to co-ordinate the work of specialists and administrators.

(f) To initiate the drafting of legislation and advise on the drafting of important elements of legislation.

(g) To represent the department on inter-departmental committees and in major negotiations with outside bodies.

(h) To examine draft answers to Parliamentary questions and Ministerial briefs and speeches.

The Fulton Committee saw grounds for criticism in the concentration of the top civil servant on the co-ordination and review of policy, on sensitive cases and issues rather than on managerial systems. Even at that time, however, the criticism was fairly superficial: in departments which directly manage large projects (such as Defence) high-level administration has for years had a strong systems element, involving the establishment of management programmes and budgets and monitoring project expenditures against performance. Elsewhere, the administrative view of the top management job has directly reflected the preoccupations of Ministers, who generally have had little interest in the management systems operated by their departments. The professionalism of administration has lain in being able to deal effectively with critical and sensitive cases, to construct and help the Minister to pilot legislation through to enactment, to handle hostile debate and to react rapidly to crises. The climate at the top of a politically exposed department has been described by Mr Roy Jenkins in a recent reminiscence of his time as Home Secretary as one in which 'tropical storms blow up with speed and violence out of a blue sky, dominate the political landscape for a short time and then disappear as suddenly as they arrive. When they are on, it is difficult to think of much else. When they are over it is difficult to recall what the fuss was about.'[12] In this situation, primacy is given to political instinct, rapidity of reaction and dialectical skill rather than to managerial or analytical skills: 'The ultimate test of success in administration is that they [administrators] should give their Minister a case which stands up to criticism by expert debaters in public.'[13] This has led to the observation that departments are directed and controlled by a secretariat of 'politicians' politicians'[14] or 'statesmen in disguise'[15] whose members see all issues as political 'in the sense of responding to those air currents in the upper atmosphere in which ministers exist most of the time – the reactions of their fellow Ministers, the attitude of conventionally powerful pressure groups, the kind of action that will cope with the immediate situation in Parliament and constitute a defensible position in the country'.[16]

In an environment in which political awareness has a higher valuation than managerial skill, esteem and preferment go to the man who is articulate, diplomatic, quick-thinking, skilful at drafting, politically sensitive and alert to prospective crises and who gets on well with his peers. Such men are drawn from those who 'show talents for neat and tactful drafting, good manners, presence of mind in conversation, general good sense and some flair for politics'[17] and who have been given a wide, but somewhat superficial, experience of a variety of activities in the department and a general grounding in the ways of handling political issues. The embryo administrator has to learn to be, in R. G. S. Brown's analysis,[18] first a *facilitator*, someone who insures that political or expert ideas are properly recorded, processed and implemented; secondly, a *mediator*, someone who links the specialist to the rest of the system; and thirdly, an *arbiter*, someone who uses his judgement to compare and reconcile conflicting priorities. He has to learn to play the role of 'a rarified kind of layman'[19] with 'a mind open to the point of agnosticism'[20] so that he can synthesize the points of view of professionaly qualified advisers and of executive managers with his own sense of what is politically feasible. Eulogists of this view of administration, which has been almost as common in British industry as in government, have laid great emphasis upon the superiority of the well-educated layman in the work. 'He will, of course, take all the advice he can get from the specialists: he may even lean heavily upon them. All this advice, however, will tend to be tinted . . . The administrator's job is to recognize these tints, tone them down if they are too bright, see when advice of another tint is required, and combine them so that the final result is of the white or clear character desired.'[21] His special technique or art is that 'he knows where, how and when to go to find reliable knowledge, can assess the expertise of others at its true worth, can spot the strong and weak points in any situation at short notice and can advise on how to handle a complex situation'.[22]

The conventional background for the development of the skills of the administrator has been a good Oxbridge arts degree and a familiarity with the working of the departmental machine. He has obtained this familiarity by serving a long apprenticeship as a supernumerary in assistance to a wide variety of senior administrators. As his career has progressed, he has continued to change from job to job with great frequency (on average, spending less than three years in each completed job). 'Too long a period in one job produces staleness, a drying up in the flow of new ideas and a loss of detachment. This detachment is particularly prized and many administrators said that it tends to disappear when the administrator has too great a familiarity with, or is too closely involved with, the problems in hand. This attitude was exemplified in an extreme way by the view that it is dangerous to know too much about the job.'[23] Sir Edward Bridges thought that it was a healthy practice that administrators change jobs every three years or so: 'When a man has done five jobs in fifteen years and has done them all with a measure of success, he is afraid of nothing and welcomes change.'[24] An administrator has thereby been taught to absorb a department's traditions rather than being trained for a particular job or in specific technical or analytical skills: 'No amount of training however carefully and elaborately devised, can instil that spark of artistic genius that good administrators seem to be born with.'[25] Sisson quotes an 'authoritative Treasury source' as commending 'the long-established tradition of regarding members of me Administrative Class as intelligent amateurs who form their judgements on the basis of experience rather than as a result of a prescribed course of theoretical training' and notes that the British administrator travelling abroad is shocked to discover that many countries are administered by men who read books about public administration. 'This, in the British view, is not only a surprising but a very unfortunate state of affairs, and goes some way to explain the difficulties under which foreigners, in the matter of government, notoriously suffer.'[26]

Though roughly forty per cent of the members of the former Administrative Class had joined it from other classes (mostly the Executive) and some exceptional individuals have risen to it from the lowest Clerical and Executive grades (particularly in wartime), top administrators have come from a fairly narrow social and educational background (see Chapter 2). Indeed this homogeneity of origin and experience, this 'fraternity'[27] has been claimed as a valuable integrating mechanism: 'Members [of the Administrative Class] are so selected and trained as to be able to work together flexibly and correctly. Socially, there is no gap between a Permanent Secretary and an Assistant Principal.'[28]

In sum, the effects of the distinction made by Northcote and

Trevelyan between intellectual and mechanical labour and the convention of total Ministerial accountability together created a concept of administration in which power was held by the lay administrator (the 'amateur-gentleman-politician' in the view of his critics) who applied great intelligence and experience, common sense and political judgement to the views of professional experts and managers.

We shall see in the next chapter that this concept came under fire from most of the critics of the higher Civil Service and was entirely rejected by the Fulton Committee as an out-moded product of the nineteenth century. The administrators were accused of amateurism, dilettantism, arrogance and elitism. Much of this criticism was unfair and ill-informed. In the light of their (and Ministers') view of their role as a political secretariat, the administrators are a highly professional group. If their central task is to be aware of Ministerial responsibility and to see that the Minister can account in public and Parliamentary debate for the way in which he discharges his responsibilities, then the requirement is that they should be fluent and articulate generalists, widely experienced in the ways of Whitehall and in the operation of the government machine. It also helps if they are intimately linked to their peers in other departments by a network of social and educational connections and a sense of corporate identity.

The argument of the critics was that the management of today's huge departments and expenditure programmes calls for a top management group with a wider role than that of a political secretariat and that the tendency of administrators 'to give a low valuation to management, specialization and "investigation as a preliminary to action" constitute attitudes more appropriate to the service of a Regulatory State than that charged with administering the Welfare State and managing the economy'.[29]

There is substance in this argument, as the Civil Service was having to recognize before Fulton reported. The administrative style is not well suited to a situation in which complex technical evaluations are required to precede decision-making. A generalist administrator with no formal education beyond an arts degree is rarely able to see the value of, let alone carry out, the statistical analysis and social research required to evaluate, for example, welfare or housing legislation; a study of the 1967 Rent Act has shown that that particularly counter-productive piece of legislation was prepared by a Ministry which actively discouraged research into the housing problem and preferred to reach decisions unencumbered by too much information.[30] Without formal training in investment appraisal or analytical cost accounting, he is not well prepared to pass judgement on the capital programmes of a nationalized industry or the investment in an aerospace or construction or computer project, or to assess the likely costs and benefits of alternative schemes to aid industry or agriculture. An example of this weakness is provided by the millions poured into the shipbuilding industry, largely, said the Minister of Trade and Industry in May 1971, 'siphoned off into unproductive uses instead of contributing to the strengthening of the industry'.[31] The department which handed out all this wasted money apparently not only carried out no preliminary analysis of its prospective use, but had no clear idea of how to judge the benefit of the expenditure.* The indications are that many of the government's great industrial investments in recent years – in Rolls-Royce, Concorde, the Upper Clyde shipyards, the Multi-Role Combat Aircraft – have been out of control since the first penny was spent and that they were neither properly evaluated at the outset nor subsequently monitored with any professional rigour.

The evaluation of such issues will inevitably become an increasingly important part of the work of the higher Civil Service. It will call for more expertise than the well-rounded arts graduate can bring to bear, particularly in measurement, analysis and research. As Herman Kahn observed, while experts may be bad at large issues they are not as bad as what he called 'your gentleman amateurs' are on expert issues.[32] The administrative style is also ill-suited to developing and making the best use of junior staff.

*The Permanent Secretary, Ministry of Technology, to the Select Committee on Procedure in March 1969: 'Take as an example the Shipbuilding Industry Board Programme for the reconstruction of the shipbuilding industry. Thirty-two million pounds has been voted by Parliament for that purpose. How one measures the benefit from doing that I do not know. I would not know how to start that calculation.' Select Committee on Procedure 1968–9, H.C.410, para. 236.

Inexperience of man-management too often leads to an impersonal attitude to members of the lower grades, who are seen as rightly restricted to the stations predetermined for them by the points at which they happen to have left the education system.

Many young administrators are dissatisfied with the conventions of the administrative style and feel that it has lost relevance to the work of managing today's great departments. They want to be trained and developed as managers, analysts and planners. The conventions of the career class system froze their prospects as much as those of any other group. The innovations discussed in the following chapters will offer new opportunities to them as to others. The pity is that most of these innovations were proposed in the course of a violent and pointless argument about 'amateurs' and 'professionals', both before and after the Fulton Committee reported, which so soured the general debate as to reduce the likelihood of their acceptance. This debate is described in Chapter 2.

The New Structure of the Administration Group

Salary scales* for new grades (as from 1.1.71)	New Structure	Former Grades		
		Administrative Class	Executive Class	Clerical Class
£5,000–£6,300	Assistant Secretary	Assistant Secretary	Principal Executive Officer	—
£4,600–£5,200	Senior Principal	—	Senior Chief Executive Officer	—
£3,250–£4,400	Principal	Principal	Chief Executive Officer	—
£2,775–£3,400	Senior Executive Officer	—	Senior Executive Officer	—
£2,150–£2,625	Higher Executive Officer / Higher Executive Officer A	Assistant Principal	Higher Executive Officer	—
£1,260–£2,000	Administration Trainee	Assistant Principal	—	—
£800–£2,000	Executive Officer	—	Executive Officer	—
£507–£1,385	Clerical Officer	—	—	Clerical Officer
£7.19–£19.95 (weekly rate)	Clerical Assistant	—	—	Clerical Assistant

*Note: All salary figures given in this Appendix are national rates.
Source: CSD Report, 1970–71, (H.M.S.O. December 1971)

29

CHAPTER 2

Fulton: The Establishment, The System and
The Amateur

THE report of the Fulton Committee came at the end of a decade
of increasing criticism of the Civil Service in general and the
Administrative Class in particular. Prior to this period, there had
been occasional demands for reform, some of them causing a
brief flurry of interest at the time. One of the most interesting and
well argued of these irruptions occurred in an introduction by
H. J. Laski to a book on the Civil Service written by J. P. Mallalieu in 1942.[1] Laski made many of the criticisms of the Service
which became fashionable twenty years later and proposed most
of the reforms recommended by Fulton in 1968. He accused the
Administrative Class of a lack of imagination and audacity and
an unwillingness to experiment and saw them as regarding 'all
principles to which they are unaccustomed, all experience alien
from their own, as dangerous and impractical'.[2] 'Innovation on
the grand scale, utter frankness, relentless attack upon obstructive
interests, rapid adaptation to the unexpected, the ruthless rejection of the men who do not rise to the occasion . . . are pretty
exactly the qualities against which the main genius of our Civil
Service has been directed.'[3]

He went on to make twenty recommendations for change,[4]
proposing arrangements for late entry into the Administrative
Class; the removal of personnel work from the Treasury to a new
Minister of Personnel; the establishment of a staff college and
training for the lower grades; the removal of the barrier between
the administrative side and the scientific and technical sides; the
establishment of the right of direct access to Ministers by specialists on specialist matters; and a 'humanization' of public relations.

In the book Mallalieu commented upon the extreme social
exclusivity of the senior civil servant of the day, the failure to
make full use of experts ('the expert tends to be treated as a
necessary hack rather than as a colleague'[5]) and the lack of train-

ing in administration: 'The ruling class, at least in this country, has a curious belief in the amateur, whether in sport or in running an industry.'[6]

In the early 1950s the topic of Civil Service reform was raised in the context of attacks upon 'The Establishment'. The term is said to have first been used in print by Mr Henry Fairlie in 1955 in his articles in the *Spectator* discussing the Burgess and Maclean affair, and quickly entered into popular usage as descriptive of a kind of public school and Oxbridge-educated Mafia whose members were in control of the key institutions of our society. Members of the Establishment were accused of gentlemanly amateurism, arrogance, unwillingness to innovate and total failure to understand the needs of the times. Bound together by common social origins and shared values, they were said to conspire to prevent the assumption of power by the technically trained 'professionals' who were needed to bring Britain up to date.

In 1959 all these criticisms were focused in a collection of essays, *The Establishment*,[7] which examined the characteristics of what were said to be the 'socially gifted amateurs' who controlled the Army, the BBC, Parliament, the City and the Civil Service and whose common values were nourished in the public schools. The essay on the Civil Service, by Dr Thomas Balogh, was entitled: 'The Apotheosis of the Dilettante: The Establishment of Mandarins.'[8] In this essay Dr Balogh concentrated upon the lack of technical expertise of top administrators in the Civil Service and discussed the attitude of effortless superiority, combined with cultured scepticism, upon which 'that mysterious art, Administrative Capacity', was said to depend. He accused administrators of a lack of knowledge of the present world and its problems and the Treasury of using its patronage to insure the acceptance of administrators who had no professional training and the inferiority in status and pay of the technical and specialist classes. His view was that the recurring crises and creeping paralysis of the British economy had taken the authorities unawares because Ministers had not been supplied with all the facts by their civil servants: he asked how much of British influence and power could have been saved by a little more tact, a little more imagination and a lot more expert knowledge.

In 1962, an American writer, David Granick, in a book on the characteristics of the industrial management of different European countries, devoted a chapter to 'Great Britain – Home of the Amateur'. 'While the Civil Service Administrative Class has been recruited almost exclusively from among university graduates, this has never been due to the belief that they possess specific desirable skills and knowledge. To the contrary. The task of the schools and universities is to develop character (an imponderable which no one seriously tries to define), provide a common social experience so that independent-minded men can later work together in harness and train the intellect . . . it matters little in which subject the degree is taken. In fact, to the extent that there is a preference, it is for a student of the classics.'[9] Granick went on to observe that the great advantage of a subject like classics was that its study could never bring the charge of professionalism against the student – 'the graduate preserves his amateur status'.[10]

In 1963 Professor Brian Chapman wrote 'British Government Observed', an essay attributing much of the humiliating decline of British influence in the preceding ten years to the signal lack of success of the institutions of British government to keep pace with the modern world and to a series of misconceived or calamitous decisions made by their senior officials. He made unfavourable comparisons between the training and experience of the British Administrative Class ('a closed society' . . . 'sheltered spinsters') and those of their French counterparts. He concluded that 'at the very heart of British government there is a luxuriant amateurism and a voluntary exclusion of talent'.[11]

By 1964 some prominent politicians had become interested in the management of the Civil Service. In that year, Dr Norman Hunt questioned Mr Harold Wilson, Mr Jo Grimond and Mr Enoch Powell on B.B.C. radio (in a series of interviews published as *Whitehall and Beyond*[12]) on the topic of the modernization of the machinery of government. Mr Wilson spoke of combing the Civil Service for specialists, bringing in outside experts and of building up a powerful Cabinet secretariat ('I am very worried about what I feel is the amateurism of the central direction of Government'). This secretariat would include staff with experience of science and economic administration and groups of experts from inside and outside the Service who would undertake long-term studies. Mr Grimond thought that far too many top civil servants were brought up in the old disciplines of Greats and History and found it wholly wrong that scientists and technologists were kept as advisers in a comparatively humble capacity. To keep the balance, Mr Powell, as former Minister of Health, thought that having administrators with medical training in that department would illustrate that a little learning is a dangerous thing and, surprisingly for a famous logician, thought that since Ministers were laymen then it was best if top administrators should have lay minds as well . . . 'the professional advice should be in a sense subordinate to the administrative advice'.[13]

Also in 1964 the Fabian Society published a tract called *The Administrators*[14] which was believed at the time to have been written by a group of senior civil servants. This dealt specifically with the Administrative Class, which it described as isolated from industry, local government and other fields of society; as containing omniscient all-rounders capable of formulating policy in any field; as closed as a monastic order with no inward or outward movement; and as having no provision for appointments from outside. This description led to three main criticisms of the system: amateurism (the tradition of the all-rounder or generalist); a negative approach by civil servants, who concentrated too readily on procedure rather than the substance of problems and too much secrecy in the formulation of policy. These defects were thought to spring from features of the way the system was run: a concentration upon Oxbridge graduates with arts degrees; inadequate training; the lack of movement in and out of Whitehall; the rapid switching of senior officials from one job to another so that they could not master a subject; the lack of specialists at a senior level; and the refusal to give such specialists equality of status with the generalists who ran departments. The authors of *The Administrators* pointed to the need for civil servants to be able 'to assess costs, risks, interactions' in quantitative terms and to the need for a reform of the personnel management function in government departments and the Treasury, in view of its emphasis upon economy and its treatment of personnel work as a by-product of controlling expenditure.

The main proposals put forward in *The Administrators* were for the establishment of an enlarged Civil Service Commission to include not only service-wide recruitment but the Treasury's personnel management functions; the widening of the field of recruitment of administrators; free movement in and out of the service aided by the institution of contributory pensions; the establishment of a central school of administrative studies; the better articulation of careers, so that people acquired a progressively widening range of experience and were not jumped about between unrelated jobs; the abolition of career classes above the Assistant Secretary level, so that specialists and administrators could compete for the top jobs on an equal footing; an increase in the number of specialists and the appointment of outside experts to assist Ministers.

The run-up to the 1964 election was marked by the emphasis of the Labour Party leadership upon managerial and technological efficiency. The Labour election manifesto 'Signposts for the Sixties' said that our economy was dominated by a small ruling caste and that the dead wood should be cut out of Britain's boardrooms and replaced by keen young executives, production engineers and scientists who hitherto had been denied their legitimate prospects of promotion. Mr Wilson had long been interested in science and technology and this interest 'was encouraged during the 1950s by his two close friends and advisers, Dr Tom (later Lord) Balogh and Roy (later Lord) Fulton'.[15]

In early 1965 the Estimates Committee of the House of Commons considered the question of recruitment to the Civil Service. In the course of taking evidence, a sub-committee, with Dr Jeremy Bray, M.P., as chairman, examined the problems of recruitment to the Executive and Administrative Classes and paid particular attention to student attitudes to the Civil Service, the disinclination of graduates from red-brick universities to join the Service and the shortage of economists and other specialists. The Committee's report [16] concluded that both the structure and the public image of the Civil Service needed to be reviewed in the light of modern needs and recommended that a committee of officials, aided by members from outside the Civil Service, should be appointed to initiate research and to examine and to report upon the structure, recruitment and management of the Civil Service and that, on receipt of this report, the government should consider the need to appoint a Royal Commission.

In the event, the government decided to set up a committee with a chairman and a majority of its members from outside the Civil Service. In February 1966, Lord Fulton was appointed chairman of the Committee on the Civil Service with terms of reference 'to examine the structure, recruitment and management, including training, of the Civil Service and to make recommendations'. The Prime Minister, Mr Wilson, in his introductory statement to the House of Commons, said that the decision to set up a committee was reached in view of the changes which had taken place in the demands placed upon the Civil Service and of the changes in the country's educational system and that the time had come to insure that the Service was properly equipped for its role in the modern state.

While the Committee was sitting Mr Max Nicholson sounded a particularly loud blast against the higher Civil Service. In *The System*[17] (subtitled *The Misgovernment of Modern Britain*) he maintained that command of the mechanism of central government was in the hands of an irrelevant and outdated elite who sustained a 'system' of antiquated principles, aims, policies and codes of conduct. He traced the trouble to the reform of the Civil Service in 1854, which replaced a corrupt and patronage-ridden service with the products of Arnold's public schools and Jowett's Oxbridge – 'a new model service based on academic amateurism rather than a professional training'.[18]

'To say that the Civil Service today is characterized by shoddiness of thinking, feebleness of imagination and foresight, intellectual inertia, distaste for and distrust of research, technical and scientific illiteracy, reluctance to admit mistakes and proficiency in covering them up as far as possible, timidity in venturing beyond past precedent and routine, caste consciousness and departmental pettiness is merely to recapitulate some among the defects which the service itself has placed on the record.'[19]

The commissioning of the Fulton Committee therefore came as the culmination of a growing, and increasingly vocal, dissatisfaction with the higher Civil Service. This dissatisfaction was part of a wider demand by journalists, academics and radical politicians for the modernization of British institutions. The movement was fuelled by a feeling that the management of these institutions was socially exclusive and closed to outside scrutiny, and that they were accountable only to themselves.

As a final flourish, within a few weeks of the publication of the Fulton Report a group of American and Canadian economists reported on *Britain's Economic Prospects* for the Brookings Institute.[20] Commenting on the widespread distrust of specialists and specialist training in British industry, they said: 'The trouble with the public school and Oxbridge graduates lies not in the "old boy" network of recruitment but rather in their amateurism and their frequent acceptance of business as second choice when they fail to qualify for a Civil Service career. They tend to retain the Civil Service as their model and settle into a trustee role of gentlemanly responsibility that hardly conduces to rapid innovation.[21]

THE EVIDENCE TO FULTON

Over 150 memoranda were presented in evidence to the Fulton Committee by the Treasury, other government departments, outside organizations and individuals, and these were published in three volumes. In addition, the Committee published three volumes of surveys and investigations. Few of the memoranda of evidence contributed significantly to the discussion. The main battle was fought between the Treasury and the Association of First Division Civil Servants on one side and the Institution of Professional Civil Servants and a Management Consultancy Group on the other.

The Treasury's main suggestion for a reform of the structure of the Civil Service[22] was that the Executive and Administrative Classes should be combined so as to give one line of promotion through a managerial class from the level of clerical supervisor to the top posts in a department. There should be an enlarged graduate entry, a portion of which ('roughly equivalent in size to the present Assistant Principal entry') might be 'starred' on the basis of academic record and performance at the selection stage. The necessity for identifying an elite group arose from the need to give the most able an especially attractive career and because departments could give special training to only a few The Treasury also suggested the merger of the Administrative with the Specialist Classes above the level of the top of the Assistant Secretary scale and the provision of training for senior specialists so as to fit them for general management. However, it pointed out that those who had spent their careers in general management and administration would look to the general policy posts in the Higher Civil Service, because these required a high degree of expertise in government administrative processes and in the working of a very complex machine.

In other words, the Treasury could see no need for any radical change. Although it was willing to give the appearance of opening the top jobs to executives and specialists, in fact its proposals for a 'starred' entry of suitably academically qualified graduates meant the retention of the Administrative Class in all but name. The Treasury's inability or unwillingness to comprehend the depth of feeling against administrative elitism and its bland assumption that the system needed only a slight adjustment rather than a fundamental reappraisal provided a telling example of its remoteness from attitudes within the Service.

The First Division Association,[23] representing the Administrative Class, found even the Treasury's proposals too radical to stomach. 'Starring' the right kind of graduate they found insufficiently exclusive for their members – 'many of our assistant principal members . . . assure us they would not have been interested in joining under these conditions. They saw a real incentive in seeking to join what they regarded as an elite . . . They will only see a lowering of the graduate entry standards and, in place of membership of an elite, a vague promise of preferential treatment.' On the question of the primacy of the lay administrator, the F.D.A. said that he had to bring to bear on any issue all the wider considerations that were relevant, while the role of the specialist was to speak on the scientific or technical merits of a particular course of action: 'We do not believe these roles can be combined.' It went on to say that any specialist who became fully able to perform the administrative role would thereby cease to be a specialist and would have to turn to other specialists for expert knowledge.

The Institution of Professional Civil Servants, representing most of the specialist classes in the Civil Service, presented an impressive body of evidence to Fulton in eight memoranda.[24] At the outset, the I.P.C.S. attacked the Treasury's evidence as inadequate and unreal in seeking to keep the specialist in a subservient role and to perpetuate the mystique of the lay administrator. It proposed the abolition of all the class divisions above the level of administrative Principal and proposed three broad career groups: the Technology Group, the Science Group and the Administrative Group with unified structures replacing all the technical and junior classes. Responsibility should be placed on the man doing the job – for instance the specialist engineer should be responsible for seeing his work through, rather than having it vetted and approved by an unqualified administrator. Jobs should be open to the best man available rather than one from a particular academic or career background: in future no man should be effectively barred from any level or from participating in policy or from giving advice directly to the Minister because of his profession. The work of formulating policy and of management should be open to all talents.

Some individual specialists, principally economists, gave evidence to Fulton on their experience of the Administrative Class at work. Mr Dudley Seers, formerly planning director of the Ministry of Overseas Development, observed in them 'an almost unanimous reliance on intuition and a distrust of systematic argument, especially where the context is highly quantitative' ... 'some Civil Servants feel a surprising confidence in their own ability to decide technical subjects – lack of any education or even systematic reading on economic questions does not stop them from expressing strong, even if vague, views on subjects such as international liquidity, views based on the fashionable journalism of a few years previously'.[25] A group of economists from the same Ministry wrote of the imposition by administrators of strong intuitive opinions on complex economic questions, of 'amateur' and 'ineffective' analysis and presentation of statistical material by administrators and of their inability to understand the contribution of modern methods of statistical analysis to policy problems.[26] Mr D. L. Munby, a former assistant director in the Department of Economic Affairs, had found his administrative colleagues 'extremely competent in the construction of well-argued, precise documents which sound convincing to anyone not expert in the subject matter'.[27]

The Society of Civil Servants, the staff association representing the Executive Class, approved the amalgamation of the Administrative and Executive Classes, opposed starring for selected graduates and also thought that the Administrative, Executive and Specialist Classes should be combined at the upper levels into a higher Civil Service.[28]

The evidence submitted by the *Guardian* newspaper contended that the change in the responsibilities of the Civil Service had not been matched by a widening of the field of recruitment of men to handle them: 'The Accounting Officer (Permanent Secretary) of the Ministry of Power handles the biggest investment programme in Europe. His successor will have to be chosen from among a relatively small number of men . . . who graduated during the late 1930s or 1940s (probably at Oxford or Cambridge and probably in an Arts subject) and who have had no subsequent experience outside the Civil Service.'[29]

The evidence sent to the Committee by the Labour Party[30] was widely interpreted at the time as a list of complaints against the Civil Service which the government had accumulated in two years of office. It drew attention to the fact that the Civil Service now managed a highly complex techno-industrial society – a job calling for more specialized technical skill than the generalist could provide. In a highly publicized section, it criticized the amount of information withheld from Ministers which made some of them 'tools of their departments a good deal of the time' and said that 'inter-departmental committees of officials are a particularly effective way of undermining the authority of Ministers'. It proposed that an incoming Minister should have the right to appoint a personal cabinet of assistants who would have access to him and to all the information in his department. 'Its function would be to act as a political brains trust to the Minister, to act as an extra pair of eyes and ears, to stimulate him.' It also proposed the temporary appointment of expert advisers in 'posts of confidence' who would have direct access to the Minister. It opposed the Treasury's proposal for 'starring' an elite group of graduates and supported the merger of the Administrative and Executive Classes and the upper levels of these with the Professional Classes. It recommended that 'administrative' training should be given to professionally qualified entrants to fit them for administrative jobs; that improved training should also be given to non-graduates so that they could also compete for the highest posts; that the personnel-management function of the Treasury should be transferred to the Civil Service Commission; that careers should be better planned so that an official acquired a steadily widening range of experience and was not expected to move between totally unrelated jobs. It proposed a more vigorous and determined attempt to recruit people from universities other than Oxbridge and with other than arts degrees, an enlarged Centre for Administrative Studies and the provision of middle and senior management courses for both administrative and professional staff.

THE EVIDENCE OF THE MANAGEMENT CONSULTANCY GROUP

In the early stages of the Committee's work, one of its members, Dr Norman Hunt, proposed that a team of civil servants, businessmen, members of the Committee and management consultants should be set up to examine in detail a number of blocks of work in the Civil Service. The team would examine the management and organization of each block, comparing these with the best practice in business firms, and would consider the responsibilities held by the staff, the tasks performed, the skills the work called for and the relationship between specialists and administrators.[31] The Committee approved the formation of such a team (the Management Consultancy Group) under Dr Hunt. The group started work in 1966 and consisted of a senior official from the O. & M. Division of the Treasury, an executive from British

Petroleum Ltd, and the author, from Associated Industrial Consultants Ltd. Its members interviewed nearly 600 civil servants from clerical assistant to Under Secretary in twenty-three 'blocks' in twelve different departments. The sections to be examined were selected under the guidance of the Permanent Secretaries on the Fulton Committee, so as to be as representative as possible.

The Management Consultancy Group's report, published as Volume II of the Fulton Report, began with a discussion of the strengths of the Civil Service and the complexity of its working environment. It then set out descriptions of the work and characteristics of the Administrative, Executive, Clerical and four Specialist Classes (Accountants, Scientists, Research Officers, the Works Group) as the group had seen them. They went on to describe the relationships between specialists and administrators, the work of establishment and organization divisions and Civil Service conventions of management and organization. This last section ended with suggestions for possible lines of reform and observations on the need for a new style of management.

The group found that over half of the direct-entry administrators they had interviewed had degrees in history or classics. They found that most lacked training or experience of management techniques and they commented on their rapid movement from job to job. They concluded that the work of the Administrative Class suffered because of lack of continuity in the job, lack of management skills and experience and largely irrelevant educational background. They gave the Executive Class a fairly clean bill of health, being impressed by the way in which its members had taken on the new managerial tasks of government, but condemned the exclusion from the posts occupied by this class of such specialists as accountants, economists and engineers. They found that the division of clerical workers into different classes was unnecessary and wasteful of ability.

The group paid particular attention to the relationships between administrators (both Administrative and Executive) and specialists. They discussed all the standard arguments for excluding specialists from the line of management and from financial control. These were that administrators were more cost-conscious than specialists; that they relieved scarce specialists of non-specialist work; that they could best co-ordinate the work of different specialists; that they could set specialist matters in the context of Ministerial policy and their knowledge of the administrative machine; that they had the fluency to synthesize various specialist and administrative views in a form on which decisions could be based; that the work of specialists benefited from critical scrutiny by the intelligent layman who, by virtue of his detached viewpoint, could spot unnecessary expenditure. They then put the opposing arguments. They had found that, particularly in matters of financial control, administrators did not have the competence to challenge the specialists except on obvious or relatively trivial points; that the division of decision-making between specialists and administrators resulted in delay and inefficiency (misunderstandings arose, papers were sent to and fro, time was occupied by explanation); that since administrators frequently changed jobs, specialists often found themselves having to explain the technical background to laymen. They observed that in industry specialists were frequently empowered to spend funds without having their decisions under continuous scrutiny by laymen – cost-control was a feature of the training of architects, engineers and surveyors; that there was no evidence that specialists were unsuited to the role of policy-makers – accountants and engineers were prominent in the policy areas of large companies; that there was no evidence that specialists could not quickly assimilate knowledge of the working of the government machine; that specialists resented their subordinate status and this hindered the recruitment of top-class professionals and that where the common task was divided between specialists and administrators, no one individual had clear management responsibility. They concluded that in administrative/technical areas the manager should usually be a specialist who had acquired training and experience in the administrative procedures of government and that it was essential that top posts should be open to specialists with the appropriate qualifications.

The Consultancy Group also commented upon elitism within the specialist classes. They observed that the Scientific Officer class had, in some respects, even more privileged conditions than the Administrative Class: they occupied a position at the head of a number of technical classes whose members were effectively prevented from reaching managerial positions. It was therefore vastly more difficult than in industry for a very able man without the appropriate academic qualifications to reach top posts in areas of scientific and technical activity.

The group went on to point out that though personnel work was laid to establishments divisions in the Service, these divisions were mainly concerned with controlling the numbers employed rather than with the more constructive aspects of developing the human resources of the Service, hindered though this was by the class system. As part of their role of controllers of staff expenditure, establishments divisions were also responsible for staff inspection (seeing that particular posts were justified and properly graded: a mandatory imposition) and O. &. M. (efficiency studies: a service by request). The group considered that the separation of these two functions was wrong and that O. &. M. operated at too low a level to be effective – that is, it never examined the jobs of administrators nor was it allowed to question the basic purpose and efficiency of major organizational units.

In its final chapter, 'Management and Organization', the Consultancy Group concluded that the career class structure was a major obstacle to efficient management in the Service and proposed the replacement of all classes by a system of pay bands covering all Civil Servants: a 'unified grading structure' based on job evaluation. The group then went on to suggest lines of research into a new managerial style for the Service based on the definition of objectives and priorities for organizational units; forms of organization derived not from the hierarchies of career classes but from the definition of managerial objectives; rewards related more to merit than to seniority; more sophisticated forms of management accounting and control; greater delegation of responsibility to individual managers supported by procedures for assessing accountability and for measuring managerial effectiveness. To establish the long-term policy framework for these systems of objective-setting and control, new high-level departmental planning units were required.

The Consultancy Group finally referred to the future top managers of departments. It saw them as being drawn from a wider range of education and background than in the past and as having deep knowledge of management of at least one function at lower levels. Preferably they should have entered the Service with relevant qualifications and should be given the greatest possible encouragement to acquire post-entry qualifications. It saw them as having to use sophisticated tools of management and being required 'to handle more variables than can be expressed in the traditional essay by which the top echelons of the Service now usually analyse, and judge, policy options'. It called for a new breed of management: numerate, trained in technique and experienced in working within the unique constraints of the public service. It supported equality of opportunity for all staff in a classless Service and opposed a royal route to the top for a selected few 'crown princes'. It concluded by saying that its investigation had led it to the belief that the Civil Service had outgrown current conventions of management and organization and the need was now for a flexible organization, directed by highly professional and self-critical managers.

THE FULTON REPORT, VOLUME I:
CONCLUSIONS AND RECOMMENDATIONS

The Fulton Committee reported in June 1968.[32] The first chapter of its report began: 'The Home Civil Service today is still fundamentally the product of the nineteenth-century philosophy of the Northcote–Trevelyan Report. The tasks it faces are those of the second half of the twentieth century. This is what we have found; it is what we seek to remedy.'

Drawing heavily upon the evidence of the Management Consultancy Group, it concluded that the structure and practices of the Service had not kept up with its vastly increased responsibilities. The Service was inadequate in six main respects:

First, it was still essentially based on the philosophy of the amateur (or 'generalist' or 'all-rounder'). This was most evident in the Administrative Class, which held the dominant positions in the Service. 'The ideal administrator is still too often seen as the gifted layman who, moving frequently from job to job within the Service, can take a practical view of any problem, irrespective of its subject matter, in the light of his knowledge and experience of the government machine.'[33]

Secondly, the system of classes in the Service seriously hindered its work.

Thirdly, many scientists, engineers and other specialists were not given the responsibilities, authority or opportunities they ought to have.

Fourthly, too few civil servants were skilled managers. Members of the Administrative Class, in particular, who were allotted the major managerial role in the Service did not see themselves as managers of departments but as advisers on policy to those above them.

Fifthly, there was not enough contact between the Service and the rest of the community. There was not enough awareness in the Service of how the world outside Whitehall worked, how government policies would affect it and of the new ideas and methods which were developing in the universities, in business and in other walks of life.

Finally, the Committee had serious criticisms of personnel management. Career planning was rare, civil servants were moved too frequently between unrelated jobs and there was insufficient encouragement and reward for individual initiative and performance.

Chapter 1 concluded by saying that the Committee had sought to devise a form of management for the Civil Service which would insure that it was better run and able to generate its own self-criticism and forward drive. One of the main troubles of the Service had been that, in achieving immunity from political intervention, a system had been evolved which until recently had been virtually immune from outside pressures for change. 'Since it was not immune from inside resistance to change, inertia was perhaps predictable.'[34]

After discussing the tasks of the modern Civil Service, recruitment and the class structure, the promotion of efficiency, the central management of the Service and relationships with the community, Fulton made 158 recommendations. The most important of these were:

1. A classless service should be created. The Committee recommended the abolition of all occupational classes and their replacement by a unified pay structure based on job evaluation (that is, the relative value of every job in the Civil Service should be analysed and fitted into about twenty pay grades).

2. Administrators should specialize, particularly in their early years of service, in specific subjects; for example, in economic and financial affairs or in social affairs. The basic principle of career management should be progressive development within a specialism. In the recruitment of graduates for administrative work the relevance of their university studies to their future work should be an important criterion. Those graduates appointed without relevant qualifications should be required to take a special training course.

3. Specialists should be allowed to carry more responsibility and the obstacles preventing them from reaching the top should be removed.

4. A Civil Service College should be created to provide training in administration for specialists, post-entry training for graduates recruited for administrative work, courses for the best school leavers, post-experience courses in management and in particular management techniques.

5. Movement in and out of the Service should be facilitated by arrangements for transfer, temporary appointment and transferable pensions.

6. The principles of accountable management should be applied to the Service; that is, individual managers should be held responsible for their performance, measured as objectively as possible.

7. Each department should have a management services unit capable of carrying out efficiency audits involving all aspects of the department's work at all levels.

8. Departments should have planning and research units with responsibility for long-term policy planning. These units should be headed by Senior Policy Advisers who would have direct and unrestricted access to the Minister.

9. The central management of the Service should be made the responsibility of a new department, the Civil Service Department, which should absorb the functions of the Pay and Management side of the Treasury and those of the Civil Service Commission. Its official head should be designated Head of the Home Civil Service.

10. The government should set up an inquiry to make recommendations for getting rid of unnecessary secrecy.

THE DEBATE ON THE FULTON REPORT

The report had a generally poor reception, though a few journals supported it wholeheartedly. Predictably in the *New Statesman* Roger Opie wrote 'implement at once!' and Dr Thomas Balogh greeted 'The End of the Amateur'.[35] The *Daily Telegraph* thought that it would 'almost certainly become a landmark on the road to a regenerated Britain'.[36] The *Guardian* thought that Dr Hunt's management studies could have destroyed the myth of the Administrative Class.[37] The *Evening Standard* headline was 'Civil Service Amateurs Blasted by Fulton' – 'The Civil Service, product of an obsolete nineteenth-century philosophy, is run with the most damaging consequences for the nation by a small elite of gifted amateurs never properly trained for their jobs.'[38]

Criticism of the report fell into four main categories. First, and most frequently expressed, the charge of amateurism was thought intemperate and unfair. Secondly, the Committee was thought to have had the wrong terms of reference: it should have tackled such fundamental questions as the machinery of government and what functions and activities were appropriate to departments, rather than such second-order questions as the management of departments and the career structure of civil servants. Thirdly, it had naïvely assumed that the practices of business management could be applied to the Civil Service and failed to understand the problems unique to public administration. Fourthly, it dressed up a number of simple improvements – many of which the Treasury had in hand anyway – as radical reforms.

In addition, there were suggestions that it was all a plot, stage-

managed by Mr Wilson and starring Dr Hunt, who had somehow
written the report while the rest of the Committee were looking
the other way: 'How Dr Hunt – aided and abetted by Harold
Wilson – took over Fulton' ... 'the product of one man's
totally-geared energies'.[39]

The passages which caused all the excitement about amateurism read fairly mildly. On its first page the report referred to 'the
tradition of the "all-rounder" as he has been called by his
champions, or "amateur" as he as been called by his critics' and
there was one further reference to 'the philosophy of the amateur
(or "generalist", or "all-rounder")'. Sir James Dunnett, one of
the Permanent Secretaries on the Committee, said later in a
lecture on the report that the first of these references 'seems to me
to be a fair statement of fact'.[40] At the time, these references were
said to be close to rudeness, abrasive, undiscriminating, notorious,
sweeping ('again and again the epithet of amateurism is hurled at
the Service,' wrote William Robson),[41] and to show the substitu-
tion of slogans for thought.

Some observers thought the report not at all radical: Lord
Helsby, a former head of the Civil Service, thought it 'natural
that the Committee should be tempted to divert attention from
the relative modesty of its proposals by presenting its criticisms in
a somewhat ferocious way'.[42] Mr Eric Hobsbawm wrote it off
as a 'compendium of commonplaces of the 1960s'.[43] Mr F. A.
Bishop, a former Permanent Secretary, wrote that it was for the
most part neither controversial nor original and that it merely
assisted trends already in evolution.[44]

Fulton's new breed of professional managers were seen in a
fairly jaundiced light. In the *Daily Telegraph* Lord Redcliffe-Maud
wrote 'give me the first-class man in *any* honours school, provided
he has character as well,'[45] while in the *Daily Express* Wilfred
Sendall wanted to be 'saved from the experts': 'The Fulton
Report . . . could fortify the present trend towards the production
of experts as against men of all-round wisdom. I would far rather
be ruled by men who were familiar with the tragedies of Sopho-
cles, who had a grounding in the wisdom of Socrates and Plato
and then topped it up by a wide reading of Shakespeare, Hobbes,
Locke and Stuart Mill, than by one who was an expert electronics

engineer or a first-class nuclear physicist. By acquiring all this expertise in the most modern sciences, a man is bound to cut himself off from the wisdom of the ages.'[46]

In the debate in the House of Lords which soon followed the publication of the report, their Lordships concentrated almost exclusively upon the criticisms of amateurism in the Administrative Class.[47] These criticisms were greeted with 'shame and outrage' (Lord Robbins); they had the 'wrong tone' (Lord Brooke of Cumnor); they were 'untrue and unfair' (Lord Plowden). Lord Ritchie Calder warned against the tyranny of experts and Lord Helsby pointed out that technical competence was no substitute for true outstanding ability; Lord Trevelyan was afraid of levelling down and thought that the Committee's analysis of selection procedures was Marxist. The British Civil Service was widely praised as the best in the world by their Lordships and many of them reminisced about its work during the war. Lord Sinclair of Cleeve took comfort in the belief that the elite which was in the past drawn in the main from the Administrative Class would still come to the top. The Lord Bishop of Leicester welcomed the provision of the text of the Northcote–Trevelyan report in the Fulton Report and paid tribute to the way in which the Registrar-General's department handled the regular returns of weddings made by churches. The distinguished former civil servants who took part in the debate were congratulated, and congratulated each other, on the excellence of their speeches, and Lord Brooke of Cumnor summed up the outstanding feature of the debate as 'its unequivocal assertion of the ultimate value of fineness of mind and the exposure of iconoclasm dressed up as advanced thinking'.

Interestingly, Lord Arran (a former Senior Executive Officer), apparently the only peer who had had experience of Civil Service other than as a member of the Administrative Class, spoke in favour of the report, particularly welcoming the abolition of the classes and the removal of snobbery based on grade. He recalled that a Principal talking to an S.E.O. was an unparalleled experience in patronising insult and asked their Lordships if they know what it was like 'to be what's called below the salt'. He referred to the purely arbitrary grading system whereby a man from

Winchester became 'Admin' and above 'the trogs' of the Executive Class.

Lord Shackleton, the newly appointed Minister for the Civil Service Department, in a defensive speech, confessed that he was unhappy with some aspects of the report but commended the Management Consultancy Group's Volume II to the House as 'far and away a more important background document. Indeed, in some ways it is really more important than Part 1 . . . in Part 2 noble Lords will find many of the answers as to reasons for particular recommendations.'

Compared to the House of Lords debate (which had roused a weight of opinion not seen in the House since the debate on the British Museum, according to Lord Shackleton) the Commons debate[48] four months later was very uneventful. The Prime Minister, who had earlier accepted the Fulton recommendations for the abolition of the classes, the setting-up of a Civil Service Department and a new Civil Service College, announced in the debate that the Fulton recommendation that preference should be given to graduates with relevant degrees was not to be accepted. This was generally greeted with approval. Mr Heath accepted what he saw as a recommendation to divide the Service into administrators trained in management on one hand and specialists on the other. He was worried that the abolition of the Administrative Class might discourage the best brains from coming into the Service and favoured a special list of 'high flyers' who would receive especially rapid promotion. He attributed the lack of success of some businessmen in government to the fact that they had to hold their own with men of great intellectual calibre. The Prime Minister suggested that the real problem was that businessmen were not sufficiently articulate. Most other speakers welcomed the report but many regretted the critical tone of Volume 1.

A SOCIAL SURVEY AND THE DAVIES REPORT

The last of the special studies commissioned by the Committee, the Social Survey of the Civil Service by Dr A. H. Halsey, head of the Department of Social and Administrative Studies at Oxford, and Mr I. M. Crewe of the University of Lancaster, was published in September 1969.[49] This survey was based upon nearly 5,000 replies to questionnaires. It found that until very recently the Administrative Class had tended to be more, rather than less, socially exclusive, with an increasing proportion of its direct entrants coming from the middle classes and having been to public schools. No fewer than 85 per cent of those directly recruited between 1961 and 1965 were middle class in background (as compared with 64 per cent in 1951–5) in a period when the universities were drawing an increasing proportion of their students from working-class backgrounds. The Survey also found that 'the type of subject studied at university by graduate recruits to the Administrative Class is remarkable when compared with foreign experience and with British business and professions'.[50] No less than 71 per cent had arts degrees, mainly in history and classics, in marked contrast to their equivalents in the U.S. government service, who mostly had degrees in science or social studies, and in France, where administrators were trained in economics, law, public administration, finance and statistics. Some 73 per cent of direct entrant Administrators in 1961–6 had been to Oxford or Cambridge – nearly the same as the immediate post-war period and considerably higher than during the war. In contrast, the proportion of all students graduating from Oxbridge had declined from 22 per cent before the war to 14 per cent in the early sixties. The survey also found a marked decline in the quality of recruits to the Administrative Class (as measured by class of degree). The authors of the survey concluded that 'there is reasonable ground for questioning the effectiveness of Civil Service recruitment'.

On the day this 'damning survey'[51] was published, the Civil Service Department chose to publish a report on the interview system by which most direct-entrant administrators are selected, made by a Committee under the chairmanship of Mr J. G. W. Davies, an assistant to the Governor of the Bank of England.[52] The Davies Report said that the selection system was one to which the public service could point with pride; that there had been a distinct and progressive change in the type of candidate entering the competition since 1964; that there was no evidence of bias in the system and that there was no fundamental weakness in it. It said that the selection board provided equality of opportunity and maintained an appropriate balance between the personal and intellectual qualities which were needed in the Administrative Class. The *Financial Times* reported that 'senior civil servants are clearly delighted and relieved that the Davies Report has come down so overwhelmingly in favour of the present selection system'.[53]

Lord Balogh struck back at the Davies Report a year later.[54] 'How,' he asked 'could an employee of The Old Lady, sitting in the innermost nook of the old boy network, impartially adjudicate whether an interview (with the old boy network) would or would not yield the happiest of results? By condemning it, he would condemn himself.' Lord Balogh considered that the gradual encroachment of the interview system (as against written examinations) was weighing the chances in favour of the self-confident, 'outward-going' man and in favour of upper-class origin against academic quality. 'The violence of the reaction to the critical Fulton report shows the fear of the vested interests menaced.'

THE FULTON REPORT: A REVIEW

At first reading, the imperfections of the Fulton Report obscure the value and significance of the reforms it proposed. The remarks on the amateurism of the Administrative Class opened the report on a sour note and gave the defenders of the *status quo* an opportunity to cry injustice and so obscure much more important criticisms. It failed to give adequate recognition to the very real achievements of the Service in coping with a vast expansion of the tasks of government. It criticized the characteristics and attitudes of the higher Civil Service without adequately recognizing the extent to which they had been shaped by the concept of Ministerial accountability and by the conventions of Ministerial, Cabinet and Parliamentary practice. Much of it was written in a hortatory and superficial style which rested heavily on the proclamation of principles for which very little supporting discussion was provided. Such principles as 'accountable management', 'career specialization', 'professionalism' were not adequately discussed or defined. Many of its ideas were taken from the Management Consultancy Group's report, but in the translation from one report to another these ideas often suffered substantial distortion. For example, changes which the Consultancy Group suggested should be the subject of research programmes (new forms of organization, new management controls, performance auditing) were promulgated by the Committee as full-blown principles of management without any further evidence or deeper discussion. The Consultancy Group's proposed management planning units became Fulton's policy planning groups in which a planning function and a Ministerial cabinet were confused; the Consultancy Group's job evaluation scheme was mixed up with 'end results analysis'; the Consultancy Group's classless service was overlain by highly obscure occupational groups.

Perhaps more important, the Fulton Committee missed two areas of inquiry which were central to its field of interest. First, it made no reference to the audit of departmental efficiency other than that carried out by departments themselves or by the proposed Civil Service Department. Secondly, it hardly touched upon departmental systems of budgeting and expenditure control. This topic, one of fundamental importance to the modernization of government, was dismissed in one gnomic half-line: 'public spending means public control.'[55]

In sum, the Fulton Committee bore out most of the accusations levelled at the higher Civil Service by its critics in the preceding thirty years. It did, however, present its analysis and its proposals for change in a self-defeating way. If implementation was to succeed it had to have some support among the administrators in command at the time, yet its tone and style alienated them from the outset. Rapid and effective implementation also depended on the clear and precise specification of a programme of change, yet the Committee left confusion surrounding most of its proposals. It did, however, spot most of the cracks, pressure points and distortions which had appeared in the management systems of the Civil Service and it gave the initial impetus to a number of overdue reforms which may eventually substantially change the practice of management in British government.

THE IMPLEMENTATION OF FULTON

Progress in the implementation of the recommendations of the Fulton Report in the period 1968–72 cannot be considered in isolation from all the other developments which have taken place and which are in prospect as a result of the change of government in 1970. These are discussed in later chapters and at this stage it is relevant only to consider the developments arising from Fulton's main proposals.

The Civil Service Department came into existence on 1 November 1968 It took over the activities, the management and the staffs of the Civil Service Commission and the Pay and Management Divisions of the Treasury. The Department was headed by Sir William Armstrong, a Civil Servant of outstanding ability and a radical turn of mind, who soon made a very favourable impression with his informal and approachable style and his elucidation of the tasks that the Department faced.

On the whole, and considering the new burdens placed upon the Department by change of government in 1970, reasonable progress has been made on the implementation of some of the Fulton Committee's recommendations.

On 1 January 1971 the Clerical, Executive and Administrative Classes were merged into a single 'vertical' structure, the Administration Group. It is proposed that other classes (such as Economists and Statisticians) will be associated with this group in a 'General Category'. This group accounts for 40 per cent of the total employment of the non-industrial Civil Service. In March 1971 a scheme was unveiled for producing a single 'horizontal' structure for the 650 higher Civil Servants at the level of Under Secretary and above. This scheme was the second choice of the Civil Service Department team (of officials and management consultants) which carried out the feasibility study. Their first choice was one based on two linked grading systems – one for 'direct' executive and technical management posts, the other for 'policy and headquarters management'. The joint committee of staff and official representatives charged with supervising the work felt, however, that the recommended scheme was too similar to the existing structure and rejected it. At the time of writing it was expected that arrangements for a vertical merger of the Scientific Class and the Works Group with their supporting technical classes (into a 'Science Category' and a 'General Professional Category') would soon be announced. We shall see from Chapter 7 that these arrangements (which correspond to the Treasury's recommendations to the Fulton Committee) do not yet open up the higher Civil Service to specialists and that this depends upon further horizontal mergers at levels lower than Under Secretary: a feasibility study on producing a unified structure down to the level of Principal is being undertaken at the time of writing.

The Assistant Principal grade is to be replaced by a new grade of Administration Trainee. Every year about 175 new graduates and 125 inside candidates who joined the Service as school leavers will compete for entry to this training grade. The most able of these trainees will then be marked out for accelerated promotion, and after two to three years in a second training grade, during which they will take a long advanced course, they will be promoted to the Principal grade (after a total service of four to five years, as Assistant Principals were). These arrangements are ostensibly a substantial improvement, but they could represent the Treasury's proposals for 'starring', revived under a new guise. If the selection criteria are such that those chosen for accelerated promotion turn out to be arts graduates of the kind who have been so successful in the past, then the Fulton Committee's aims will not have been met. Another weakness in this arrangement is that, in advance of a merger of the specialist categories with the Administration Group, it will create an accelerated promotion stream from which specialists are excluded: that is, the bright young generalist will be given such an early lead that he is unlikely to be overtaken by the bright young specialist.

Training has been greatly expanded since Fulton reported and a Civil Service College was opened in April 1969. Eventually it will have a capacity of 800 places in three centres. The prime training need is for programmes to meet the requirements of departments for new management specialisms: cost accounting and control, planning and programming, management consultancy, advanced personnel work. These are the specialisms for which the members of the former Executive Class will have to be trained. Increasingly the jobs formerly reserved to them will be opened up to those who were confined to the specialist classes – accountants, engineers social scientists. In addition, they will now have to compete for many of the top posts which were formerly exclusively theirs with graduate entrants keen to gain experience of executive management. A high-priority requirement is therefore a programme for turning those who entered the Service straight from school into technically qualified managers.

A number of improvements have been proposed for the personnel management of the Service – in the areas of career development and staff appraisal for example – but Fulton's ideas for 'occupational categories' and 'administrative specialization' have proved very difficult to disentangle. These problems are dealt with in Chapter 8.

A start has been made on conducting experiments into management accountability and on new planning systems. These are described in later chapters. These experiments were given a new urgency by the change of government in 1970. A reported feature of the 'new style of government' espoused by the incoming administration was a determination to reduce Civil Service employment[56] not only by terminating some functions of government (the Land Commission, the National Agricultural Advisory Service) but by the widespread application of 'businesslike' methods of government. These methods appear to relate to the creation of 'giant' departments, to new forms of resource planning (see Chapter 4); securing accountability by 'hiving off' pieces of departments and establishing 'agencies' within them (see chapter 6); and the employment of a team of businessmen to study particular management problems.

The Fulton Committee set the scene for the adoption of some useful management practices in central government. Many of these would probably have had to have been adopted ultimately, as departments grew in spending and manpower, took on increasingly complex technical projects and merged into today's conglomerate giants. Its report can be criticized for an insensitive presentation, for overemphasizing some weaknesses in the management of the Civil service and for ignoring others. It did perform an important service, however, in looking at public administration as management in a political dimension and thereby paving the way for experiment and inquiry into new managerial structures and techniques, the most important of which are discussed in the following chapters.

CHAPTER 3

Organization

THIS chapter touches briefly on the development of the theory of organization. It goes on to consider the conventions of the organization of government departments and the observations upon them made by the Fulton Committee. It concludes by discussing the forces at work for change in departmental forms of organization and likely developments in the future.

THE THEORISTS

Max Weber, in his seminal work on 'economic sociology',[1] written at the turn of the century, considered the types of authority in society: 'traditional' in feudal communities; 'charismatic' in religious and political communities; 'legal' in public and business administration. He developed a partly descriptive, partly idealized model of the administrative staff or 'bureaucracy' which had grown up in support of legal authority. Weber considered that a purely bureaucratic form of organization was the most efficient and rational means of 'carrying out imperative control over human beings',[2] being precise, stable, disciplined, reliable and applicable to all kinds of administration. 'Its development is, to take the most striking case, the most crucial phenomenon of the modern Western state.'[3]

The main features of organization characterized by Weber as bureaucratic were:

1. 'A continuous organization of official functions bound by rules' and the subjection of officials to strict discipline and control over their actions.

2. The specification of the obligations and authority of each position established as a result of a systematic division of labour.

3. The arrangement of positions in a hierarchy, with each official responsible for his subordinate's actions and in turn responsible to his superior.

4. The occupation of each position by trained officials on a free contractual relationship, typically appointed after passing qualifying examinations and remunerated by fixed salaries and pension rights.

5. The provision of careers for officials, with promotion based on seniority or achievement or both.[4]

Weber's description of bureaucracies, though recognized as an important attempt to establish a set of principles of organization, was later criticized[5] as a mixture of definition and hypothesis and a concept of the ideal which failed to take account of the conflicts inherent in bureaucracies (such as those arising from the responsibility of a superior for the actions of his subordinates). It also implied that superiors always possessed a technical competence superior to that of their subordinates and that the formal lines of authority and responsibility were the only human relationships that existed in an organization.

Many of Weber's ideas reappeared in the writing of the classical or 'scientific management' school of organization, among whose leading proponents were Fayol,[6] Taylor,[7] Graicunas,[8] Mooney and Reiley,[9] Webster Robinson[10] and Gulick and Urwick.[11] These ideas have collectively been called 'machine theory' because of their insistence that an organization could be constructed according to a set of impersonal rules. A significant feature of the classical school was that they were concerned to describe organizational forms based on principles 'which would govern arrangements for human associations of any kind'.* The classical principles of organization, as codified by Urwick,[12] were:

1. All organizations are the expression of a purpose – The Principle of the Objective.

2. Formal authority and responsibility must be co-terminous and co-equal – The Principle of Correspondence.

3. The responsibility of a higher authority for the acts of its subordinates is absolute – The Principle of Responsibility.

*Urwick later called these principles 'flexible guidelines'.

4. There must be a clear line of formal authority running from top to bottom of the organization – The Scalar Principle.

5. No superior can supervise directly the work of more than five or six subordinates whose work interlocks – The Principle of the Span of Control.

6. The work of every person in the organization should be confined as far as possible to the performance of a single leading function – The Principle of Specialization.

7. The final objective of all organization is smooth and effective co-ordination – The Principle of Co-ordination.

8. Every position in the organization should be clearly prescribed in writing – The Principle of Definition.

The classicists took the view that the tasks that had to be carried out by an enterprise in order to achieve its objectives should be clearly allocated to organizational units and that within those units individual jobs should be specified in great detail. The whole structure should be held together by the delegation of authority from the chief executive at the top of the organization to his immediate subordinates and from them to their subordinates and so on down the hierarchy and by equal ties of responsibility which bound each subordinate to his superior. Urwick, in particular, dwelt upon the supreme authority of the man at the top and his absolute responsibility for the actions of his subordinates; he placed heavy emphasis upon the attributes of leadership and saw the leader as one 'who can focus and thereby magnify the wills of all associated with him . . . so that his will and theirs are one'.[13] Carried to their ultimate development, classical organization structures progressively divided the activities of the enterprise into specialisms so narrow that only the leader could view and comprehend the operation of the organization as a whole. Among some people who were heavily influenced by the ideas of the classical school, descriptions of the role and characteristics of the leader tended to take on strong inspirational and mystical overtones.

A classical organization is highly authoritarian in concept, implying in its extreme forms the close control of the actions of subordinates by their superiors; standardized roles and tasks; the detailed specification of standards of performance; motivation by performance-related payments and disciplinary action; uniform practices and procedures – all ultimately directed and controlled by an omniscient figure at the top.

It was not long before the principles of the classical school, 'a collection of ambiguous and mutually contradictory proverbs',[14] in the view of one of its foremost critics, H. A. Simon, came under such severe attack as to be discredited for the time being, at least in academic circles. They were shown to be heavily influenced by military models; to be derived from a narrow range of experience mostly in long-established heavy industries rather than from systematic research in a variety of industries; to be markedly over-simplified, failing to take account of the complexity and fluidity of relationships and roles within an organization of any size; to fail to take account of the needs for organizations to adjust to their changing environments and, particularly, to fail to recognize that organizations are social institutions whose members have values, aspirations, needs and personal relationships which cannot be defined or prescribed by the imposition of a set of rules by superior authority. Nevertheless, most organizations in business and government are still designed or maintained on classical lines and most managers and administrators, wittingly or not, would describe a 'good' or efficient organization in terms not unlike Urwick's principles. They would, perhaps, temper Fayol's 'for social order to prevail in a concern there must . . . be an appointed place for every employee and every employee "be in his appointed place" ',[15] with some lip service to the idea of 'communication' with the staff, or even a modicum of 'participation', but the old ideas of tight central control, specialization, formal specification of authority and responsibility and detailed job descriptions (Mooney: 'The exact definition of every job . . . is justified by all practical experience') would still generally be thought to be the right ideas.

The persistent influence of classical theory has been attributed[16] to a number of its features. First, it is pro-management; that is, managers like the idea of authoritarian, decisive leadership and do not take to later concepts which emphasize consultation with subordinates and even their participation in decision-making. In addition, the principles of classical theory are simple and direct and free of sociological jargon; they are prescriptive and tell the manager how to behave; they are impersonal, conveniently considering people as objects to be manipulated; they provide a dogma which gives the manager a sense of destiny and purpose; they enable conflicts to be attributed to subordinates who are not behaving 'correctly'.

The simple, prescriptive and orderly world of the classicists came under attack from two directions: from those who examined organizations as social institutions (the 'Human Relations School') and those who examined their machinery for sensing, adapting to, and controlling change (the 'Systems School').

The foundations of the human relations school was laid by the Hawthorne studies of the late 1920s (Mayo, Roethlisberger and Dickson[17]) which showed that the motivation to work and efficiency and productivity were primarily determined by social relationships between workers, between informal worker groups and between workers and their bosses. Mayo[18] concluded that man is basically motivated by social needs, and finds meaning in his work mainly through social relationships with his fellow workers, to whose attitudes he is more responsive than to the direction, control and incentives operated by management.

These and further studies of people at work led to the concept of the informal organization: that is, the relationships formed between groups of individuals arising from their need to express common loyalties and to defend common interests. This informal organization was contrasted with the formal arrangement of relationships prescribed by those in authority as necessary for the achievement of group tasks and meeting the objectives of the enterprise. The informal organization, supported by its communications 'grape-vine' had the power to oppose authority and frustrate the demands of those formally in command if, as frequently happened, the objectives of the group and those of the enterprise conflicted. A large number of research studies (for example Whyte,[19] Walker and Guest,[20] Seashore[21]) underlined the crucial significance of group cohesiveness and the fulfilment of social needs as a determinant of organizational 'health'. Chris Argyris[22] drew attention to the tendency for organizations structured on rigidly classical lines to frustrate the development of individuals by requiring them to adopt passive, dependent roles and to lead them to react by forming defensive informal groups. The narrow specialization inherent in classical models, reinforced by rewards and controls, caused the individual to focus exclusively on his specified tasks rather than to relate his activities to those of the organization as a whole. Argyris advocated the adoption of organizational arrangements which would allow the individual to develop and exploit his abilities and to make the fullest possible contribution to the plans and decisions that affect him.

Rensis Likert[23] and others demonstrated the increases in productivity and the improvement in employee morale that could be gained by the adoption of a style and structure which encouraged employee participation, in which controls were relaxed, decision-making was delegated as far down the line as possible and the supervisor concentrated less on agitating for increased production and more on being a support to the group he led. Likert advocated organizations arranged as systems of overlapping groups connected by managers who each belonged to a higher and a lower group and thus acted as 'linking pins'. The linking individuals could transmit corporate aims, policies and objectives downwards and the needs, aims and attitudes of the staff upwards through the organizational levels. Such a manager operated with his group on the 'interaction-influence' principle: sharing responsibility, aiming at decisions by concensus, setting objectives after mutual discussion and agreement.

The writers of the human relations school were not primarily concerned to prescribe ideal forms of organizational structure, as the classicists were. Their focus was upon the small group in the working situation and the need to relate the loyalties, aspirations and concerns of such a group to the formal aims and objectives and the authority system of the enterprise as a whole. Nevertheless, it is possible to draw structural implications from their work. These are that the 'tall' hierarchical form and the closely defined authorities and responsibilities of the classical organization could often with advantage be replaced by fewer management levels and wider spans of control arising from greater delegation; that more loosely specified jobs would leave room for the personal development of the job holder and enable him to define his job by interaction with fellow members of his group; that the binding force should be commitment to, and identification with, the aims of the enterprise rather than formally imposed ties of responsibility, sanction and obligation.

Both the classical and the human relations schools can legitimately be criticized for taking too narrow a view of the functioning of organizations. The criteria of success that the classical school applied to an organization were in terms of production: volume of output, productivity, profit; those applied by the human relations school were in terms of employee satisfaction: morale, job satisfaction, attitudes to the boss. These sets of criteria were often unrelated, and they also failed to take any account of the pressures and constraints imposed upon the organization by its external environment.

The systems approach to organization takes from work in the physical sciences (for instance by von Bertalanffy[24]) the concept of the living system surviving in its environment by a process of sensing, and adapting to, external changes and thus continually controlling and adjusting its internal economy in pursuit of a state of equilibrium. Thus Simon[25] and March and Simon[26] viewed the organization as a living, organic system attempting to survive by making the correct responses both to the movements in its economic and political environment and to the changing relationships in its internal sub-systems. If the enterprise was to survive and grow it had to have a mechanism for testing the 'real properties' of the field in which it existed and for enabling it to take action to secure itself against environmental pressures. It had also to have mechanisms for attaining internal balance – that is for ensuring a common identity of purpose among its members and for maintaining the stability and continuity of the processes of policy and decision-making.

A related concept evolved at the Tavistock Institute in London in the course of studies of operations in the coal-mining industry in Britain and the textile industry in India. These experiments (by Trist and Bamforth[27] and Rice[28]) showed that, from an analysis of the demands and constraints implied by a changing technology and of the human need for commitment to a task group, forms of worker-group organization could be developed which could achieve significant improvements in morale, job satisfaction and productivity. The Tavistock 'model' embodied the idea of a socio-technical system in which technology (the task, the equipment, the operating schedule) and social relationships mutually interacted to determine the organizational form appropriate to the situation, at least at the supervisor/operative level. This idea was developed into the 'open-system' concept (Rice,[29] Emery and Trist,[30] Katz and Kahn[31]) by taking into account the organizational pressures and constraints of the external environment. The open-system view of an organization sees it as importing energy from its environment, transforming this energy into a product, exporting that product into the environment and re-energizing itself from environmental sources. This interaction with the environment requires the organization continually to adapt to the stresses caused by environmental change. This in turn requires the organization to have the capability to grow, to elaborate some activities and diminish others, integrate some functions and differentiate others according to its perception of the information streaming back from its environment.

A further significant development arose in Britain from investigations of the organizational effects of different industrial environments. Tom Burns[32] and Burns and Stalker[33] concluded from studies in the textile and electronics industries that management style and structure could be summarized at two extremes. At one extreme, there was the 'mechanistic' in which tasks were broken down into narrow specialisms, roles were precisely defined, operations were governed by instructions issued down the command hierarchy and only the head of the firm was in a position to know everything that was going on (that is, the ideal organization of the classicists). The mechanistic form of organization appeared to work well in enterprises which were operating under relatively stable conditions. At the other extreme there was the 'organic' form of organization in which jobs lost much of their formal definition, duties and powers had continually to be re-defined by interaction between co-workers, the hierarchy was loosely defined, each member of the group had to perform his tasks in the light of knowledge of the firm's objectives which was not confined to the chief executive alone. The indications were that the organic form appeared to be best adapted to conditions of rapid technological change and an unstable environment.

Joan Woodward,[34] in a study of a hundred manufacturing companies, found that the production process had a marked organizational influence: successful firms engaged on unit production had one dominant organizational form, those on batch (assembly-line) production had another and those on process (or flow) production had yet another. She concluded that there was an organization structure suitable to each type of production: for instance, success in batch production was associated with mechanistic forms of organization, while in process production these forms and conventions were associated with failure; success in unit production was associated with wide spans of control and relatively few levels of management. Woodward concluded that the classical principles still taught in management schools appeared to apply primarily to businesses in batch production and that there was no relationship between business success and the classical conventions of 'sound' organizational structure. Later research into the Woodward thesis confirmed its application to small firms and those levels of management closely concerned with shop floor processes but indicated that at the higher levels of administration in large firms the influence of technology upon organizational form tended to disappear.[35]

In recent years, studies of organization have developed towards the description and typification of sub-systems and structures within the enterprise. Katz and Kahn[36] have characterized the sub-structures of the firm as production and technical, concerned to manage themselves by regulation, definition and rational analysis of the process; maintenance, concerned to establish rules and precedents and formalize all aspects of behaviour; boundary, concerned with influencing the outside world in such matters as the procurement of materials and the disposal of products; adaptive, concerned to help the organization adjust to change through planning and research. Each of these sub-systems call for different organizational arrangements. Lawrence and

Lorsch[37] and Morse and Lorsch[38] have carried the analysis of the internal characteristics and the environments of different functional units in an enterprise to the point of evolving a 'contingency theory' concerned to describe 'the fit between task, organization and people': 'the appropriate pattern of organization is contingent on the nature of the work to be done and the particular needs of the people involved.' It is inevitable in complex organizations that different functions and activities (such as sales, production, research, accounting) will develop different organization structures, procedures, conventions, attitudes and social systems: they will show differentiation. Contingency theory indicates that successful organizations are those that can find effective devices for integrating appropriately differentiated functional departments. Integrating or mediating devices can be units or committees, or individual integrators of the appropriate status and influence using methods of conflict-resolution appropriate to the situation, or they can be communications or reporting arrangements or consultative procedures.

STAFF AND PROJECT GROUPS

Two features of increasing significance in the development of large organizations are the proliferation of groups of specialist 'functional' staff and the development of arrangements for managing projects or programmes which conflict with hierarchical arrangements of authority.

The concept of line and staff was originally a product of the classical school. 'Line management' describes the main chain of command, the hierarchy of managers in direct superior/subordinate relationship from the chief executive to the lowest level of supervision. 'Staff' describes individuals or units who either provide a service to line management or exercise 'functional' or technical authority over it in a prescribed field. A service staff, such as market researchers or policy planners, exist to provide assistance and advice to line managers. A functional staff, such as a central legal, accounting or personnel group, usually has mandatory authority or the power of veto in its field and can require line managers to comply with the standards, policies and procedures that it has laid down. Confusion is frequently caused by a failure to clarify the respective roles of service and functional staffs or to recognize that functional authority is just as binding on the manager as the authority he recognizes as emanating from his line superior.

As the complexity of the internal processes of the firm or of its environment increases the need arises for the creation of centres of specialist expertise. At a fairly low level of development a business requires an accounting specialist; as it grows it requires specialists in legal/secretarial work, personnel, productivity, planning and market research. The proliferation of staff groups is a feature of the large corporation, particularly if it is highly diversified. Such a corporation might have corporate staff groups for finance, marketing, planning, legal affairs, efficiency services, personnel, purchasing, engineering, research, planning and community relations. Many such groups have functional authority. A great deal of tension and internal litigation is created by this limitation of the freedom of action of line managers, who are often expected to be accountable for results but who are subjected to progressively increasing control by corporate staffs over a wide area of their responsibilities.

It is difficult to handle complex multi-functional projects in a hierarchical structure (particularly one based on the separation of specialists from line management) because no one manager can be held responsible for managing them or can see the total project in perspective; because divisions are jealous of their prerogatives and fight to maintain their status and receive recognition for their specialisms (inter-divisional conflicts have to be referred up to top management for resolution); and because units organized to perform repetitive tasks often lack the flexibility to cope with rapidly changing project needs.[39] An increasingly common organizational solution to this problem is to set up a project team of members seconded from their parent units to work for a project manager for the duration of the project. Such an arrangement is typically used where there is a specific objective (such as launching a new product, designing and installing new equipment, carrying out an engineering or construction project, undertaking an acquisition or diversification); where there is a time limit; and where the problem is so complex as to require the assignment of a wider range of skills than can be provided from any one unit. Where a number of project groups co-exist with the conventional structure of divisions and branches, a matrix organization results, so called because the teams are superimposed in a horizontal management structure upon the vertical departmental structure. Matrix organization has long been common in businesses which undertake series of assignments calling for the deployment of different skills for varying periods of time (for instance in the fields of contract engineering, management consultancy), but in recent years it has become popular in industry for dealing with such problems as new product planning and research and development. Recently publicized examples of its use on a very large scale have been in NASA (the Apollo programmes) and the Department of Defense (the Polaris project) in the United States.

As Donald Schon has pointed out, in matrix organizations 'most of the standard rules of management go down the drain'[40] and people accustomed to operating in conventional organization structures often find the adjustment to life in such organizations extremely difficult. For example, a member of a project team is under the direct authority of the project leader but still 'belongs' to his department for his long-term personal development. Thus he has at least two bosses and may have more if he works part time on a number of projects. The project leader has a highly responsible and very exposed position for a limited period and then may revert to a relatively lowly position in his parent department on the conclusion of the project. He is usually under great pressure to produce a specified result against a deadline and has to secure the commitment to his objectives of team members who may be of equal or superior status, who are specialists in their fields and who may feel they represent the powerful line departments to which they still owe allegiance. Argyris,[41] in a study of matrix organizations, observed that they oppose the established power structure by breaking down the monopolies of departments; that they call for a participative management style which conflicts with, and may eventually eliminate, established superior–

subordinate relationships; and that the dual allegiances they require is a fruitful ground for inter-group tension and conflict. He sees the organization of the future as combinations of project teams and conventional hierarchies; the future executive must be able to decide the conditions appropriate to each form and will 'need to become skilful in several different kinds of leadership styles, each of which is consistent with a particular form'.[42]

THE ORGANIZATION OF GOVERNMENT DEPARTMENTS

Government departments are headed by Permanent Secretaries and reporting to them are, in some departments, Second Permanent Secretaries, but more usually Deputy Secretaries. Before the establishment of the modern conglomerate or giant department the general arrangement was that a department had four to six Deputy Secretaries, and this is still the case in the smaller departments (such as Education, Home Office, Employment, Agriculture). Giant departments (such as Environment, Health and Social Security, Trade and Industry, Defence) have a dozen or more Deputy Secretaries. Some departments have top specialist posts (for instance economic, legal, scientific advisers) at or around Deputy Secretary level.

All departments have three 'corporate staff' groups. The first is the Minister's private office, headed by the Minister's Private Secretary, which provides a secretariat through which briefs, speeches and answers to Parliamentary questions are routed to and from departmental managers. The two other staff groups have functional authority over operating divisions and are headed by Under Secretaries, who report direct to the Permanent Secretary. The first of these is the Establishments and Organization Division (the activities of which are described in Chapter 8), concerned with controlling the numbers employed in the department; employment and welfare matters; training; relations with staff associations; the provision of office equipment and services and usually with efficiency ('Organization and Methods') studies and data-processing. The second is the Finance Division, usually divided into a policy branch, under an Assistant Secretary concerned with the preparation of annual estimates and five-year public expenditure forecasts, sanctioning and controlling expenditure and dealing with the Treasury on financial procedures and major cases; and an accounts branch, under a senior member of the executive grades, concerned with keeping books of account and records of financial transactions and liaising with the auditors. Both of these divisions operate according to regulations and procedures laid down by central functional departments – in the establishments and organization field by the Civil Service Department and in the financial field by the Treasury.

Deputy Secretaries co-ordinate and generally oversee the work of Under Secretaries, or their equivalents, who head the major units of organization. These units (which may be called divisions or departments) deal with a major aspect of the department's business (for example in the Home Office: Fire, Police, Criminal, Children, Prisons, Probation, etc.; in Agriculture: Horticulture, Animal Health, Economic Policy, External Relations, Land Use, etc.). In a very large department, such as the Department of Trade and Industry, there may be seventy or more of these divisions.

Within a department, divisions are the primary centres of responsibility: 'The head of a division is the authority on his subject, and recommends to his Minister directly, seeking the advice or approval of his seniors if he thinks this necessary. The Permanent and Deputy Secretaries guide and direct and co-ordinate their divisions' work; but the real weight is on the heads of the divisions, for the Department's detailed work cannot sensibly be funnelled to the Minister through a handful of top officials ... the heads of the division are the anchor men.'[43] In some departments there are divisions of specialist staff sufficiently large to be headed by a scientific or professional civil servant at the Under Secretary level (for example Directorates of Economics and Statistics, Information, Building or Design, Research) and most sizeable research establishments are headed by scientists at this level (Chief Scientific Officer).

The sub-unit of the division is headed by an Assistant Secretary or his equivalent in the specialist grades. (In some departments the unit headed by an Assistant Secretary is called a division.) It is at and below this level that the organizational separation of career classes becomes apparent. The general convention has been to separate 'policy' work from executive and specialist work in different hierarchies. Thus, reporting to a divisional Under Secretary there might be *policy or administrative branches* headed by Assistant Secretaries and staffed by Principals and members of the executive and clerical grades; *executive branches* managed and staffed by members of the executive and clerical grades; and *specialist branches*, *directorates* and *inspectorates* staffed by members of the specialist classes (for example engineers, research officers, scientists, planners, architects, technical officers).* This separation of administrative work from specialist and executive work gives rise to the organizational phenomena known as parallel and joint hierarchies which were described by Fulton's Consultancy Group[44]:

'The parallel hierarchy can be defined as one where specialists and administrators (including executives) each run separate units concerned with their respective aspects of the same business. The organizational form can be represented thus [see diagram, *Parallel Hierarchy*, opposite]:

'In this form of organization, the administrative group report to the administrative divisional head and the specialist group to an equivalent level in a separate specialist chain . . .'

A joint hierarchy is one in which specialists and administrators jointly run a single unit. The Consultancy Group gave two examples of this form (see diagrams on p. 74) and commented[45]:

'Both parallel and joint hierarchies operate in the same way. The line of managerial and financial authority runs through the administrative group, while the specialist group act, when and where required, as advisers on the professional and technical aspects of the case or project in hand. Such structures are usual, for example, in organizations concerned with construction projects. A request for new buildings comes from Department X to the administrators in the Ministry of Public Buildings and Works.† The administrators establish the requirements of the client de-

* Some of these specialist branches have a regional organization.
† Now part of the Department of the Environment.

Parallel Hierarchy

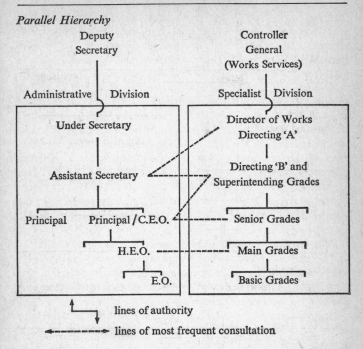

partment and decide which should be met, when, where and at what cost; this will involve the administrators in consultations with the specialists, who are organized in parallel, to obtain from them their technical advice and cost estimates. The final decision whether to erect a new building and its type and cost, or whether to lease, buy or modify an existing one is taken by the administrators. If the decision is to build, the specialists will then have detailed charge of the project, but all developments of it and expenditure on it have to be approved by the administrators.' The Consultancy Group found in a motorway construction division that administrators made the decisions on routes, the tenability of objections, and on costs and contracts after receiving advice from the engineers in the neighbouring hierarchy. In a school-building division main and senior-grade architects examined the technical

Joint Hierarchy I

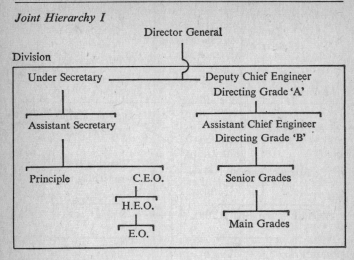

Joint Hierarchy II

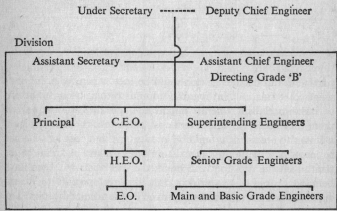

aspects of proposals and briefed Higher Executive Officers, who made the final decisions on schemes.

Parallel hierarchies can take more elaborate forms than those illustrated. It is not unusual in an Under Secretary's division to find administrative, executive and specialist branches dealing with, in order, Ministerial matters, aspects of policy and high-level casework; routine casework and clerical processing; technical inspection of compliance with legislation. There are examples of five or six parallel branches with a division organized on class lines (such as administrative, executive/clerical and several different technical and professional groups). The organizational basis is to divide the total range of activities required to operate a particular piece of legislation according to characteristics of education and experience represented by the career classes. In general, members of the administrative and executive grades with wide general experience of the department handle the Ministerial, Parliamentary and financial aspects of a case: executives operate the machinery by which routine cases are processed; specialists and professionally qualified staff contribute advice and technical ground work.

Branch organization varies according to whether the branch is administrative, executive or specialist. Administrative branches are typically small, with each level assisting the one above and with each official defining his job by interaction with his superiors and subordinates, the whole unit operating at its best as a multi-level team. The work load of such a branch is unpredictable, since it has to deal with an uneven flow of Parliamentary questions, Ministers' cases (inquiries addressed directly to Ministers), Ministerial briefs and speeches, precedent-setting cases, amendments to legislation and regulations, liaison with other branches, divisions and departments and papers on the development of policy. Typically, a paper on one of the subjects handled by such a branch is started by an H.E.O. producing a first draft after supporting material has been assembled by an E.O. The paper then passes up the line via Principal to the Assistant Secretary, being improved and amended and filled out, with further supporting material being drawn from other branches in the division or other divisions in the department, and finally passed to the Minister's private office via the Under Secretary and, in some cases, the Deputy Secretary. Administrative branch organization is frequently tall and narrow, with perhaps only one or two posts at each level. These branches have 'organic' and participative features which have evolved in response to an unpredictable environment and the overriding requirement for rapid reaction and political sensitivity and judgement.

A typical executive/clerical branch operates in a markedly different situation. Its job is to handle routine cases, transactions and applications rapidly and equitably as prescribed by law, regulation and precedent. Its authority is strictly prescribed, its area of discretion carefully delineated and supported by precedent, its procedures usually covered by written rules. These are the areas in which the executive grades supervise the clerical grades. The basic unit is the clerical section of around six clerks (clerical officers and clerical assistants) supervised by an Executive Officer. Two or three Executive Officers report to an H.E.O., two or three H.E.O.s to an S.E.O., two or three S.E.O.s to a Principal (formerly a C.E.O.). Sometimes these executive/clerical pyramids are very large, becoming divisions or sub-departments and employing several thousand staff. Most departments have groups of at least some hundreds of executive and clerical staff organized in these classical bureaucratic hierarchies. They provide fine examples of machine theory at work – narrow spans of control and close supervision, detailed job definition, the narrowest possible specialization and division of labour, the completion of simple repetitive tasks according to explicit instructions set out in manuals, a clear line of authority with each official responsible to his superior for the actions of his subordinates. It is not unusual to find a clerical section organized as a flow line, with one clerk filling in one part of a form and handing it on to his neighbour who fills in another and hands it on to his neighbour who attaches an explanatory leaflet and so on, until the outgoing letters are sealed at the end of the line by the junior clerk who opened the incoming letters in the morning. Some of these clerical factories are being replaced by computer installations, but these also usually have data-preparation and verification units organized in much the same way.

The structure and style of technical and specialist branches or other units varies between the two preceding extremes. Though formally arranged by class and grade (for example basic grade engineer, main grade, senior grade, superintending grade;

Scientific Officer, S.S.O., P.S.O., S.P.S.O., D.C.S.O., C.S.O.), their work, particularly in design and engineering and in social and scientific research, frequently requires the formation of project teams in which a man's contribution to the work of the team may not be related to his rank. In fact, the relationship may well be inverse, since rank mainly reflects age and seniority. Problems arise when members of different classes with different conditions of service and career expectations work together in project teams.

The professional classes of scientists and the Works Group (engineers, architects, surveyors) are supported by various classes of technicians (Experimental Officers, Scientific Assistants, Draughtsmen, Technical Officers) so that in some units surprisingly long chains of command are built up (for example, in an area of applied scientific research – Tech IV, Tech III, Tech II, Tech I, Tech A or Tech B or S.S.O., P.S.O., S.P.S.O., D.C.S.O., C.S.O. – nine grade levels between the bench and the head of a medium-sized research establishment). Interestingly, the conflict between a highly formalized hierarchical grading system and the changing manpower demands of research projects enabled the powerful Scientific Officer Class to negotiate for itself two major breaches in Civil Service-wide establishments rules. The first of these arrangements, fluid complementing, in effect permits the promotion of an officer 'in post' – that is without changing his job. This enables recognition to be given to the scientist whose personal contribution to research grows as he does the job better. The second is called individual merit promotion and allows for an outstanding scientist to be promoted and continue to undertake individual research instead of being burdened with the managerial responsibilities that are normally part of the higher rank. 'These two arrangements introduce a valuable measure of organizational flexibility appropriate for areas of work where individual capacities and skills are of paramount importance.'[46]

Just as the 'vertical' arrangement of departments into divisions, branches and sections is heavily influenced by definitions of the work of the classes, so the number of 'horizontal' levels within divisions is influenced by the number of grades within a class. Comment has already been made upon the frequency of tall thin pyramidal forms of organization with many levels and spans of control averaging only two or three. In part, these forms can be attributed to the 'constitutional' requirement for vesting financial authority in one Permanent Secretary, which, at least in theory, limits the scope for delegation; to public accountability and its requirement for careful drafting and scrutiny of Ministerial briefs and replies and for the meticulous checking of financial transactions by rank above rank of officials. They may also reflect the need to provide support in depth for frequently moving officials of the Administration Group. One obvious determinant of the long hierarchical chain of command is the convention that organization structure must reflect the grading structure of the classes concerned. Thus there is an assumption that administrative divisions require the Assistant Secretary level between Principal and Under Secretary whether or not the work could be carried out without this level. Similarly, it is assumed that the E.O. (or H.C.O.) grade is inevitably required between C.O. and H.E.O. If the task clearly calls for the use of the E.O., S.E.O. and Principal grades the tendency is to use the H.E.O. grade as well – particularly necessary because the only promotion route from E.O. to S.E.O. is via the H.E.O. grade.[47] The omission of any grade from the hierarchy not only upsets the career progression of those within it but also affects promotion prospects for that grade throughout the department, so that all interests are best served by filling every available grade level whether the work demands it or not. The occupant of an unnecessary level can soon find work for himself in commenting on the flow of papers flowing between his superiors and his subordinates. Further oddities appear when the hierarchy crosses class boundaries and when, for instance, an Experimental Officer is debarred from promotion in his section because to advance any further would take him into the preserve of the Scientific Officer Class, to qualify for which he has to have a degree or show 'graduate ability'.

In organizations as rigorously hierarchical as Civil Service departments the problem arises how to integrate decisions and operations on subjects which cross unit boundaries. The usual mechanism for doing this is the committee or working party, which assembles and synthesizes departmental views and opinions. Such committees are often as much representational as working bodies, so that every division which could possibly have an interest in the matter feels obliged to field someone of the appropriate rank to keep an eye on developments. The result is that long meetings, of a score or more senior officials whose rank is determined by that of the convenor, take place with all those present empowered to do no more than report back to their superiors.

Establishments divisions are responsible for matters of organization, under the guidance of the Civil Service Department. As we shall see in Chapter 8, their officers usually have had very little training in this field. They very rarely study departmental organization anyway, except at the level of the Organization and Methods assignment, which is usually concerned mainly with the arrangement of junior posts. Establishments divisions also employ a small group of 'staff inspectors' whose job it is to see that posts are correctly graded and that staff are properly employed, usually using a set of rough and ready rules and precedents based on experience of the work appropriate to the grades employed in the department.

Establishments officers are primarily concerned to limit the growth in manpower and to slot everybody into a job that looks right for his grade while preserving the relativities between classes and the ratios between higher and lower jobs which make for a neat promotion chain and which satisfy the staff associations. The adjustment to increases in work load is usually made by a request for more staff, which is inspected and approved or refused by the Establishments Division. A decrease in work load is not easily detected. There is no mechanism for requiring a department, a sub-department or a division to submit to a thoroughgoing organizational audit, concerned not only to determine the size of the organization but its internal arrangement of sections and posts and the continuing relevance of the systems it has to operate (see Chapter 7).

FULTON ON ORGANIZATION

The Fulton Report had relatively little to say about the organization structure of departments. One major change it recommended in this field was that departments and major sub-departments should have planning units headed by senior policy advisers who, on matters of long-term policy development, should report direct to Ministers. This recommendation is discussed in Chapter 4. The Committee also recommended that departmental O. &. M. sections should be upgraded in scope and quality so that they could take on 'efficiency audits involving all aspects of the department's work at all levels ... in particular, special attention should be paid to studies designed to improve organizational efficiency'.[48] This recommendation is discussed in Chapter 7. The Committee considered that in more departments there might be a case for the creation of the post of chief scientist or chief engineer. 'His job would be to take the chief responsibility for the direction of the department's technical work; he would have direct access to the Minister as his main adviser in these matters; he would be the professional head of the specialist staff.'[49]

The Fulton recommendation with potentially the most far-reaching organizational effects was that 'accountable units' should be established within departments. Accountable units were described as units of organization 'where output can be measured against costs or other criteria, and where individuals can be held personally responsible for their performance'.[50] The problems of defining managerial accountability are discussed at length in Chapter 6. Here it is sufficient to note that Fulton suggested that 'executive' areas of work should be designated as separate managerial commands or 'centres' and that the managers of these centres should be made accountable for the results they achieved as compared with pre-determined budgets or standards. In 'administrative' areas, concerned with policy and administrative matters, a similar concept of centres based on 'management by objective' should be introduced. The Committee thought that to enable organization by centre to be introduced certain other reforms would have to be undertaken. First, responsibilities which were diffused when several departments or branches had a substantial interest in the same matter should be concentrated in one man or a team, who would have the responsibility for assembling the relevant material and putting forward observations. Secondly, there was scope for reducing the number of levels in the hierarchy of most departments. With 'flatter' structures, there could be a more precise allocation of responsibility and authority. Thirdly, the separation of administrators and specialists in parallel and joint hierarchies not only prevented the specialists from exercising the full range of responsibilities normally associated with their professions but also obscured individual responsibility and accountability: no single person at any level had clear-cut managerial responsibility for the whole task. The best organization for this kind of work was a single integrated organization (or centre) under a single head, who should be the man with the most appropriate qualifications for the job. At lower levels, administrators and specialists should be integrated in teams or unified hierarchies. Fulton therefore recommended two possibly conflicting principles in its section on organization: first, the organization of executive and administrative work in separate commands; secondly, the amalgamation of specialist and administrative work in integrated commands.

Fulton's Consultancy Group[51] advocated *experiments* in new organizational forms related not to the traditional structure of class and grade but to operational needs as demonstrated by an analysis of the objectives and key functions of departments. It then outlined an approach to organization based on teams, groups and 'centres' of staff of mixed backgrounds and qualifications. There appeared to be the need for high-level functional and service staffs serving the top management of departments – certainly for planning and possibly in some departments for management services: data processing, operational research, efficiency studies, training and development. At operating levels, the Group proposed the creation of managerial units or 'centres' based upon accountability for costs: 'budget centres' in areas where output could be measured; 'responsibility centres' in areas where the measurement of output was difficult or impossible. Within these centres, analysis might show scope for some modification of the rigid hierarchy in favour of 'looser' team groupings and less closely prescribed individual jobs. These ideas for functional groups and management centres would work, the Group suggested, only within a framework of greater delegation to managers of responsibility for resources and if supported by entirely new systems of information, planning and control.

THE BUREAUCRACY
AND ORGANIZATIONAL CHANGE

Though the focus of present-day organization theory is on the construction and evaluation of models of the sub-structures and integrating mechanisms of complex organizations[52] rather than on the search for universal principles, the principles of the classicists still determine the form of most organizations in public administration. The present view, summarized by Rhenman,[53] is that the classical form is most appropriate in a situation in which organizational units are relatively independent; each level in the hierarchy represents successively greater technical and administrative competence; there are relatively few specialists in the organization; an authoritarian type of management prevails and is accepted; the organization functions in a community where stable values pertain and technological development is slow. The conventional department bureaucracy is therefore particularly well suited to applying long-established and well-defined regulations and precedents to a regular flow of routine transactions. This work will doubtless continue to be typical of many, perhaps most, areas of departmental activity for as far ahead as we can see, though the way in which it is organized will be increasingly influenced by developments in data processing.

However, today most departments are also engaged in the management of complex operations in an environment of rapid technical change. In these situations, the bureaucracy's standardization of roles and behaviour, its 'ritualist attitudes',[54] hinder a rapid and flexible response to new demands. Thompson[55] considered that the most symptomatic characteristic of modern bureaucracy is 'the growing imbalance between ability and authority'; the conflict, in areas of technological development, between specialists and their less well-trained superiors which cannot be solved in the context of a strict hierarchy of authority. In a study of bureaucracy in one of its most extreme forms (in two French national agencies) Michel Crozier observed that 'by and large, the common underlying pattern of all the vicious circles that characterize bureaucratic systems is this: the rigidity of task definition, task arrangements and the human relations network results in a lack of communication with the environment and a lack of communication among the group'.[56] He concluded that because the tendency of a bureaucracy is to leave nothing to the initiative of the individual but to produce ever more binding and precise rules and because excessive centralization leads to a situation in which those who make decisions cannot have first-hand knowledge of the problems faced by the organization, 'a bureaucratic system of organization is not only a system that does not correct its behaviour in view of its errors; it is also too rigid to adjust without crisis to the transformations that the accelerated evolution of industrial society makes more and more imperative'[57]

Perrow, discussing experience of bureaucratic forms of organization in U.S. public administration, has taken a less extreme view. He acknowledges the success of the bureaucratic model in promoting efficiency and competency and in controlling and adjusting to many of the uncertainties and variabilities in the environment, but concludes that, 'in some cases, the rate of change is so rapid, the new techniques so unproven and so uncertain, the number of contingencies so enormous, that the bureaucratic model is only partly applicable'.[58]

Though they were never so closed or entrenched as Crozier's examples, British departmental bureaucracies were, by the time Fulton reported, finding increasing difficulty in comprehending and responding to changes in their external environments, in fitting a growing army of specialists into the strict hierarchy of authority and in developing a style of human relations which met the aspirations of their junior staffs. Fulton's solutions for these difficulties were to give greater status and weight to policy planning and research; to abolish the career class compartments and integrate specialists and administrators in mixed hierarchies; and to counteract bureaucratic centralism by establishing units of managerial accountability (it paid relatively little attention to problems of human relations). We shall see in Chapter 6 that managerial accountability poses the greatest problems of implementation because, while attractive in principle, and often practicable in industry, it acts in opposition to the conventions of public accountability. The accountability of Ministers to Parliament and Permanent Secretaries to the Public Accounts Committee, the need for the meticulous stewardship of public property and funds and for the equitable application of policy and legislation generally tend to centralize the direction and control of key aspects of a department's activity, particularly in the fields of finance, manpower, and public and Parliamentary relations. Managerial accountability pulls the other way, towards greater delegation of authority and responsibility to unit managers. The organizational problem posed by the proposed units of accountability lies in the need to specify the responsibility and authority which can be properly defined as managerial while maintaining an integrating framework which enforces the over-riding importance of the public accountability of Ministers and Permanent Secretaries. We shall see from later chapters that the development of such a framework implies the construction of greatly improved systems for planning, defining objectives and marshalling control information.

The development of information technology will itself have substantial organizational effects. All departments are data-intensive and some of them handle information on a scale rarely equalled in business. The first computer was installed in a government department a decade ago; today there are 200 computer installations. In the past five years installed computer power has been increasing at an average rate of 50 per cent per annum and a fifteen-fold increase in computer power is a reasonable expectation by 1980.[59]

So far computers have been used mainly to mechanize existing repetitive clerical work and for scientific work, but already they are beginning to affect managerial processes. Investigations are now being made into programming simple case work and the application of case law, regulations or settled practice – in the Paymaster General's office, for example, and in the enormous Social Security system for the payment and recording of short-term benefits. In the future, attention will have to be given to recasting all existing casework procedures so that much of it can be processed by computers.[60] A Civil Service Department publication has said that 'computers will certainly be used increasingly in all departments over the next ten years to provide information for high-level decision-taking in the fields of management and policy. Two examples are:

(a) Computer-processed network analysis;

(b) Model-building and simulation studies, e.g. the development of a health service system; economic and fiscal planning (the latter through the development of a tax model); urban planning.

Management decision-taking assisted by computers is a complex operation involving the simultaneous consideration of a very large number of variables, frequently interrelated. Development of the models will have to be undertaken by operational research specialists, economists and statisticians and automatic data-processing staff in close consultation with senior management.'[61]

-The same publication also pointed to the integrating effects of computer installations in terms of the requirement for the interchange of data between departments and between departments and external organizations, though hitherto each department has embarked on installing computers virtually independently. Data transfers will have to take place between the vehicle-licensing system and the proposed police system for identifying vehicles; between local education authorities and the proposed register of students to be maintained by the Department of Education and Science; between the Department of Employment and the regional computing centres of the Department of Health and Social Security. The integration of information systems may eventually involve linking the social-service departments of local authorities to a central intelligence system which would span some of the present fields of activity of the D.H.S.S., the Home Office, the D.E.S. and the Department of the Environment. Ultimately, an integrated information system can be foreseen for the D.H.S.S. and Inland Revenue, which together account for a significant part of the total volume of cash transactions between central government and the public and who both require declarations of income and personal circumstances from individuals. The integration of the information systems required by these two departments would be an essential first step towards the rationalization of government transactions with taxpayers and recipients of benefits. By 1975, the Export Credits Guarantee Department plans to have the whole of its daily office work on computer, its records organized as a 'data base' (see p. 181) and a network of regional terminals.

Within departments, the use of computers is creating a new sub-profession. There are already well over 2,000 systems analysts and programmers now employed by government departments and the number has been increasing at a mean rate of 30 per cent per annum.[62] By 1980 there will be more than 20,000 of them. They will be one of the largest occupational groups in the service, with expertise, training and career characteristics as distinctive as any of the present classes. In industry and commerce, data-processing staffs (and the closely associated operational research specialists) have all the non-hierarchical features of specialist and innovatory groups. In the Civil Service, however, non-scientific computers are the province of the executive grades – markedly hierarchical in structure, non-specialist and originally organized to manage clerical operations. Though the attempt is made to fit these grade levels to computer work – Executive Officer programmer, H.E.O. and S.E.O. systems analyst – such arrangements are under considerable strain. Rigid gradings often do not reflect the contribution of different individuals to a computer team: a good programmer may very well be ready to take the lead on the design of advanced systems long before the fifteen years or so that he might have to wait for promotion to S.E.O. A programming/systems team on a large computer installation (perhaps twenty or thirty strong) may well require an internal organizational form that conflicts with the neat pyramid which the department requires to provide an orderly career progression for its middle management: it may require more S.E.O.s and H.E.O.s for example, or a disproportionate number of Principals. Already these, and other, conflicts are being demonstrated by the serious loss of data-processing staff from the Civil Service and by the difficulties of retaining experienced men in data-processing teams.[63]

The effects of computers on departmental organizations has yet hardly been felt. From industrial experience we may expect data-processing installations to become powerful nodal points in departments and to have marked effects on the balance of authority: some computer centres in companies have had the effect of replacing much of middle management and markedly 'flattening' the organizational pyramid.[64] The traditional executive/clerical hierarchy will, under the influence of the computer, tend to become nucleated into specialist groups each highly differentiated from the other by task, skill, specialism and attitudes. We can expect large groups of staff engaged on data preparation, verification and coding as highly industrialized as a pie factory; groups of skilled staff operating the computer; small clerical hierarchies handling exceptional cases; loosely organized systems design, analysis and research groups of programmers, systems analysts, social scientists, statisticians, engineers, accountants, managers and administrators assembling and reforming in constantly changing and adapting teams. Such teams will be engaged on studies ranging from the maintenance and updating of current accounting routines to the construction of enormously complex models of the transaction – processing and information requirements of proposed policies and legislation. In future the data-processing implications of a change of policy will become increasingly important and the data-processing facility will inevitably develop into a 'corporate staff' with substantial functional authority over the heads of operating divisions.

NEW ORGANIZATIONAL FORMS

Accepting that to question the Permanent Secretary's role as the Accounting Officer would take the discussion beyond the bounds of this book and into deep constitutional waters, we are obliged to assume the continuation of the arrangement whereby each department is headed by a single official who is answerable not only to his Minister but also directly to a committee of the Legislature for the propriety of all voted expenditure and for the efficient and economical administration of the department. However, it is reasonable to suppose that if the present emphasis upon accountable management and upon the use of new specialisms continues, new skills will have to be represented at very senior levels in the departments. It seems very likely, for instance, that the department of the future will have a data-processing and management-information facility so large and so central to its operations as to warrant full-time management by an official of the level of today's Deputy Secretary. In a large spending department many of whose operations and expenditure programmes interact directly with the client communities (such as Health and Social Security, Agriculture), the planning, cost-benefit analysis, programming and policy research activities described in Chapter 4 are likely to assume equally great importance.

In addition, we shall see in Chapter 6 that if any significant move is to be made towards establishing managerial accountability, it will have to be accompanied by greater delegation to, and within, departments in respect of both finance and manpower and by a budgetary control system which demonstrates managerial performance in the deployment of both resources. Such a system points to merging the establishments control operated by Establishments Divisions with the financial control operated by Finance Divisions and the establishment of one control or budgetary centre concerned to organize, analyse and issue the information on which accountability can be judged, to argue the department's case for money and manpower with the central departments and to supervise the application of Service-wide regulations on expenditure. It will also be argued in Chapter 7 that internal consulting services will have to be given much greater weight than in the past, and in Chapter 8 that new procedures and concepts will have to replace much of what passes for personnel management in departments today.

These trends could eventually have substantial effects upon the organization and activities of Finance and Establishments Divisions. The general effect would be to distinguish five 'corporate' service or functional staffs in replacement of those two:

1. A central computer facility engaged on processing information for vote and management accounting and 'control' (see Chapter 5) and providing computing power for planning, modelling and programme analysis carried out by:

2. A planning and policy research unit, concerned with environmental studies, research into community needs, studies of new and long-term policy options and alternative programmes, studies of departmental effectiveness and the preparation of long-term plans.

3. A management consultancy group, undertaking assignments to review and improve the organization and operations of the department, pursuing innovations in management and acting as a window on the world of new management techniques.

4. A personnel division, concerned with supplying managers with the staff they need, planning and developing the human resources of the organization, with the working environment and conditions of employment: a centre of expertise in the applied social sciences.

5. The control or budgetary centre, concerned with applying budgetary control systems (see Chapter 5), with accountability and with expenditure regulations. A concept similar to this has been advocated by Sir Richard Clarke[65], who sees Finance Divisions reconstituted as Budget Divisions.

A reconsideration of the organization of Finance and Establishments Divisions bears out some misgivings about Fulton's division of responsibilities between the Treasury and the Civil Service Department. It has been suggested as absurd that the Treasury should be responsible for the efficient use of financial resources while the CSD is responsible for efficient management.[66] As things stand at the moment, both departments are responsible for the design and maintenance of expenditure planning systems; accountable management and management by objectives are laid to the CSD, the management accounting procedures which are required to support them to the Treasury; computer policy is a matter for the CSD, while H.M.S.O., which reports to the Treasury, buys the computers.* A more logical solution, in the light of the likely development of management techniques, may have been to have left the Treasury with ultimate

---

*In March 1972 it was announced that a Central Computer Agency in the CSD would take over the responsibilities of H.M.S.O. for buying computers.

responsibility for planning, expenditure control, data processing and 'efficiency' and to have created the CSD as a Department of Personnel, as Laski suggested thirty years ago. This would at least remove the anomalous situation in which the CSD is expected both to 'argue for the Civil Servant' and to be the sponsor of efficient management and manpower control. The risk that this leaves too much power in the hands of the Treasury could be countered by other means: for example, a powerful and independent external state audit body (see Chapter 7). An alternative suggestion, by Sir Richard Clarke,[67] is that responsibility for all management functions (including expenditure planning and control) should be located in a new Central Management Department and that the Treasury should become a department for National Economy and Finance.

Beneath the five departmental corporate staffs, we might expect operating centres (perhaps 'agencies' – see p. 194) which merge today's separate administrative, executive and specialist divisions into unified hierarchies. Many of these centres will be less rigidly bureaucratic than at present. Apart from the effects of advancing office automation, the re-definition of jobs in the terms of a classless service, greater delegation, the application of accountability and the use of some formal participative system, such as management by objectives, will tend to widen spans of control and reduce the number of levels in the organization.

The likelihood is that the use of *ad hoc* project teams will become more common in civil departments, for instance for planning, cost-benefit studies and consultancy assignments. One of the principles of the new style of government advocated by David Howell, M.P. (now Parliamentary Secretary to the Civil Service Department), and apparently behind much of the present government's thinking on organization, was the project approach – seeking 'to define as many projects of government as possible with clear goals or end results. Once the goal has been defined then the organization, or project team, can be set up to achieve it. And once the team has been set up then someone can be placed in charge and held responsible for success or failure or continuing performance. And above all, once the objective has been achieved the project team can be wound up.'[68]

Inevitably, the general tendency towards a nucleated pattern of organization, of staff groups, centres and project teams, rather than the rigid scalar hierarchy, will lead to a higher degree of organizational differentiation than in the past. If detailed central control and supervision is relaxed in favour of greater delegation to managers, then the groups, centres and teams will tend to develop individual operating methods, organizational arrangements and management styles. This will underline the crucial importance of integrative systems for planning, information and performance review, that is for ensuring the congruence of unit and departmental objectives and programmes. In some cases it is likely that integrating structures will also have to be adopted: 'boards' or management committees of top-tier officials and heads of functional staffs, as in the late Ministry of Technology.[69] A particularly useful device in industry are 'junior boards', or committees of middle management, chaired by members of the main board, of which the heads of operating units are members. Such an arrangement interlocks policy direction and operating management on the linking-pin model and provides a mechanism for the resolution of operational problems, the regular review of performance and a filter for policy issues on their way to top management.

Some of these developments are already discernible: the Management Review of Prison Department in 1968-9 produced a Controllerate of Planning and Development which included a 'corporate' planning unit and units for research and development and management information and Controllerates of Operations and Administration staffed by members of the prison governor, administrative, executive and specialist grades. A recent account of this review showed the influence of contingency theory in that the proposed organization structure within major units at headquarters varied according to the nature of their activities, the specialist content of the work and the environmental pressures to which they were subjected: in other words, there was a high degree of internal differentiation. This ranged from the bureaucratic hierarchy in areas processing routine transactions, to loose 'organic' structures in research and development areas in which project team members were to have considerable freedom to define their own roles. It was proposed that the integration of these various structures should be accomplished at middle management levels by a Prison Department Committee of divisional heads, by an annual planning conference and by new management information systems.[70]

The reorganization of the former Ministry of Public Buildings and Works in September 1969 'in accordance with the general principles recommended by the Fulton Committee' ended the separate hierarchies of specialist and administrative staff and replaced them with a unified structure in which each block of functions is under a manager responsible for all aspects of its work. Under a top echelon of three deputy secretaries and a specialist controller there are twenty-one directorates, half of them headed by specialists.[71]

In May 1970 an announcement was made of the intention to introduce a 'line management' structure into the regional organization of the Ministry of Agriculture, Fisheries and Food. Formerly each of the seven headquarters divisions was headed by a controller who co-ordinated the activities of the heads of specialist groups (the veterinary service, the land-drainage service, etc.) but had no authority over them. The proposal was that 'the controller will become a manager and in charge of the specialist branches. This should prevent overlapping and the consideration of problems in isolation. One benefit for the members of professional services is that they will have greater promotional possibilities.'[72]

The government which took office in 1970 has laid emphasis upon its determination to introduce 'accountable units of management' as a means to securing greater departmental efficiency. The first such unit was the Supplies Division of the Department of the Environment, the reorganization of which was announced in January 1971. The division procures and supplies goods and equipment to government departments, embassies and education authorities, museums and some other public bodies. The proposed changes appeared to be a development of what the division had been doing over a number of years: that is, reducing the variety of goods it purchased, laying down tighter specifications for suppliers, adopting trading accounts and statistical measures of performance and making realistic service charges to its customers. It now has to 'demonstrate its commercial viability'.[73] It is not clear from published reports if the division could operate its own personnel policy or was in any way directly accountable to Parliament for its vote or whether its customers could go elsewhere if they did not like its service charges or the goods it offered.

The second experiment in accountability was more of a break with tradition. In April 1971 a White Paper announced a new Government Organization for Defence Procurement and Civil Aerospace[74] combining defence research and development, equipment-buying and support for civil aerospace activities of the Ministries of Defence and of Aviation Supply. This organization was to be headed by a chief executive who was to be an accounting officer for the vote (i.e. the purchasing agency was to be responsible for the vote and not the user of the equipment or the customer for the research). Four of his subordinate Controllers of weapons systems were also to be accounting officers. Within the organization there were to be project managers with full responsibility for the specialists assigned to them: these specialists would also have a functional line of responsibility within their own specialization (i.e. there was to be a matrix organization). There was something of a break with establishments conventions in that the organization was to be 'largely autonomous' in personnel management matters.[75] However, in spite of a lucid analysis of what had been wrong with defence procurement in the past (fragmentation of responsibility, duplication of effort, lack of clear accountability, lack of cost awareness, lack of professionalism) the solution still appeared to dodge the problem of integrating specialist and administrative staff. In fact, it appeared to create a parallel hierarchy of specialists (four controllers of weapons systems and a controller of research and development) and administrators (a Secretary and controllers of 'policy', finance, personnel and sales). The roles of secretary and the Controller of Finance were described in familiar administrative terms. The Secretary was to provide 'the rounded advice of a senior civil servant' and was to advise on 'the reconciliation of procurement policies with the broader requirements of government policy and accountability'. The Controller of Policy was to relieve the systems controllers of the detailed work in thinking through policies, procedures and methods. In other words, specialists were to be confined to specialist matters.

In 1971, the employment services of the Department of Employment were constituted as an agency within the department under a chief executive 'with complete control over all the resources of his section' – that is, with responsibility for staff numbers and a 'single management budget'.[76] Studies on similar lines are being carried out for the Royal Ordnance Factories, the Dockyards and various units of government concerned with construction projects. In the D.H.S.S. local, regional and national social security offices are being placed under one command. The movement is clearly towards the reconstitution of those departments with substantial executive activities into federal structures consisting of small policy divisions and large executive agencies with delegated control over their own manpower and expenditure (see Chapter 6).

An important trend in government organization has been the creation of giant departments. This began with the formation of the Ministry of Defence and continued with the creation of the Foreign and Commonwealth Office, the Department of Health and Social Security and, in 1970, the establishment of the Department of Trade and Industry, the Department of the Environment (formerly the Ministries of Transport, Public Buildings and Works and Housing and Local Government) and the merging of the Ministry of Overseas Development with the Foreign and Commonwealth Office. The reasons for the 1970 wave of amalgamations were stated in the White Paper announcing them[77] as being to develop a single strategy for clearly defined objectives; to resolve conflicts within the line of management rather than by interdepartmental compromise; to manage large programmes within departmental boundaries, making possible more effective delegation; to facilitate the application of analytic techniques; to offer more direct identification to the community of Ministers and departments responsible for defined functions; and to contribute more effectively to the government's overall strategy. These changes were to be accompanied by the creation of a central policy review body (see Chapter 4). The indications are so far that the Department of the Environment and the enlarged Foreign Office have achieved greater effectiveness through the closer integration of formerly separate but allied functions. The marriage of Health with Social Security in the D.H.S.S. does not appear to have brought any benefits: the two sides of the department are reported to have little to do with one another.[78] They were two very different organizations – Social Security highly managerial, accustomed to running a network of local and regional offices and processing vast numbers of transactions; Health, a policy-making and advisory body with few managerial responsibilities and with strongly entrenched parallel hierarchies of administrators and medical men. The Department of Trade and Industry, however, seems to have reached the point in size where the load and range of work which is expected to be handled only by the Secretary of State has exceeded the capacity of a single human being, even when he is supported by three Ministers and three Parliamentary Under Secretaries.*

The growth of 'accountable' agencies within giant departments will pose some formidable management problems. They could come increasingly to resemble those conglomerate corporations which were so fashionable a few years ago, particularly in the U.S.A., and which have been falling apart ever since. This form of large-scale organization can be made to work effectively but it requires a continuous flow of first-class top managers and highly developed control systems. There is also no indication that these giant departments have assembled the planning, research and consultancy staffs which can help to prevent the likelihood that a big bureaucracy will get even more out of touch with its environment and more inefficient than a small one. In addition, there is a pressing need in the Civil Service for some systematic programmes of organizational research: for studies into the relevance of

* 'There was that memorable week last April when Mr Davies (Secretary of State at the D.T.I.) had to make major Parliamentary statements or speeches on four successive days on the Vehicle and General (insurance) affair, the decision to site the third London airport at Foulness, the future structure of the Steel Corporation and Government Policy for dealing with unemployment' (Colin Jones, 'The Question of Size', *Financial Times*, 23 February 1972).

the conventions of bureaucratic organization to the tasks now faced by modern government and the skills they now have to deploy and for systematic training in handling organizational change for the senior staff of establishments divisions.

CHAPTER 4

Planning

THIS chapter deals with the 'strategic' planning systems operated by departments. It considers existing and developing procedures for the allocation of departmental expenditures and for establishing management objectives and programmes. Here planning is taken as relating to the medium-term and long-term future of the organization, from the end of the current budget period to as far ahead as any reliable estimates can be made of its environment and operations. The discussion begins with a background description of the main features of corporate planning in industry and of policy and expenditure planning procedures in government departments. It then goes on to consider Programme Budgeting, which appears to be the basis of the new planning systems which are currently being developed in departments. It concludes with a consideration of a major problem of planning in government departments: how to link decisions on policy and the broad allocation of resources to specific programmes of action for accountable managers.

CORPORATE PLANNING

Most managers in industry have long operated procedures whereby the objectives of the business and the deployment of its resources for the coming year are quantified as budgets and made the responsibility of a manager or 'budget-holder'. In many cases planning is still limited to the preparation of annual budgets but, increasingly, the budget is the detailed first-year element of a multi-year plan. Once agreed and authorized, the budget provides the foundation of a control system, that is, the process of arranging information so that the performance of the organization can be monitored and decisions can be taken to keep it on course.

Many organizations have also been obliged by the nature of

their activities to take operating decisions in the context of a long-term forward view. The directors of plantation and mining companies, public utilities and many other capital-intensive industries frequently take decisions now that commit and constrain their successors twenty or more years hence. In such organizations there usually exists some arrangement for estimating demand, prices, costs and profits well into the future. The significant developments in business planning in recent years, however, have been the growth of such arrangements in most large companies, whatever the distance of their time horizons, and the development of formal procedures for systematic planning. These procedures are usually called 'long-range', 'strategic' or 'corporate' planning. Though most of the techniques of corporate planning are said to have been in use in the largest American companies for many years, their development in Britain was heavily influenced by a book by Dr Igor Ansoff (formerly of the Rand Corporation and Lockheed) published in 1965.[1]

Typical corporate planning systems have three main elements: first, a cyclical routine for establishing and reviewing the long-term objectives of the enterprise; secondly, arrangements for carrying out studies of alternative courses of action and selecting the most promising; thirdly, the establishment of short-term programmes of action and budgets for managers.

These elements are linked together in the following steps:

1. A statement of aims – that is, of the purpose or fields of activity of the enterprise, the level of economic return which is sought – is endorsed and usually originated, by the board of directors.

2. Based on this statement of aims, the systematic examination and ranking of possible alternative long-term strategies is carried out by a corporate planning unit, usually reporting directly to the head of the enterprise. This strategic analysis is based on an evaluation of the company's present market standing and its particular strengths and weaknesses; on likely political, economic, technical and social changes in its environment in the foreseeable future and the implications of these changes for the company's development; on the opportunities and risks associated with the company's current activities; and on the costs and revenues likely

to result from various strategies that could be adopted to fill the 'gap' between prospective returns from current activities and the returns required to meet company aims. The corporate planning unit is typically engaged in the appraisal of a variety of investment opportunities; in research into the future demands for present products and possible new products; in studies of the opportunities for diversification, acquisition and divestment and in gathering and sifting intelligence on the behaviour of competitors, proposed new legislation and other developments in the community served by the company. The more highly developed corporate planning units are engaged on using mathematical models to simulate the effects of varying values assigned to each important variable or response mechanism of the market.[2] A system of inter-related equations is constructed to represent supply and demand, investment, production and inventory, competition, profit and price. The inputs to such models vary from fairly well-understood economic relationships to managerial estimates of, for example, the probable outcome of competitors' pricing policies or of the effect of advertising. To this extent the estimates of outcome can rarely be more exact than the attachment of various levels of probability to proposed courses of action – 'profiles of risk' – but computers can provide the capability for rapidly updating the model in the light of experience and for recalculating the risks and potential benefits attaching to any number of prospective policy options.

When properly used and trusted by the board, the corporate planning unit can be the initiator of debate and thought about the company's future. It should also be the company's antenna, continually scanning the furthest corners of its environment for the first signals of significant changes for which the company has to be prepared.

3. In parallel with this process of policy evaluation by a staff group at the top of the organization, the line management budget holders also participate in the planning procedure by setting down the prospective problems and opportunities they can see as a result of their day-to-day operations and by putting forward proposals to deal with them. These analyses are passed up the line of management for scrutiny and comment and finally referred

to the corporate planning unit for reconciliation with the strategic studies which its staff has been carrying out.

4. After the integration of the views of both the corporate planning staff and the line management, often carried out in a formal conference of planners and senior managers, the board selects a strategy expressed as a long-term plan (say for five to ten years ahead) setting out specific objectives (such as growth, profit, share of the market) for key areas of the business to be attained within the planning period.

5. These objectives are then expressed as agreed sub-objectives and programmes of work for individual managers and translated into annual budgets and standards of performance as the basis for control.

6. Financial and statistical control information is then organized in a form and frequency which allows regular comparison with budgets and standards.

7. Formal annual procedures are set up for reviewing the past year's performance of the business as a whole and of each manager, for restating corporate aims, revising corporate objectives, authorizing the next sequence of short-term programmes and budgets and casting the long-term plan ahead by another year.

Experience in industry has shown that corporate planning on these lines can work only if a number of preconditions are met, and from this experience we can learn a number of lessons for planning in government. First, and most important, the top management group has to be persuaded of the value of the exercise and has to be convinced of the credibility of the corporate planners. Time and again, attempts to introduce corporate planning have failed because the board of directors have never really been persuaded that systematic planning has any relevance to their business, preferring to rely on their own gifts of intuition and entrepreneurial flair, and because the young graduates typically employed in corporate planning units have not been acceptable as advisers. British company directors often have a strong anti-intellectual bias and a marked preference for hunch over systematic analysis, particularly if this analysis involves complicated calculations. Young graduates, on the other hand, often put into planning units because they quickly take to analytical work and because they like the idea of surveying the activities of the business as a whole, frequently suffer from intellectual arrogance and a lack of understanding of the perceptions of the practical men on the board. The result can be that the two parties glare at each other across an educational, experience and generation gap and a dialogue is impossible. It is therefore crucial that before embarking on corporate planning top management should be convinced of the need to base its long-term decisions on careful analysis and that it should be able and willing to examine, question and restate the basic aims of the business and to articulate these as planned objectives for specific periods ahead. It is also important that a corporate planning unit should include senior and experienced managers as well as young analysts; that there should be frequent movement of staff between line management and the corporate planning unit in addition to a small core of professional planners: that the initiative should be seen to lie with the board and not with the planners; and that the planners should advance cautiously in gaining the confidence of the board.

Secondly, the links between planners and managers should run through the organization to the lowest levels of management. While many environmental studies can be carried out only by the planner because of the time he can devote to assembling the data, 'the basic problem of every planner is that of trying to persuade otherwise distracted people not only to buy his product, but to help him fabricate it'.[3] The greatest resource of practical knowledge of what options are open to the company lies with line management. A corporate planning unit exists to organize this knowledge, to bring to bear specialist skills in evaluation and appraisal and to display the options to those who have the ultimate responsibility for setting the future course of the enterprise. In order to prevent the planners from becoming occupants of an academic backwater and to close the incipient gap between planners and doers, some businesses give operating executives or committees of executives the responsibility for the supervision of planning studies. Once the corporate plan has been established, it is important that the organization should possess a consultative system to enable corporate aims and objectives to be explained to every level of management, so that each manager can see his tasks in relation to the plan.

Thirdly, a plan should have an organizational expression, so that its elements are clearly the responsibility of managers who can be held accountable for producing results and so that planning and control are integral parts of a single management system. This implies an organization based on units of accountability, described in the last chapter, to which objectives, budgets and programmes of work can be allocated.

Finally, before undertaking corporate planning on any scale, an organization must have a management information system which supplies accurate and timely information about its current operations. A business must have some idea of the costs and returns associated with its present activities if it is to make systematic decisions on alternative uses of its resources. In industrial terms, it is necessary to go through the budgetary control stage in order to get to corporate planning, that is, there has to be a foundation of budgets, standards and indicators of performance if choices are to be made between alternative options and if plans are to be broken down into management programmes. This is particularly important in the Civil Service context where less effort has been put into management accounting, which tends to be thought of as an 'executive' and low-status activity, than into strategic planning.

EXPENDITURE PLANNING IN GOVERNMENT

As government has moved from purely regulatory activities into direct intervention in economic and social processes and as the complexity of its tasks and machinery have increased, its time horizon has inevitably receded. The development of a weapon system, a motorway network, a nuclear-power generation programme, a data-processing system, a school or hospital building programme all involve the commitment of resources for many years ahead. Departments have therefore been faced with having to establish procedures for planning the expenditures associated with their current and prospective policies over periods in the future well beyond the one-year span on which government expenditure estimating has traditionally been based. The first impetus towards the establishment of formal multi-year planning systems was provided by this lengthening of the time scale on which decisions have to be made, particularly in the defence field. The increase in total public expenditure, from 5 per cent of gross national product at the turn of the century to over 40 per cent today, has also faced governments with a widening choice of alternative demands for public money. Whatever the total of revenue that has been raised by taxes, duties, insurance contributions or borrowing, the government of the day has had to reconcile competing claims for funds which, in aggregate, far outstrip available resources. If orderly decisions are to be taken about the priorities for spending, governments are therefore obliged to forecast the total claims on public expenditure made by departments and to relate these to forecast economic growth.

An impetus towards formal planning systems has also been provided by Parliament. It has become clear to M.P.s that the process of debating the annual estimates of expenditure (the 'supply procedure' – see Chapter 5) has had little point when these show only the items to be purchased rather than the purpose of the expenditure, when most of the policy decisions which the estimates represent are irreversible and when the estimates account for about only half of all public expenditure. Committees of the House of Commons have therefore agitated in the last decade or so to be given access to long-term plans for public expenditure and to the economic forecasts and policy assumptions on which these plans are based.

In addition, the widespread adoption of planning, programming, budgeting (PPB) systems in the United States, Canada and some European countries has led to some attention being paid in Whitehall to their application in a British context. These systems are described below.

Finally, and most recently, pressure for a greater refinement in the planning process has arisen from those who, taking their cue from the Fulton Report, want to see the introduction of modern systems of management planning, control and accountability.

These systems can work only where there are formal procedures for choosing between alternative courses of action, setting objectives and establishing management programmes.

THE PUBLIC EXPENDITURE SURVEY

The inadequacy of a single year as a time-span over which to plan the expenditures of modern government became apparent in the early 1950s and led to the establishment of a variety of longer-term 'forward looks' in departments, particularly in the fields of defence, education and road building. In 1957–8 the Select Committee on Estimates[4] examined, and commented very critically on, Treasury planning and control of expenditure. It found 'somewhat disturbing' the fact that the Treasury did not sufficiently appreciate the need to review established policies involving expenditure and appeared to lack a constructive approach to the matter.[5] It called for a systematic and regular review of existing policies in terms of their prospective expenditure. It expressed 'grave disquiet' over the extent to which departments underestimated their expenditures and the willingness with which the Treasury accepted supplementary estimates when the original ones were exceeded.[6]

The Committee also criticized the 'natural tendency, within the present system of estimates and accounts, to concentrate too much attention on the policy and expenditure proposals for the coming financial year with too little regard to the commitments and consequences for future years . . . an obsession with annual expenditure can stultify forward planning',[7] and recommended that longer-term forecasts should be carried out in civil departments. It also thought that the Treasury should be interested in 'programme control': planning and controlling, expenditure in advance of estimates, by specific spending programmes such as those for research and development, aircraft and weapons.[8] The Committee concluded by recommending that a small independent committee be appointed to report on the theory and practice of Treasury control of expenditure. The government did not accept the Estimates Committee's recommendation for an external committee of inquiry but set up a body led by Lord Plowden under the authority of the Chancellor of the Exchequer, which reported in July 1961.[9]

The Plowden Committee made its most important recommendations in the field of long-term expenditure planning. It noted that in the areas of defence, nationalized industries, education and pensions the practice of regular 'forward looks' had already become established and that long-term programmes for hospital building and five-year programmes for motorways were in existence. However, the traditional system of piecemeal decisions persisted in most departments and no criteria existed to permit a rational choice between different kinds of expenditure. The Committee proposed that in future: 'Public expenditure decisions whether they be in defence or education or overseas aid or agriculture or pensions or anything else, should never be taken without consideration of (a) what the country can afford over a period of years having regard to prospective resources and (b) the relative importance of one kind of expenditure against another.'[10] The Committee then recommended that: 'Regular surveys should be made of public expenditure as a whole, over a period of years ahead, and in relation to prospective resources; decisions involving substantial future expenditure should be taken in the light of these surveys.'[11] It also called for improvements in the tools for measuring and handling public expenditure problems and recommended the more widespread use of quantiative methods of dealing with these problems. Finally, Plowden recommended that there should be more effective machinery to enable Ministers to take collective decisions and bear collective responsibility on matters of public expenditure.[12]

The field to be covered by Plowden's proposed regular surveys of public expenditure was far wider than that covered by the supply procedure. The supply procedure excludes, among other items, expenditure by local authorities and nationalized industries, the national insurance fund and debt interest. In 1969–70 the supply estimates amounted to £8,172m. while total public expenditure came to nearly £20,000m. Thus the Plowden proposals were not only for a further look ahead than was the practice in most departments but for the totality of spending in the public sector to be considered at one time so that priorities could be systematically ordered and decided upon.

From 1961 onwards annual surveys of public expenditure have been prepared for Ministers on the lines proposed by Plowden. These were described in the 1966 White Paper *Public Expenditure: Planning and Control*.[13] They look five years ahead and are prepared in an annual cycle which runs parallel to the preparation of the supply estimates. In February the Finance Divisions of the spending departments must submit their five-year expenditure forecasts to the Treasury, showing the cost of present policies, divided between existing basic programmes – that is, those to which they are already committed by past policy decisions – and additional programmes which could be undertaken if more resources were made available. In March and April discussions take place between the Treasury and individual departments on the policy and statistical assumptions made by the departments. In May a draft report on public expenditure is assembled by the Treasury and submitted to the official Public Expenditure Survey Committee (P.E.S.C.) on which sit the Principal Finance Officers of the major spending departments. The Committee prepare a report to Ministers 'showing where present policies are likely to lead in terms of public expenditure at constant prices if they remain unchanged over the ensuing five years and what would be implied by a range of possible alternative policies'.[14] In April and May, the Treasury prepares a Medium-Term Assessment of the economy, relating to the same period as the P.E.S.C. survey and covering the forecast balance of payments, the estimated rate of economic growth and other key economic indicators. Both the P.E.S.C. report and the Medium-Term Assessment are submitted to Ministers in June, and between July and October decisions are taken on the total of public expenditure for the next five years and its broad allocation to major 'functional' categories.

As a Treasury memorandum[15] has pointed out, 'allocation' describes a highly complex network of interactions. Any government inherits programmes which have a momentum of their own and which can be changed only gradually. Many major capital-investment and construction programmes run for ten years or more, and some of these cannot be adjusted in the short term without serious loss of efficiency. Some government commitments are open ended (for that year at least) in that once the policy has been settled the government has to meet the claims of all those who qualify (for example agricultural support grants). In any year, therefore, Ministers can make only limited changes in major sectors of public expenditure. Nevertheless, with the availability of P.E.S.C. and the Medium-Term Assessment of the economy, Ministers do have an opportunity to review their priorities in the context of the total public resources that are likely to be available.

In April 1969, the government proposed[16] a new presentation for the public expenditure survey as a basis for Parliamentary debates. This document would show figures for each functional sector of public expenditure (such as law and order, defence, health and welfare) for the year preceding publication, the year of publication (year 1) and each of the four following years (years 2 to 5). Year 3 would be the one on which the government would focus the attention of its annual survey because this is the first point in time at which there is real scope for substantial changes of policy.

In December 1969, the public expenditure survey was published in the new form.[17] £20,000m. of public expenditure was displayed under twenty-five main functional headings, showing the average annual percentage increase planned for each between 1968–9 and 1971–2. It was supported by publication of elements of the medium-term economic assessment for 1968–72.[18] Publication of the survey was greeted as a major advance for Parliamentary democracy ('The Treasury lifts its veil at last . . . one of the most radical documents produced by any recent British government'[19]) but for the debate on it in the House of Commons, 'this great occasion heralded as of prime constitutional and economic importance', fewer than fifty M.P.s appeared.[20]

POLICY RESEARCH AND PLANNING UNITS

The Haldane Report on the Machinery of Government of 1918 observed that: 'In the spheres of civil government the duty of investigation and thought, as preliminary to action, might with great advantage be more widely recognized. It appears to us that adequate provision has not been made in the past for the organized acquisition of facts and information and for the systematic application of thought as preliminary to the settlement of policy and its subsequent administration.'[21]

Very few departments had specialist staff engaged on the organized acquisition of facts and information before the late 1950s and it was not until the arrival of the 'technological revolution' of 1964 that research and planning staffs became common in Whitehall. They were not always welcomed by the higher Civil Service and were sometimes radically weakened when their Ministerial protectors moved on. Policy research was also firmly separated from policy implementation by the career class system.

'This research effort has been on a very small scale and most research units have been seriously understaffed. Their staffs have usually been members of the Research Officer class (only 230 strong) with limited career prospects, very little hope of transfer into the ranks of top management and confined to a purely advisory role, well away from the main stream of policy making . . . Similarly, there has been virtually no involvement by administrators in the research process and therefore little familiarity in top management with the contribution that systematic research could make to the formulation of policy. The result has been that policy research has tended to be divorced from management and management planning has hardly existed: there is not the same strong link as there is in well-managed industry between long-term policy studies, long-term plans for the deployment of resources and the establishment of short-term budgets and programmes of work for individual managers.'[22]

Not only are administrators usually not involved in formal policy research but neither are line managers from the executive grades, nor engineers, scientists and, very noticeable to an outsider, nor are accountants. Whereas in a big company it would be customary to set up a multi-disciplinary team including management, accountancy, economic and technical expertise to study a new policy venture, in the Civil Service the reservation of most research to specialist classes (research officers, economists, statisticians) has meant that it has been isolated from direct management experience. The Economic Planning Division of the short-lived D.E.A. and the large and long-established Home Office Research Unit have been quoted as illustrating the detachment and academicism of some of these research and planning units.[23]

The isolation of research groups from top management is reinforced by the low status of research officers. Fulton's Management Consultancy Group compared the prospects of a young research officer (who might expect promotion to a grade carrying a maximum at that time of £2,155 p.a.) with a young administrator (who could expect to reach Assistant Secretary at a maximum at that time of £4,500 p.a.) and pointed out that since the research officer was required to have a degree appropriate to the work of his department and the administrator was not, this amounted to 'discrimination against expertise'.[24]

Much policy evaluation and development takes place in administrative divisions where administrators who are operating current policy and dealing with high-level case work and Ministerial matters have been expected to find time to write papers on future policy. Time and again, administrators complain of 'what they really ought to be doing' – considering the development of future policy in their field – being driven out by the daily pressure of Ministerial cases and Parliamentary questions, by the necessity of attending committees simply to show the flag for their departments, and by Ministerial preoccupation with the short term, the crisis and the expedient. Even if there were time, policy evaluation and planning as a side activity for those concerned with policy execution would always suffer from gradualism, subjectivity and a weak analytical base.

There always has been a body of opinion in the higher Civil Service, though it is now diminishing, that systematic research and planning has little relevance to its work. Concentration upon the awareness of Ministerial responsibility tends to put a low valuation on systematic research-based planning and a high one on rapid reaction to the topic of the day. Their emphasis upon the turbulence of political life and the intangibility of high-level administrative work often gives the impression that highly quantified planning and evaluation could be applied only to the most routine executive acivities of their departments. At all levels, however, government officials are operating in social and economic environments in which broad trends can be detected now which are likely to become the specific policy issues to be faced by future Ministers. 'Topics which spring to mind are race relations, problems of the concentration of industry into groups of enormous economic power; declining industries, automation, pollution and conservation; transport and traffic; drugs and delinquency; student revolt; an ageing population; child neglect and poverty; regionalism; the implications of world famine and nationalism. Research and forecasting studies on these and many other such major policy problems should be carried out or at least co-ordinated by departments because the Civil Service has to understand them well enough to be prepared when the Minister of the day requires legislation and executive action.'[25]

DEPARTMENTAL PLANNING ARRANGEMENTS: A SUMMARY

The public expenditure surveys cover all public expenditure, span five years, are linked to an assessment of economic prospects over the same period and display information in a way that permits decisions to be taken on the allocation of resources between major functions of government. Their introduction was an important and, by international standards, a pioneering step in the strategic planning of government expenditure as a whole. However, as a recent White Paper[26] has pointed out, they have failed in two respects to provide Ministers with the information they needed to balance the claims of competing blocks of public expenditure: they do not call for explicit statements of the objectives of expenditure in a way that would enable a Minister's plans to be tested against general government strategy, nor do they embody detailed analysis of existing programmes and of major policy options on them. Departmental surveys have been inadequately supported by analytical studies of alternative programmes or of the justification for continuing programmes, and they have not generally been accompanied by any post-audit of the results of past expenditure.

One former senior government economist, in giving evidence to the Fulton Committee, referred to the Treasury's annual review of expenditure plans as 'just departmental horse-trading' and pointed to the difficulty, under this arrangement, of providing any rational method of cutting expenditure. 'A global figure is decided in advance and the allocation betweeen departments is worked out hurriedly, in the first place by Treasury officials, without estimating how much a departmental economy will improve the next year's balance of payments (the ostensible purpose of the exercise) . . . The objective is to achieve a certain level of expenditure, not certain economic goals, and for this purpose all expenditures are equal.'[27]

The Brookings Report on Britain's economic prospects (1966) commented on the lack of an economic base for allocating resources to social programmes: '. . . a wide variety of technical standards, rules of thumb and political factors, – "needs" and "requirements" – appear to prevail. Also a tendency to set social services at "last year plus x per cent" makes adjustments sluggish, even in cases where a large change (especially an increase) is called for. Since there do appear to be some such cases, the present Treasury methods may need revision as well as refinement. Even in housing, education and, to some extent, health services, where economic appraisal is possible, little research has been done either in Whitehall or independently and what has been done does not always influence Treasury decisions. This may cause random imbalance among these programmes (as, for example, there probably was between housing and hospitals during the 1950s). More important, it may systematically favour the programmes of the nationalized industries in the competition with social services for public funds.' The Brookings Report concluded that 'the need is for major revisions within and among programmes, not for cuts alone . . . More co-ordination is needed among programmes to combat deprivation, in place of the present tendency towards over reliance on separate programmes, particularly in education and housing.'[28]

The recent introduction of 'programme reviews' and the establishment of a central analytical unit attached to the Cabinet Office (see p. 145) have been taken to meet these criticisms. However, these additions to the public expenditure survey system still do not make it an adequate basis for management planning in departments.

First, in contrast to the arrangements in corporate planning systems by which short-term budgets and controls are directly derived from long-term plans, the surveys do not project the future, in terms of total expenditure, of individual managerial units. The planning system is therefore not supported by a structure of budget accountability.

Secondly, the surveys do not establish any criteria by which departmental effectiveness or efficiency can be judged.

Thirdly, an important element of the corporate planning process, the examination of the attitudes and likely reactions of the client community, has had virtually no part in public expenditure planning. Very rarely do departments carry out 'market research', attitude surveys or studies of need in the communities they serve and regulate and, as a result, they sometimes misjudge the requirements of those communities and also assume that the values, assumptions and perceptions of Whitehall are general in the community. Thus investment allowance schemes are introduced which industrialists cannot understand, social security programmes are introduced which are incomprehensible to pensioners, tax allowances intended to benefit the poor in fact benefit teenagers and working wives. As might be expected from the administrative style described in Chapter 1, departments have been far more acutely attuned to their political than to their social and economic environments. A department is alert to the slightest tremor from the House of Commons but too often insufficiently perceptive of major trends and developments in society at large. There is a precise and highly responsive mechanism for dealing with the Parliamentary question or Minister's case but often no mechanism at all for identifying, analysing and indicating ways of adjusting to current or future developments of significance in the external community.

Finally, an air of unreality is cast over the five-year P.E.S.C. forecasts by the fact that five-year manpower planning is not carried out in the same degree of detail. Within a general long-term forecast the Civil Service Department and Establishments Divisions of departments operate 'establishments control', that is, control over the numbers and grades of staff employed, by the imposition of annual staff ceilings and by *ad hoc* cuts in manpower allocations (see Chapter 8). A department may therefore have a long-term expenditure plan but may have no idea of whether it will ever be allowed to recruit the staff which are allowed for in the plan and on which its attainment will depend. Indeed, there are examples of the refusal by the Civil Service Department to allow recruitment to the levels required to sustain the expenditures already approved by the Treasury.

THE FULTON PROPOSALS

The Fulton Committee commented upon the 'crowding out' of long-term thinking and planning in departments by the more immediate demands arising from the Parliamentary and public responsibilities of Ministers. It concluded that 'a department's responsibility for major long-term policy planning should be clearly allocated to a planning and research unit'. A planning unit should be equipped to assemble and analyse research information and 'its main task should be to identify and study the problems and needs of the future and the possible means to meet them; it should also be its function to see that day-to-day policy decisions are taken with as full a recognition as possible of their likely implications for the future.'[29]

The Committee thought that planning units should be staffed by younger-generation Civil Service managers and outside experts on short-term contracts and should be headed by Senior Policy Advisers. Though these advisers should be lower in status than the Permanent Secretaries who head departments, they should have direct access to Ministers on questions of long-term planning. In some cases Policy Advisers might be personally appointed by Ministers but usually they would be career civil servants. The Committee drew a distinction between the responsibilities of the Permanent Secretary (the management of the operations of a department and day-to-day Ministerial support) and those of the Senior Policy Adviser (studies of long-term departmental policy).

Fulton's Management Consultancy Group had earlier drawn the attention of the Committee to the need for planning units, which it saw as concerned not only with studies of long-term policy but also with providing a planning system for the management of department operations. 'Such units would be engaged on preparing "scenarios" of the department's situation in future years, identifying the likely policy needs and the associated demands for resources. On this basis the allocation of resources can be planned and can be adjusted to meet changing situations, programmes of work can be initiated and objectives set for various parts of the organization.'[30] Significantly, the Management Consultancy Group then went on to suggest systems of objective setting, control and accountability. The Fulton Committee saw planning as concentrating upon research into the definition of long-term policy objectives; the Consultancy Group's planning units were seen as doing not only this but becoming deeply involved in new accounting and information systems and the definition of management programmes.

The Fulton concept of planning units, though right in seeing the need for specialized groups concentrating upon the study of future problems, had one major weakness. It envisaged the separation of planning from control: first, by failing to take the Consultancy Group's point that policy research should lead to the statement of departmental and unit objectives and then to programmes of work for accountable managers; and secondly, by recommending that planning units should be headed by Senior Policy Advisers reporting direct to the Minister and not to the Permanent Secretary. As we shall see later in this chapter, a major problem of planning in departments is how to link the plan with a system for seeing that it is carried out: the Committee's proposal simply accentuated the problem. Furthermore, the removal of responsibility for long-term planning from the official head of the department would perpetuate the isolation of present research units. The Fulton proposals would actually confirm and institutionalize the gap between planners and managers by establishing a structure in which the planning group reported directly to the political master and the managers reported to the top permanent official. The suspicion must be that the Committee wrapped two quite different ideas into one proposal: first, the concept of a corporate planning unit, and secondly the idea of an independent *cabinet* of Ministerial advisers influenced partly by French and American practice and partly by the Labour Party's complaint that Ministers had insufficient knowledge of what was going on in their departments.

The Consultancy Group's view of a planning unit was influenced by industrial experience of corporate planning. In government these processes pose far more complex problems than in industry as we can see from considering recent American experience with programming, planning and budgeting systems.

PLANNING-PROGRAMMING-BUDGETING SYSTEMS (PPB)

PPB is a planning system in which expenditures are displayed in a way which relates them to major policy objectives and in which analysis is carried out on the cost and benefits of alternative routes to those objectives. It has been called 'potentially the most significant management improvement in the history of American government'[31] and was first applied in 1961 to the U.S. Department of Defense. The impetus for its adoption there came from Robert McNamara, then Defense Secretary, and Charles J. Hitch, his Assistant Secretary (Comptroller), who had previously been head of the economic department of RAND, a research consultancy where the early work on the design of the system had been carried out. The results of its application encouraged President Johnson to announce in August 1965 that it would in future be applied in all federal agencies.

PPB: The Classification of Accounts

At the outset, PPB requires a classification of expenditures different from that traditionally prepared by government departments.

Government accounts are prepared according to the conventions of the supply procedure by which Parliament annually authorizes estimates and receives statements of expenditure (see Chapter 5). These accounts are classified according to input, or subject of expenditure – for example, all wages and salaries, accommodation costs, equipment costs are grouped together. Thus in 1969/70 the general estimates (as distinct from estimates of grants, subsidies, price guarantees and services) for the Ministry of Agriculture were arranged into the following categories:

AGRICULTURE, FISHERIES AND FOOD
   (GENERAL)   *£m.*

A. SALARIES, etc.	27.28
B. GENERAL ADMINISTRATIVE EXPENSES	
(Travelling etc., Post Office, misc.)	3.89
C. COMMITTEES AND INQUIRIES	0.14
D. PAYMENTS FOR AGENCY SERVICES	1.51
E. FATSTOCK DEFICIENCY PAYMENTS, Sundry Expenses	0.05
F. WHITE FISH AUTHORITY: Salaries etc. for Chairman and	
members	0.02
G. ROYAL BOTANIC GARDENS, KEW, Salaries and Allowances	0.72
H. PLANT VARIETY RIGHTS OFFICE, Salaries and Allowances	0.04
I. MEAT AND LIVESTOCK COMMISSION, Salaries and Fees	1.93
Deduct: Appropriations in aid	0.87
	34.71

Additional Expenditure

(1) Maintenance, furniture, fuel, light, etc.	5.59
(2) Rental values	2.10
(3) Rates	0.60
(4) Stationery and printing	1.08
(5) Superannuation	4.23
(6) Miscellaneous	0.30
	13.90

In contrast, PPB requires the classification of expenditures into 'programmes', that is categories which display the aims of the expenditure. It focuses attention not on the inputs, or items which are to be bought, but on the purpose to which the spending is to be directed.

The 1970–71 U.S. budget included a special analysis by programme categories of the budgets of selected federal agencies. The estimates of the Department of Agriculture were arranged into the following main programme categories and sub-categories:

Program Category and Sub-Category	1970 Estimate* $000 m.
Income and abundance:	
Farm income	4.02
Agricultural production capacity	0.49
Agricultural marketing and distribution system	0.11
Growing Nations – new markets	
Food for Freedom	1.01
Export market development	0.03
Agricultural development	0.01
International agricultural services	0.01
Dimensions for living	
Diets and nutrition	1.10
Health and safety	0.13
Education and training	0.02
Services for living	0.04
Communities of tomorrow	
Community development services	0.04
Housing	0.06
Public facility and business expansion	0.37
Resource protection and environmental improvement	0.20
Recreation, wildlife and natural beauty	0.07
Timber	0.33
General support	0.05
Offsetting receipts	0.43
Total Budget Authority	7.70

*These estimates also showed comparisons with 1968 actual and 1969 estimated expenditures for each category and sub-category. Figures are rounded to the nearest $10m.

Some PPB applications have never progressed beyond this preliminary stage of reclassifying accounts, but the implementation of the system should start at this point and move through sequential stages of planning, programming and budgeting.

PPB: The Planning Stage

The planning stage of PPB typically has these processes:

1. A statement by the top decision-making authority of the purpose and aims of the organization: that is its areas of activity and the values it is seeking to establish ('the provision of recreation opportunities'; 'the reduction of infant mortality rates'; 'to help individuals select and obtain efficient counselling in manpower centres'; 'to hold those committed to custody and to provide conditions for their detention which are currently acceptable to society, . . . in dealing with convicted offenders . . . to do all that may be possible within the currency of the sentence to encourage and assist them to lead the useful life'). The aims of government departments are both more complex and diffuse than those of businesses and few have been put in writing. They usually have to be distilled from legislation and regulations, Ministerial statements and the proceedings of official inquiries and Parliamentary committees.

2. The establishment of planning and research staffs to develop the programme structure (see below), examine programme proposals, carry analytical studies and monitor, and report on, programme results. The Ministry of Defence, for example, has 'a central, "uncommitted" policy and programming unit which is not tied down by day-to-day business and has direct access to top management with the right to challenge or compel examinations of any aspect of the programme, and to propose alternative policies for study'.[32]

The central Finance department or Treasury also requires a programme evaluation, review and audit body capable of examining and challenging the definition of departmental objectives, validating the analytical basis of departmental programmes, scrutinizing the cost of departmental resource requirements and with the authority to exercise sanctions against inadequately supported bids for funds. The Treasury Board in Canada, for example, has laid down that 'unsubstantial submissions or submissions that simply summarize many unrelated requirements will continue to be exposed to arbitrary reductions'.[33] The central body should also be concerned to examine departmental submissions in aggregate for evidence of inconsistency, ambiguity and conflict and to carry out analytical studies of programmes which cross departmental boundaries (for instance in the fields of regional development and the relief of unemployment) or of major national projects (such as port development).

3. The design of a programme structure. This involves the classification of public expenditures on an output basis and their grouping into basic functions which are directed to a common purpose. Each function is then progressively subdivided into a hierarchy of programme categories, programmes and programme elements (or 'activities' and 'sub-activities'). Thus, in the nomenclature of the Public Expenditure Survey, a basic function of government is the provision of Environmental Services. Within this there is the function of Roads and Public Lighting; at the third level of classification there could be a programme category which might group all research expenditure; at the fourth, the programme, which might cover research into traffic management; at the fifth, the programme element which might relate to a specific research project. In addition to the establishment of a hierarchy of programmes and activities addressed to the needs of the general community, it may be necessary to produce special programmes aimed at particular 'target groups': that is, within a general category of preventive health care (programmes of education, immunization, communicable disease detection), specific clientele groups or disease categories may be identified as requiring separate expenditures: low-income families, pre-school children; smallpox, VD, cervical cancer.

In a series of model programmes for U.S. cities, states and counties drawn up in a research project at George Washington University, a sub-activity concerned with foster-home care for 'normal' children is located within the programme structure for 'Health' (as shown on p. 120).[34]

During the process of developing a programme structure the bulk of the current expenditure of a department should be related to its aims. There is now a basis for examining the weight of expenditure currently given to one aim as compared with another; it is

PROGRAM STRUCTURE FOR 'HEALTH'

Category I*   Promotion for General Health and Vigor

Objective: To promote a state of wellbeing by patterns of living.

Definition: Programs other than direct health programs that elevate the health status and vigor of a people and are not merely concerned with the absence of disease and injury.

A satisfactory nutrition

B satisfactory educational
  attainment

C leisure for physical and
  emotional fitness

D employment satisfaction

E income maintenance

F satisfactory social and
  inter-group relations

G satisfactory home and community environment

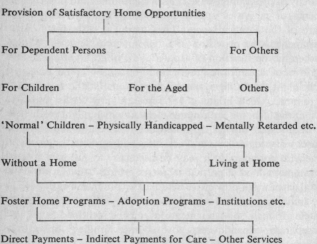

Provision of Satisfactory Home Opportunities

For Dependent Persons   For Others

For Children   For the Aged   Others

'Normal' Children – Physically Handicapped – Mentally Retarded etc.

Without a Home   Living at Home

Foster Home Programs – Adoption Programs – Institutions etc.

Direct Payments – Indirect Payments for Care – Other Services

Supporting Activities: – Finding Homes – Examination and Referral
                   of Children – Research – Evaluation and
                   Planning – General Administration.

   *Other main categories are II Environmental Health: III Preventive Health Care: IV Diagnostic Services, Treatment and Rehabilitation Care: V General Support.

possible to examine which activities contribute to more than one aim or which appear not to make a contribution to any aim; some quantitative data exists on which to display choices between programmes and activities; an examination can begin to be made on interfaces between the programmes of the department and those of other departments or external authorities.

4. The specification of measures of need and performance criteria which will allow the formulation of specific and quantified objectives for programmes and activities and the assessment of their impact on the community. The planning staff carry out preliminary research and analysis into the dimensions of the community defined by departmental aims and its present and prospective needs. This calls for surveys of population and client groups and the social and economic trends affecting them and provides the quantitative background for the translation of aims into objectives. Thus, aim: 'to provide outdoor recreation opportunities for the people of —'; objective: 'to provide for wilderness-type outdoor recreation experience accessible to 90 per cent of urban residents within x hours' drive by 1975–6.' An objective should be measurable. It should state the quantity (and quality, if possible) of benefit that is being aimed at and the period in which it is to be provided. In many areas of government activity this is not difficult. In some, however, it may be virtually impossible. At one end of the range, the objectives of a health programme for schoolchildren can be measured by such criteria as scores in physical fitness tests, the percentages of children with uncorrected chronic defects by type, mortality or hospitalization rates; the objectives of a water fluoridation programme can be expressed in terms of the average number of decayed or filled teeth by age group; those of an accident-prevention programme by rates of mortality, injury and absenteeism; those of a job-finding programme by the numbers of people of different skill levels who are found employment and the length of their period of unemployment. The objectives of more complex programmes can often only be expressed not by indicators of ultimate benefit but by 'intermediate' indicators of volume or service provided or by comparative indicators. Thus the objective of an evening-class programme will be impossible to measure in terms of the cultural or leisure enhancement or the entertainment enjoyed by its participants, and its objective can be expressed only in terms of the number of places provided or occupied; the objective of a

national parks programme may best be stated in terms of the number of acres administered or made accessible; a library programme in terms of the number of volumes in stock and on loan; a police patrol programme by the areas and frequency of patrol; a welfare programme by the average social worker case load, the number of children in care. The aim, however, should always be to attempt to specify ultimate rather than intermediate objectives. Ultimate objectives concentrate the decision-maker upon essentials – for example the number of families decently housed rather than the number of houses built.

5. The preparation of issue letters. These are letters from the director of the central programme review office to heads of departments suggesting the major problems that should receive attention during the current planning cycle. They are the product of regular discussions between the review office and each department. 'The rationale behind the identification of major issues is the need to focus the limited analytic resources on the more important problems, the importance of reaching agreement upon the nature of the problems involved and the value of analysis which can broaden the range of policy alternatives considered by the agency and the President.'[35] Thus a letter from the Director of the U.S. Bureau of the Budget to the Secretary of Transportation in April 1968 raised the following questions for the fiscal year 1970:[36]

(a) Issue: What should be the composition of the Federal-aid financing in 1970 of state highway engineering projects considering the costs and benefits in terms of reduced congestion and improved highway safety? Compare new construction and engineering improvements to existing roads in urban areas.

(b) Issue: If the Department of Transportation proposes a parking program for 1970 under what guidelines will parking facilities be evaluated and financed? What measures of the contribution of urban area parking facilities to more efficient urban transportation will be applied? What is the appropriate allocation of effort between fringe and downtown parking capacity? Should the federal role be to subsidize private initiative, finance

State and local initiatives, build capacity to be leased, or build and operate capacity?

And so on, for twenty-four issues – each accompanied by a list of the alternatives to be considered and a deadline for the answer.

At the end of the planning stage, there should exist a statement of the aims of the organization, a categorization of all its expenditures in terms of those aims, criteria by which needs can be assessed and objectives developed for many of its programmes and a delineation of the critical issues to which its attention should be directed. At this point guidance from Ministers is required for the analytical effort of the next stage – what are their attitudes to the present disposition of resources? Do they wish to swing effort from one programme category to another? What objectives appear to them to be attainable for various programmes over the next five years? Do they have a particular target group of the population in mind as warranting a particularly heavy allocation of funds? What, from their political perspectives, do they see as the key problem areas and opportunities for progress? What are their attitudes to those areas which have been specified by the central budget authority as crucial?

PPB: The Programming Stage

Programming, the definition and ranking of alternative methods of allocating resources so as to achieve the desired objectives, is the core of PPB. It includes these elements:

6. Programme analysis and special analytic studies. This is broadly comparable to the strategic studies – the gap analysis, investment appraisal, acquisition and diversification studies and simulation modelling – carried out by corporate planning units in industry. One difference is that programme analysis works within much wider tolerances of accuracy; objectives are less accurately quantifiable, the relationships between major variables are less well understood, feedback from the environment is slower, the department may be operating at arm's length from the community and the intervening organizations (local authorities, private

industry, public bodies with varying degrees of autonomy) may be beyond departmental control or not planning so far ahead anyway.

Programme analysis usually starts with a definition of the 'base case' – what is the total public programme currently being addressed to the satisfaction of a particular community need? What result is this programme achieving? If present social and economic trends continue over the next five years where then will the present programme stand in relation to the need?* Thus, a special analytic study might identify all the expenditures which are currently being devoted to closing the gap between the level of unemployment in Ulster and the average level over the rest of the country by means of taxation reliefs, investment allowances, advance factories, government retraining centres, government contracts and expenditures on public works and might try to analyse the net effect of each and all of these on meeting the objective over the periods in which they have been in operation.

Diverging from the base case, the programme-analysis staff generate an array of alternative approaches that are potentially available to meet policy objectives. For example, at the time of writing it is believed that between two and five million people in the U.K. are living in poverty according to various definitions of what constitutes a minimum standard of living. These people fall into main groups – the old, and low-paid workers with large families – though the numbers in each group and the incidence of poverty within them are not fully known (that is we do not yet have sufficient information even to develop the base case).[37]

*Advocates of 'zero-base' budgeting argue that instead of accepting or even considering the base case, departments should be required to justify the need for every existing programme, however long established, and should assume that the base is zero, that is that the case for every programme should be argued as if it were to be started afresh. This would oblige Ministers and officials to focus on the basic purposes of their organization rather than on the additional expenditures for which they were seeking authorization. There are, however, a large number of practical obstacles to zero-base budgeting: many departments are 'locked' into expenditure programmes by long-standing legislation; the public and Parliament look upon some programmes as a commitment and even to question them would be politically unacceptable; no department could mount a legislative and analytical review of its basic programmes except over a period of many years.

Programmes to relieve these conditions could take the form of additional supplementary benefits to groups in the greatest need; increased family allowances (with or without 'claw-back' through income tax); increased old-age pensions; raising the earned income allowance for wage earners by various degrees; the institution of national minimum wage; the establishment of a negative income tax at various levels of benefit to the poorly paid.

The examination of alternatives involves attempting to quantify the probable results and the costs of a manageable number of potential approaches to satisfying community needs by using analytical techniques, of which cost-benefit or cost-effectiveness analysis are the best known. Costing in this context is not the accurate and closely defined costing of the business accountant but uses very 'rough-cut' costs and focuses on the marginal or incremental values appearing to attach to different approaches to an objective. Typically, the data in aggregate is so unreliable that 'in most long-range planning problems where major uncertainties are present quantitative differences among alternatives must be *at least a factor of two* before we can have any confidence that the differences are significant'.[38] One significant risk, not unknown in corporate planning, is that the statisticians and operational researchers to whom these exercises are given may be tempted to construct bigger and bigger and increasingly expensive models on progressively deteriorating data. Most cost-benefit analyses are a mixture of accurate costings, estimates, forecasts, possible cost-ranges, and informed and uninformed guesses, and they should be displayed in a way which enables the decision-maker to assess their reliability.

There are two principal approaches to cost-benefit analysis: the fixed-utility method, in which the desired benefit is stated and the analyst tries to find the least-cost route or combination of routes to that end, and the fixed-budget method, in which the probable budget allocation is stated by the ultimate decision-maker and the analyst attempts to find the route which produces the highest level of benefit. Major uncertainties can be tested by 'exercising the model', that is, changing the values assigned to uncertain factors to see if they make a significant difference to the outcomes. Exercising usually involves some variant of sensitivity analysis in which the factors known to be highly uncertain are assigned high values during one run of the model and low values during the next, so as to see what the ultimate effect might be; or in which some external factor, such as economic growth, is assigned various values, or the evaluation criteria are changed in weight, or all the uncertainties are alternatively valued optimistically or pessimistically, or various time scales of expenditure are postulated.

The main problem in cost-benefit analysis is to establish criteria for the assessment of social and economic impact, to place a value on 'public goods'. For many prospective benefits the final assessment is entirely a matter of political value-judgement. One of the problems of the assessment of benefit which recurs in transport, health, nutrition, welfare, environmental and other programmes is the value to be placed on a human life. Professor Alan Williams has observed: 'Attempts have been made to derive the value of saving a life from compensation awards by the courts, since these are made in the name of the community at large. But in my view it is the task of our elected representatives to determine what this figure should be. That is, they should solemnly debate an issue such as "how much of the community's resources it is worth devoting to extend the expectation of the life of the average citizen by one year". Should it be £50, £500, £5,000 or what? Once determined, this figure could be used in all investment decisions involving additional life expectation . . . so that we do not find ourselves spending (say) £100,000 to prevent a loss of 100 man-years of life expectation on the railways, while on the roads (let us say) the corresponding figure is £1,000, for with the present diverse pattern we are not increasing the expectation of life of the community as a whole as much as we could even with the existing amounts of resources specifically devoted to this objective.'[39]

The problem of valuing social impact is particularly intractable in areas of government policy involving aesthetic or amenity factors. A recent case in point is the cost-benefit analysis carried out by the Roskill Commission on the third London airport – by far the biggest exercise of its kind ever carried out in this country. The cost penalty for the noise nuisance at each of the three sites was calculated at between £11m. and £24m. out of total costs which ranged from £2,200m. to £2,400m., and that for the loss of recreation amenity ranged from £0.3m. to £6.7m., yet the adverse impact upon the environment was clearly the issue which preoccupied most of the community who had an interest in the matter. As one commentator wrote at the time of the publication of the analysis: 'Essentially, economists cost what can be costed. In the case of recreation, they calculate what people would be willing to pay for the pleasure of visiting a site *if they were asked to pay* . . . It is a fair bet that on the methods the research team has used, there would be no justification for preserving Stonehenge, or Hampstead Heath, or possibly even St Paul's Cathedral.'[40] In the event, of course, the Cabinet decided that the environmental and recreational factors were worth more than the £197 million difference between the economically most desirable site and the environmentally most desirable one.

Itemizing the potential costs and benefits associated with a projected programme can call for the construction of highly complex 'balance sheets'. The typical mixture of a few hard facts and many 'unknowns' is brought out in this highly simplified balance sheet of a programme aimed at reducing school 'drop-outs' in Canada:

PROGRAM ANALYSIS

Resource cost per drop-out prevented	
Direct prevention costs	$5,814
Additional instruction costs	725
	$6,539
Internal benefits per drop-out prevented	
Increased present value of lifetime income (unadjusted)	$2,750
Minus adjustment for effects of non-educational factors	—
Improved self-esteem of student	+
External benefits per drop-out prevented	
Increased productivity of co-operating resources	+
Increased social and political consciousness and participation	+

Decreased social costs (e.g. of crime and delinquency)	+
Decreased social costs of administering transfer payment programs (e.g. of public assistance)	+
Inter-generation benefits	+
Total costs (per drop-out prevented) not covered by measured benefits	$3,800
Distributional effects	+

Source: Operations Research Ltd, Ottawa

7. Programme analysis results in the presentation of a number of programme choices to the decision-maker. 'The idea is to present the results of the formal quantitative work, interpret these results and then to say this is as far as the formal quantitative analysis *per se* will permit us to go. However, there are important *qualitative* considerations that you (the decision-maker) should try to take into account: and here they are (listed by the analyst).'[41] The political decision-maker has to compare programmes to assess their relative value for money and to specify programme objectives. He has to weigh a programme's ostensible value against his view of the reliability of the supporting analysis, its likely acceptability to other Ministers, the legislature, the electorate and pressure groups, the financial and other constraints likely to be imposed upon him, his own political values, the state of his popularity and his personal need to strike a new posture or lie low. In many sensitive areas of policy – immigration, penal policy, housing policy, major construction and aerospace projects – these judgemental factors may often outweigh the most rigorous cost-benefit analysis.

8. When programme decisions have been taken and specific objectives have been agreed, each programme is costed in much greater detail and is translated into a multi-year (usually three or five) plan showing the estimated costs and results of each year of programme implementation and supported by a programme memorandum which describes in detail:

(a) the strategic and analytical justification for the programme;

(b) year-by-year indicators of cost and achievement and acceptable limits of variance;

(c) how the programme will be funded;

(d) who will be responsible for the management of the programme and its activities;

(e) the requirements for special skills or staff training;

(f) relationships with allied programmes in other departments or institutions;

(g) major uncertainties;

(h) key issues yet unresolved;

(i) the procedure for reviewing the programme.

PPB: The Budgeting Stage

9. Financial authority has now to be sought from the Legislature for the first year's expenditures on all the department's programmes. This usually requires a translation of programme expenditures into the traditional form of annual financial estimates. All programme costs (and receipts, if any) are classified into such inputs as wages, accommodation, equipment and capital expenditure by means of an indexing arrangement called a 'crosswalk'. In some governments (for example in Canada – see Chapter 5) there is a move towards presenting annual estimates to the Legislature in both input and programme form or only in programme form on the grounds that it is in a better position to keep the Executive under surveillance if public spending is arranged in programmes with stated objectives rather than in lists of the things that it is proposed to buy. When this matter was discussed in the Select Committee on Procedure the enthusiasm of some of its members for the presentation of estimates by programme was somewhat dampened by the attitude of senior civil servants who thought that 'Parliament would be no better off if its accounts were in a better form' (Permanent Secretary, Defence), and that the 'present form of the civil estimates from the point of view of the efficiency of the governmental spending of the money does not seem very relevant ... the Comptroller and Auditor General fixes on a certain point ... he asks questions on how the department behaves, reports and then there is a discussion in the

Public Accounts Committee. This would seem the natural way of dealing with it. I do not think it turns on the accounts in a detailed point' (Permanent Secretary, MinTech).[42]

10. The budget is approved, the plan becomes a management instruction and the programmes are put into operation. This has always been the weakest part of the whole PPB process. Most authorities on the subject can describe in the greatest detail how to devise a programme structure and how to carry out cost-benefit analysis, but when it gets to the point of actually managing a programme a certain vagueness creeps into the discussion. The early theory on how to integrate the planning structure with the management structure was that, where necessary, programme costs were to be reclassified by a second cross walk into managerial elements: that is, each programme was to be broken into pieces which coincided with the structure of departments, divisions and branches. If a programme crossed departmental boundaries, then one department was to be designated the 'lead agency' and was to insure that the others made their contribution to the programme. Within departments, each manager of a contributing branch or division had to insure that his unit fulfilled each of the pieces of programmes allocated to him. We shall see that in the event this arrangement proved extremely difficult to apply and that new approaches to the problem are being devised.

11. Every year the multi-year plan and its constituent programmes are reviewed and rolled forward another year. Ideally, information on programme expenditures and results is produced during the course of the year so that operations can be tracked by programme, by appropriation category and by organizational unit, and thus the performance of the programme, the spend against the estimate authorized by the Legislature and, where possible, the efficiency of the managing or contributing units can be monitored. In some cases the feedback of results is as rapid as it usually is in industry (benefits issued, criminals apprehended, families housed), but very often the lag between the expenditure and even intermediate objectives (roads constructed, probation officer training places provided) runs to years and the lag between the expenditure and the final objectives (improvements in health, the reduction of traffic accidents, or of delinquency), may run to

decades. In the long-lag programmes, *ad hoc* research studies into the current state of progress have to take the place of a running review and evaluation of results.

PPB: An Evaluation

'This morning I have just concluded a breakfast meeting with the Cabinet and with the heads of federal agencies and I am asking each of them to immediately begin to introduce a very new and very revolutionary system of planning and programming and budgeting throughout the vast federal government, so that through the tools of modern management the full promise of a finer life can be brought to every American at the lowest possible cost' (President Johnson, 25 August 1965).

There were a number of reasons why the President was encouraged to take such an optimistic view of the benefits of PPB. The application of analysis to defence problems by a powerful Systems Analysis Office under Defense Secretary McNamara appeared to be a highly successful innovation. When McNamara arrived at the Department of Defense (in his own words 'the greatest single management complex in history'[43]) from the Ford Motor Company it was apparent that there was conflict and wasteful competition for resources between the three armed services: 'each sought to guarantee larger shares in future budgets by concentrating on dramatic new weapons'[44] and each concentrated upon its own view of the likely course of any future war: the Navy upon its new nuclear missile-equipped submarines, the Army upon anti-missile systems, the Air Force upon bombers and missiles. None of them had fully analysed the supporting resources they required and none had taken a policy view far enough into the future. McNamara saw that the central problem was 'the absence of the essential management tools needed to make sound decisions'.[45] He therefore saw the need to install a global planning system which would permit the systematic analysis of the national need for defence and would enable the department to select the programme that met that need at least cost. The emphasis had to be upon cutting across traditional service boundaries so as to find those forces and weapons that represented best value for money ('more bang per buck') in the context of a review of all the possible threats to national security. In the early years of the use of the system, the analytical processes supporting PPB permitted the rationalization of defence spending on missiles and their supporting infrastructure; established more accurately the cost of different weapons systems; defined costs in relation to the missions and objectives of different forces and established the real differences in strength between the NATO and Warsaw Pact alliances.

On a wave of enthusiasm generated by this experience, PPB was preached at civilian agencies by the Department of Defence and the Bureau of the Budget to such an effect that by 1969 it had been introduced into twenty-six agencies in the federal government at a yearly cost in extra jobs and contract consultancy services of about $60m. a year.[46]

PPB appeared to have great promise for civil agencies in U.S. government because it tackled some long-standing problems while building on earlier developments in accounting practice. One problem had been that single sectors of expenditure were divided among an unusually large number of independent and separately financed agencies and departments. The Health Budget, for example, was spread over thirteen agencies (including the Small Business Administration) and seven Cabinet Departments. In a number of cases, health expenditures were classified under other activities; in the 1965 budget, for example, only £3 billion of the total £5.4 billion allocated for health could be traced in departmental or agency accounts.[47] Similarly, federal transport expenditures were spread over nine departments and agencies.[48] There were no fewer than forty-two federal departments, agencies and bureaux spending funds on education and nearly every Committee of Congress had jurisdiction over some type of education legislation.[49]* There was also no formal system of long-term expenditure planning (though there were five-year 'previews' submitted by each agency to the Bureau of the Budget) because of the resistance of the Legislature to the idea. On the other hand,

*The Nixon Administration's Adviser on Consumer Affairs, Mrs Knaur, discovered that 413 units of the Federal Government administered 938 'consumer-related activities' (*Which*, February 1970).

many federal agencies had long-established systems of management accounting, budgetary control and efficiency measurement. The Hoover Commission of 1945 led to the Budget Accounting Procedures Act of 1950 which had required agencies to produce cost data for each organizational unit ('performance budgeting'). They therefore had a foundation of internal cost and performance information and a number of managers who were familiar with carrying out or using cost analysis.

In spite of these favourable conditions, PPB has not lived up to its early promise in U.S. government. In 1970, a survey of its use in sixteen agencies concluded that 'the planning, programming and budgeting functions are not performed much differently in most agencies than they were before the introduction of PPB'.[50] Another study concluded that 'very few budget decisions have been a product (or even a by-product) of PPB' and referred to the 'paucity of PPB success stories'.[51] It was put to the author by senior planning staff in Washington in late 1970 that PPB had led to 'disillusion and disappointment' (and in Ottawa that the mention of PPB would provoke 'critical, amused or alienated' reactions from senior officials).

Examination of PPB experience in the U.S.A. and Canada carries some lessons for the development of planning systems in British government. While some of its failures and successes are due to the characteristics of the American system of government, others are of relevance to the current attempts to introduce it in Britain. At the outset, many of the Congressional committees which examine and authorize departmental appropriations viewed PPB with suspicion as another attempt by the Executive to outsmart the Legislature. They also proved remarkably resistant to the persuasion of cost-benefit analysis. As the assistant director for programme evaluation of the Bureau of the Budget observed to a Congressional Committee: 'Because the calculus of politics and the calculus of efficient resource allocation differ so markedly, the combination of cost-benefit analysis and politics can turn out to be quite ironical, as well as explosive. It may be recalled that cost-benefit analysis was originally and most thoroughly applied to water resource projects. Yet, it is a matter of common knowledge that direct benefit/cost ratios of 0.5 or 0.8

have not precluded projects from being pushed and implemented.'[52] Time and again Congressional committees have defied
the logic of analysis in order to do right by the interests that they
represent; they have insisted on low-benefit irrigation and highway projects, on a nation-wide spread of small hospitals when
analysis showed the logic of a concentration on large ones, on
uneconomically favourable tax treatment to private flying – every
analyst in Washington has his favourite example.

The objectives of some programmes were defeated by the
intransigence of defiance of state and city governments. In
September 1970, for example, Governor Reagan of California
had to be ordered by a federal court to comply with the rules on
the payment of cost-of-living allowances under the Federal Aid
to Families with Dependant Children Program, but was reported
as saying that he would 'take on the welfare bureaucracy in
Washington' rather than comply.[53] There were also examples of
the diversion of federal poverty programme funds to unauthorized ends: it is said that many a dollar aimed at poor black schools
ended up paying for band uniforms in rich white ones.

Considerable harm was done by the way in which PPB was
introduced. It was thrust upon departments in a way which suggested a marked increase in Presidential intervention in departmental affairs. The abrasive young analysts who were introduced
into the civil departments to carry out and advise on programme
analysis greatly underrated the complexities and subtleties of
social programmes. As might be expected, the reaction of some
long-serving officials to these unwelcome invaders, bent on
quantifying every dimension of activity, took the form of darkest
negativism:

'No one was surprised to have it said that analytic treatment of
Government problems does not tell one everything, or that political factors are important or that distribution of benefits is often as
important as amount, or that analysis in many areas is difficult.
All of this could be readily agreed upon. But the idea that anyone
would *deny* any utility to rigorous thought, quantitative where
possible, about the gains, losses, and resource expenditures involved in a particular course of action was not expected.'[54]

Congress still required budget estimates to be submitted in the traditional form and this was the basis on which departments and agencies had to argue for their money. Programme structures were therefore overlaid on this system as a secondary form of expenditure analysis with lower political priority. They were 'appended to the traditional channels of budgeting supported by the appropriation accounts . . . each of these processes has data requirements, time schedules and semi-independent players with only partial overlap and communication'.[55] This, coupled with the fact that the programme structure did not coincide with the organization structure within departments, meant that the PPB system bore little relationship to decision-making or management processes.

The exponents of PPB also overestimated the capacity of departments to carry out cost-benefit analysis. Few departments could produce thorough analyses for, say, several score programmes and a dozen special issues. The Bureau of the Budget has estimated that only about 25 per cent of the analytical work could be judged adequate or better – 'most programme memorranda tend to be descriptive, verbose, nonanalytic accounts of existing and proposed programs, together with an impassioned plea for funding at the full request'.[56] In addition, the very large number of social programmes sponsored by different organizations and devoted to closely related objectives created great problems of congestion at the centre. The 1970 catalogue of federal domestic assistance (antipoverty and social improvement programmes) produced by the Office of Economic Opportunity identified 1,019 programmes administered by fifty-seven departments and agencies (of which twenty-six related to home buying and ownership schemes, for example).*

*Rural American Indian Communities are the beneficiaries of programmes for tribal operations, community development, adult education (including consumer protection), technical assistance, vocational training, employment assistance, work experience, general assistance, housing development, housing improvement, industrial and tourism development, investment, range improvement, real-estate appraisal, property management, expert-witness loans, tribal credit, conservation, arts and crafts development, sanitation facilities, Indian health, emergency foods, nutritional deficiency, clinical-laboratory upgrading, community-health representatives, rural electrification, neighbourhood facilities and tribal account services.

Cost-benefit analysis in support of a claim for funds was not the objective, detached, rational procedure that the theorists assumed: to agency management it was just another tool of advocacy. 'In most cases, their fundamental objective is not to make analysis successful. They are trying to get proposals accepted. If they find analysis useful, they will use it.'[57] It is not difficult to prove that a prized programme is essential in the national interest or to support a new project with convincing cost-benefit analysis. Thus most of the analytical effort went into justifying new programmes for which the agency wanted a budget increase: very little went into proving the value of long-standing programmes. 'The agencies that monitor old programmes, which on careful review may not be worth the money, are the ones that will do their best to fend off analysis.'[58]

In the cases where PPB was taken seriously by the top management of a department it soon loomed large in that department's incentive system. Giving a high priority to quantification and analysis became a mark of a 'good' manager and was rewarded by recognition and esteem. Unfortunately, because it is easier to quantify than to analyse, there is a risk in such a situation that measurement, using real or phony numbers, will become an end in itself. The Department of Defense, particularly in its conduct of the Vietnam war, was swept by an enthusiasm for doubtful quantification (for instance for bogus body counts and measures of pacification): 'What happened in Vietnam is that we are simply drowned in information. A very small proportion of this information was adequately analysed ... the system that was developed in Vietnam was geared to the massive outpouring of data, data that drowned all of us.'[59]

The evidence so far from U.S. federal agencies has been that the best results from the use of PPB have been obtained in organizations which produce physical assets. This is partly because the cost and benefits of alternative proposals for roads, dams and aerospace projects are more easily measurable than those for poverty, health and education programmes, but it is also because organizations which produce these goods are usually headed by engineer – or scientist – administrators. Most of the successes of PPB are quoted from agencies concerned with transportation and construction which in the U.S. are managed by technically qualified men. The case which is often quoted in support of PPB is the success of the National Aeronautics and Space Administration, which was not only headed by an outstanding engineer and teemed with technically qualified managers but also had a single specific programme objective: to get a man to the moon by 1970. It usually transpires that the other agencies in which PPB has been a success were doing cost-benefit analysis before PPB was introduced: the Corps of Engineers, the Atomic Energy Commission, various other transportation and construction groups. So far, PPB has produced fewer useful results in the civil agencies which run social programmes and which (like Whitehall departments) tend to employ administrators without a technical background.

Perhaps more important from the point of view of those concerned with the development of management systems in government departments, PPB – at least as originally conceived – often cannot easily be matched to a control system. A department may have an array of programmes, all justified by analysis, all projected as five-year plans, all endorsed by the central budget department and all funded by the legislature, but may then find that very few of its managers can be held accountable for programme results. If a department has full responsibility for programme management, from the original political decision to direct contact with the ultimate beneficiaries, and if each programme corresponds to a managerial command within the department, then the programme and the managerial structure coincide and managers can be made responsible for programme inputs and results. But this is rarely the situation.* Many programmes have to cross the internal management structure of a department (a hospital building programme in a health department requires inputs from a finance division, a manpower division, engineering and design divisions, medical divisions, supply divisions) and many organizational units must devote part of their time to a variety of programmes (a social-security office handles sickness benefit, maternity, industrial injury, retirement and other

*This situation is fairly common in British local government authorities and in some of them PPB is being adopted with encouraging results.

programmes). Furthermore many programmes have to cross departmental boundaries (a regional development programme calls for inputs from departments concerned with labour, agriculture, transport, industry, housing) and many will have to cross the boundaries between central and local government (typically in the fields of education and health) or even take the form of grants to autonomous agencies (University Grants Committee, the White Fish Authority). This has proved to be an intractable problem in U.S. federal government (twenty-six agencies still dispense aid to education through 330 programmes). The concept of the lead agency managing and controlling cross-departmental programmes had to be dropped in the face of interdepartmental rivalries, conflicting priorities and overwhelming difficulties in co-ordination.

In spite of all these disappointments PPB is credited with a number of achievements and is being developed and improved in Washington and Ottawa. For the first time departments and agencies have had to examine their fundamental aims and purposes. Either as a result of having to develop a programme structure or of being challenged on the issues referred to them by the Bureau of the Budget, some agencies have had to specify which business they are in, and why. Thus PPB is credited with causing the Bureau of Indian Affairs to discover that it was a 'people' agency and not a natural resources agency. Some British public institutions (such as the Forestry Commission, H.M.S.O., H.M. Dockyards) and policies (such as the insurance principle in social security, green-belt policy in land-use planning) would doubtless benefit from a similarly critical examination.

Secondly it has introduced analysis, or at least awareness of the value of analysis, into the decision-making and managerial processes of parts of government which were not familiar with it and has had a substantial educational value. Even the most traditionally-minded officials have come to talk in terms of objectives, alternative deployments of resources and value for money. Demands for analytic studies prior to policy formulation are beginning to form part of the regular operating routine of senior managers. As the quality of analysis improves, managers are giving it more weight in the process of policy determination:

'Some recognition is now being given that where bargaining is a vital part of any political process it operates to the benefit of the participants when there exists a better understanding of the costs, outputs and beneficiaries of alternative courses of action ... There is also a recognition that good judgement is made even better when it can operate with good analysis. The framework of PPB and the systems analysis approach necessary for its use have to a large extent achieved legitimacy.'[60] As Charles Schultze has said: PPB introduces the 'efficiency partisan' into the debate. Though the programme staff operate within the constraints and values of a department 'they are more likely to be interested in efficiency than the rest of the bureau ... the program evaluation staff can be advocates for optimizing the use of that budget from the standpoint of effectiveness and efficiency.'[61] It has also provided for the first time a means of displaying the total government effort in a particular field and of comparing related programmes in different departments or agencies. It enables a central view to be taken of allied or broadly similar programmes that are being operated by departments and can provide the basis for rationalization. Finally, the quality of information within U.S. government departments has been markedly improved. Existing information has been restructured in a more useful form and whole new areas of information have been opened up on objectives, inputs, outputs, target communities, the impact of government action.

New developments in PPB in Washington really amount to a 'second generation' of the system. A lot of low-quality analysis is being jettisoned for the analysis of key areas of activity and crucially important programmes. For the fiscal year 1971 only seventy-five major policy issues have been identified, in place of the 380 of the year before. The emphasis is now on selling PPB as a routine for better management, and each agency is being encouraged to develop PPB to suit its own needs, rather than follow a prescribed pattern. An education programme in systematic analysis is being developed to upgrade the quality of analysis in departments, and universities are being encouraged to design courses 'to serve the public need for graduates equipped with both the traditional skills of the professions (e.g. law and medicine) and the additional skills useful for evaluating public resource alternatives'.[62] In the longer run, the movement is towards the alignment of the structure of programmes and that of management responsibility within departments ('building-block programmes' – see Chapter 5). The reorganization of the U.S. Bureau of the Budget in 1970 as the Office of Management and Budget and proposals to rename PPB as 'Planning-Programming and Evaluation' or 'Planning – Programming – Management' has marked a new emphasis on relating planning to the day-to-day activities of managers.

Most of this discussion has concentrated on PPB experience in the U.S. central government, where so much effort has gone into it and where its failures and successes have been so public. In Canada, a somewhat less obtrusive, and in some ways a more successful, route to PPB has been followed. One substantial advantage of the Canadian approach to PPB was that it followed a series of reforms of the management of Canadian government rather than being introduced as an overlay to existing structures and procedures. These reforms arose from the Glassco Commission of 1960–62, which was appointed 'to inquire into the organization and methods of operation of the departments of Canadian government and to recommend changes which would promote efficiency, economy and improved service in the dispatch of public business'.[63] Most of the Commission's recommendations were incorporated in the Government Organization Act of 1966. The Glassco Commission had wider terms of reference than the Fulton Committee and went deeply into questions of the role of the Treasury Board and the accountability of units of government. It is worth noting that in Canada a PPB-type planning system was set in the context of increased delegation of control over expenditure to departments; a structure of responsibility centres within departments so that managerial responsibility for the expenditure of programme funds could be pinpointed; the preparation of schedules for each programme accompanied by analyses of alternatives and by performance indicators for many activities; the adoption of accrual accounting (see Chapter 5); and a change in the presentation of budget estimates from an input to a programme form. These reforms were accompanied by concentration in the Treasury Board on the design of 'measures of effectiveness' – that is, the establishment of yardsticks by which to measure success in attaining programme and departmental objectives. Thus in Canada PPB has been as much a managerial as a resource allocation process. The problem of establishing a locus for a top-level view of government-wide priorities and programmes was tackled by Prime Minister Trudeau in 1968 when he set up a Cabinet Committee for Planning and Priorities. Canadian government still has unresolved problems in defining programmes which cross departmental boundaries, and in making the responsibility centre concept meaningful, but the Canadian experience may have some useful lessons for Whitehall.

Developments in Britain

At the time of writing, planning systems and planning units are the focus for much attention in Whitehall. The Treasury has computerized its short-term and medium-term economic assessment models; the Public Expenditure Survey system has been further developed; new departmental planning units have appeared and some experiments in PPB have been started. The Select Committee on Procedure of 1968–9 endorsed PPB and the government which came to power in 1970 has introduced it in embryo under the title of 'Programme Analysis and Review' (PAR).

The first application of PPB (then called 'functional costing') in British government began in the Ministry of Defence in 1963 and it was in operational use by 1965. The department has a structure of fourteen major programmes and 700 programme elements and a central analytical staff concerned with programme evaluation and review. It is said that the system revealed the full cost of the TSR2 aircraft, the aircraft-carrier force and the presence East of Suez and made a major contribution to the eight reviews of the defence budget between 1964 and 1970, though apparently it has had limited success in integrating the activities of the Service Boards.[64]

A Treasury feasibility study for PPB in the Department of Education and Science was published in April 1970.[65] This divided the output of the Department into three functional blocks – Education, Research, and Cultural and Recreational Activities. Within the education block it proposed seven major programmes, for example compulsory education, nursery education, education for the sixteen–nineteen year-old and so on up to post-graduate education. On the question of the assessment of output from the education block, the authors wrote that quantitative measures 'would almost invariably be intermediate rather than final objectives: for instance, pupil/teacher ratios rather than educational standards'.[66] This was because the benefits of education usually accrue over the recipient's lifetime, because of the difficulty of measuring the 'value added' by an educational process and because of the lack of data on the different effects of lifetime earnings of people who had gained different academic qualifications. For each educational programme such criteria as the additional places provided and the improvement in pupil/teacher ratios were suggested. The *Economist* greeted this study as 'a pretty innocuous series of programmes',[67] and asked how much point there was in the department producing detailed national programme costing if the local authorities were not working on the same system. A more pointed comment on the study was made by Tyrell Burgess in *New Society*.[68] Under the headline 'Try Again, DES', he criticized the 'vacuity' of such programmes as 'education for the fifteen-year-old: to provide education suited to the age, aptitude and ability of the fifteen-year-old to the highest possible standard and for as high a proportion of the age group as possible' and the reliance on intermediate output criteria when much more meaningful objectives could have been devised. 'How about this: that every child leaving the infant schools should be able to read and write? . . . we know how many children leave the infant school actually able to read and write (between two-thirds and three-quarters). So it is open to us to propose as an objective the literacy of the remainder.' For the programme for fifteen–sixteen-year-olds, he suggested an objective of full-time education for all, defined as attendance at an educational institution for 400 sessions a year. Burgess pointed out that to meet such objectives a wide variety of alternatives could be explored (different methods of instruction, different forms of educational institution) and useful programme analyses could have been carried out.

Apart from that in Defence, the most highly advanced application of PPB sponsored by government has been developed by G. J. Wasserman, Economic Adviser at the Home Office, for local police forces. This system is 'devoted to meeting the needs of individual forces rather than to enhancing the planning capacity of the central government',[69] and is aimed at providing managers at the various levels in the police system with better information about the resources they control. It is based on the codification and analysis of all police-force expenditures into about eighty programme elements grouped into nine major programmes. This structure identifies four operational programmes (ground cover, crime investigation and control, traffic control, and additional services); three support programmes (management, training, support services), and two overhead programmes (pensions, accomodation). Programme elements can be arranged in different combinations and broken down into territorial or other organizational groupings and can also be linked to, or combined with, the programmes of other authorities (such as traffic control with a local authority's traffic management programme). Work is continuing on the most difficult part of this system, the establishment of criteria of effectiveness or performance standards for each programme element, but already the system offers an improved mechanism for enabling the management of police forces to make decisions on the alternative uses of their resources, to establish the real cost of different activities (dog sections, vice squads, task forces, etc.) and to budget. The programme structure of this system is closely aligned to the management structure of a force and so costs can also be analysed by centres of responsibility. 'In this way PPB for the police service can serve the needs of management by objectives and accountable management.'[70]

The Home Office has also been the scene of another experiment in planning systems. A planning and development division was proposed for its Prison Department in late 1969,[71] as the result of a re-organization proposed by a management review team of consultants and civil servants (see Chapter 7). It was envisaged that this division should report to the top management board of the department; that it should be staffed by specialists, administrators and executives; and that it should be concerned not only with the long-term development of penal research and policy but with seeing that management objectives and programmes were established for each sub-unit of management. The proposed planning system was designed to operate on an annual cycle linked to the public-expenditure survey and the supply procedure. The basis of the system was a consultative procedure whereby the central planning unit provided line management with prison population forecasts and with the Board's broad policy and expenditure assumptions for the period under review. On this basis each regional and divisional head was then to produce a view of his priorities and future programmes. These were to be assembled in a draft plan which identified the inconsistencies and conflicts between the divisional views. The draft plan was to be considered at an annual conference of top management at which a reconciliation of priorities and programmes would be made and expressed as a five-year plan, firm for the first year and in outline for the succeeding four. As the data on current operations was progressively upgraded by the installation of management accounting and the improvement of other management information, this cyclical routine could eventually provide the framework for both the analysis of key policy issues and programmes and for the installation of systems of accountable management. The designers of this planning system considered that before any more sophisticated PPB-type system could be introduced, the department needed far more quantified information on its current operations than existed at the time; it needed to recruit or develop staff skilled in analysis, and top management had to have time to become accustomed to formal procedures of planning and setting objectives.[74] Like the police system, the system proposed for Prison Department is much more management-orientated than 'classical' PPB, placing its initial emphasis upon the establishment of a base of much-improved management information.

The government which came to power in 1970 has emphasized the need to improve departmental and supra-departmental planning. The White Paper on the re-organization of government[72] announced that a Central Policy Review Staff (CPRS) was to be set up in the Cabinet Office to work for Ministers collectively under the supervision of the Prime Minister. Its task would be to relate individual departmental policies to the government's strategy as a whole and to see that the implications of alternative courses of action were fully considered.

To improve the analytical basis of the public expenditure survey, a team of businessmen in the Civil Service Department were developing a system (PAR – Programme Analysis and Review) which would provide more and better information to support departmental submissions in the public-expenditure survey cycle. It would provide Ministers with an opportunity to evaluate alternative policy options before final decisions were taken on expenditure programmes. The process would involve a greater emphasis on the definition of objectives and the expression of programmes as far as possible in output terms. As far as can be seen from the first annual cycle of PAR, it amounts to the 'issue letter' sequence of the PPB system.[73] A Treasury committee suggests a number of areas of departmental expenditure which are worth detailed analysis. Ministers then collectively select one or two of these areas for each department for treatment as programmes. The department produces a PAR report (= programme memorandum) to the appropriate Cabinet committee. Any policy changes which are approved as a result of the report are fed into the next departmental PESC cycle. The CPRS has been constituted to undertake a higher level of issue analysis and has carried out studies of topics which cross departmental boundaries and of fundamental matters of government policy: 'The staff makes a comparatively intensive study of a chosen topic because it runs across the frontiers of normal departmental responsibility or raises what is regarded as a basic issue of government strategy or is thought to require a second opinion to test against an entrenched departmental view.'[74] Such topics have been Concorde, regional policy, population growth, government support for the computer industry and the organization and management of government research and development. The report on government R. and D. by Lord Rothschild was published as a Green Paper in November 1971[75] and set out, in a vigorous and polemical style, the concept of the customer-contractor relationship for applied R. and D.: 'The customer says what he wants; the contractor does it (if he can) and the customer pays.' Though the report relied more on assertion than analysis, for which it was heavily criticized by leading scientists, it did represent an attempt to extend Fulton's principle of accountability into an area of public expenditure where governments had hitherto been loathe to intervene.

PLANNING: REVIEW AND CONCLUSION

Strategic planning in government departments generally poses much more complex problems than planning in industry. There are the difficulties of specifying objectives and quantifying results. There is the frequent unpredictability of the expenditure implications of existing commitments, particularly when the government engages in high-technology, high-prestige projects such as Concorde and the RB-211 engine. A planner in government is faced with having to forecast and apply analysis in a system in which corporate aims are subject to substantial periodic shifts and yet much expenditure rolls on under its own momentum. Another dimension of complexity is added by the separation, in many departments, of policy origination and funding from direct management control. Local authorities, for example, account for 25 per cent of public expenditure and though the government can affect this expenditure in total, in general it cannot direct allocations to specific sectors. It is in these areas that government planning has to diverge most markedly from corporate planning. The essence of good corporate planning is that long-term plans provide the framework for short-term budgets and management objectives which in turn provide the framework for measuring management effectiveness. There can be an unbroken line from a board decision to the operating programme of the most junior manager, from strategic planning to day-to-day control. In situations in which a department (Education, Environment, etc.) formulates and develops policy and partly or wholly funds programmes which are managed by external bodies it is not possible to integrate policy planning with control in this way. On the other hand, all departments have some programmes which are internally managed (such as headquarters administration), some directly manage the bulk of their expenditure (such as the Foreign Office, Defence, Civil Service Department) and some contain both categories (such as the Home Office, where Police programmes are external and Prisons programmes are internal; D.H.S.S., where Health is external and Social Security internal).

The advocates of planning are faced not only with these technical problems but with some opposition to the idea that any planning, except at the highest level of generality, is of value in a political environment. This opposition springs from the view that practical decisions in politics develop sequentially from the operation of current policy in conditions of uncertainty and cannot be made on the basis of analytical problem-solving; that analysis produces solutions according to criteria of efficiency when the more meaningful criterion is the achievement of consensus through the adjustment of conflicting political values and that the measurement of objectives and the weighting of alternatives is unattainable when applied to social and institutional problems.[76] Experience of the practical application of PPB lends some force to these arguments. The development of a programme structure may be politically unexceptionable, but when they attempt programme and issue analysis the planners sometimes have to simplify so greatly as to defy all political sense. Vice-Admiral Rickover, the naval chief of the Polaris submarine programme, observed in a Senate hearing: 'In the cost-effectiveness studies performed by the analysts, they compute numerical values for the effectiveness of nuclear power. However, before they make the calculation, they make certain simplifying assumptions in order to be able to do the arithmetic. These assumptions just happen to eliminate from consideration the principal military reasons for wanting nuclear power in the first place.'*[77]

---

*A more homely example of the risk of grossly oversimplifying in order to quantify is provided by the work of a research group in a County Council who attempted to measure the financial benefit to the community of introducing closed-circuit television in small secondary schools by evaluating the increased earnings that would result in an area if its economic employment pattern were brought up to the national average and then deducting the cost of closed-circuit television.[78]

The originators of PPB considered that it was essentially a system for broadly allocating resources to Ministerial objectives and for examining the collective consequences of the activities of different departments, rather than a basis for control.[79] They expected that some subsidiary system could be devised for the measurement of management performance. It is true that for those expenditures which are managed by external bodies, departments can do relatively little to insure the efficiency of management other than to encourage them to adopt planning routines that are compatible (in time span, accounting conventions) with the departmental system and to instal and monitor broad indicators which demonstrate the effectiveness of policy implementation and enable the department to forecast and justify future expenditure. In situations in which departments wholly or partly manage their expenditure programmes, however, it is necessary not only to specify and evaluate expenditure on a programme basis but to relate programmes to the internal management structure and to its system of control. Thus a departmental planning unit should prepare an array of programmes which enabled the Minister to make policy decisions on the general direction of the department's effort. The programmes which were internally managed should then be expressed as expenditure and operational plans for departmental management and should be developed into budgets, staff quotas and measures of effectiveness and efficiency for unit managers within the department.

We have seen from an earlier discussion that the public expenditure survey does not yet provide the basis for management planning and control. PAR is not designed to solve this problem, but to improve the analytical background for some expenditure decisions while avoiding the problems of analytical over-kill encountered by the practitioners of PPB in American federal government. It appears to examine the justification for a few key programmes on a once-for-all basis rather than to be concerned with the improvement of departmental planning, budgeting and management processes.

If PESC/PAR is to be developed into a procedure akin to corporate planning, the first steps should be to put together greatly improved arrangements for gathering and organizing information; to reclassify the accounts into programme terms; to construct measures of need and impact; to establish the standing of departments in each of their programme areas; and to identify accountability for results. These problems are discussed in the next two chapters.

CHAPTER 5

Control

To the manager, control means the collection, analysis, comparison and distribution of information to permit the performance of the organization and its constituent parts to be regularly compared with pre-determined standards so that action can be taken when the variance between achievement and standard exceeds acceptable limits. The aim of control information technology is to provide the organization with a nervous system which enables it to perceive and react to internal and external events in time to correct deviations from plan. An effective control system requires, first, a strategic *plan* which expresses policy decisions about the allocation of resources in, and the results that are required from, the enterprise as a whole and its major managerial sub-units; secondly, *information* so organized that the disposition of resources can be expressed as budgets and standards and subsequent performance can be measured against them; thirdly, arrangements which establish the *accountability* of managers for results.

In the last chapter we discussed strategic planning in a Civil Service context. In this we shall discuss the requirement for control information and in the next, managerial accountability.

FROM TIME AND MOTION STUDY TO CYBERNETICS

The concept of control has dominated management thinking from the earliest days of 'scientific management' over seventy years ago. In recent years, the study of self-regulating control systems, drawing upon evidence of such phenomena in the natural sciences, has achieved recognition as the new sub-science of cybernetics.

The first control systems in industry were developed from attempts to describe and measure the work of production workers in factories and mines by the use of what was called, until about 1911, 'Taylorism' and for many years afterwards was called time and motion study. F. W. Taylor,[1] 'the father of scientific management', began his studies of production management and work measurement in a Philadelphia steelworks in the 1880s. In order to arrive at some objective assessment of what constituted a fair day's work he carefully analysed and described the activities of lathe operators in his charge. By studying and timing each action of the operator he was able to find the most efficient sequence of movements, to write instructions describing the 'standard' method and to set a 'standard' time for carrying out each process. His work was taken up and refined by others, notably the Gilbreths,[2] and led to the widespread use of procedures for the study of working methods and for recording, analysing, timing and setting standards for manual operations and to the establishment of targets or norms of output for individual workers, worker gangs, sections, departments and whole factories. Production managers employed teams of rate fixers to measure the time taken to do a job by trained workers using the most efficient methods and thus established a standard time for that job. Production planning and control systems were also devised to measure the output of sections and machine groups, by reference to manuals of standard times and machine capacities, and to enable management to monitor production and correct deviations from production plans.

Taylorism included arrangements for paying piece-work bonuses, and between the wars numerous payments by results schemes based on work measurement were used in manufacturing industry. The attachment of bonus payments to work measurement made it the subject of considerable controversy and also led workers and managers to adopt a variety of measures to manipulate or invalidate the control information derived from it. In recent years, work study (the name for time and motion study since the 1940s) has paid more attention to the environment and organization in which the worker is employed and to providing him with better-designed machines, less tiring operating methods and more mechanical aids. The use of methods of payment in which individual bonuses are linked directly to time-study-based standards is declining in the face of arrangements for sharing profits or sharing savings in the labour content of production. The use of direct measurement by stop-watch is giving way to less subjective methods of work measurement and rating using, for example predetermined motion time (PMT) systems.[3]

The first manual of work measurement for clerical operations was written in 1917 by W. H. Leffingwell,[4] though it is only in the last decade or so that work measurement and method study has become at all usual in offices. In 1922 a highly significant development in the field of management information took place with the publication of the first standard work on budgetary control by the American business school professor and consultant, James O. McKinsey.[5]

Budgetary control has the object of comparing actual income and expenditure with forecast or budgeted income and expenditure under headings which permit the analysis of the efficiency of the various units in an organization. It involves organizing financial information in such a way as to identify managerial responsibility for costs, expenditure and revenues; to provide a basis for the formulation of plans; and to permit the identification of deviations from plans in the course of their operation. An additional level of financial control is provided by 'standard costing'. This involves pre-determination of the costs of labour and material (and sometimes overhead costs) of performing a task by the standard method at a stated level of output and permits analysis of the reasons for departures from standard. It also provides a cost model which can be used to show the effect of changing such variables as materials and processes. 'Management accounting' is a generic term for the arrangement and presentation of accounting data for use in these systems of short-term planning and control.

Budgetary control (like work study) can be wrongly used as a device to 'needle' junior management and supervisors,[6] to create competition and force up production. This leads to the fairly widespread practice of sub-optimization: rigging the figures so as to produce good results compared with the budget or concentrating exclusively upon those elements which show up in the control returns rather than those which do not (for instance the factory manager who concentrates upon maximizing output but neglects machine maintenance; the salesman who concentrates upon drumming up business from his regular customers because no credit is given for going to look for new ones). Just as workers will endeavour to manipulate a harshly applied work-study scheme, so managers who are made responsible for unrealistic budgets will attempt to defeat budgetary control, particularly when bonus payments are involved. Trouble also often arises at the interface between control systems, for example between a production shop heavily orientated towards high output and a quality control system further down the line based on rigorous inspection and the rejection of sub-standard work. Inevitably, informal procedures for getting round the system are devised in the interests of peace and survival. It has been suggested,[7] on fairly slight evidence, that *all* control routines provoke those whose performance is being controlled into setting up counter-systems designed to ameliorate their worst effects and to adapt them to the real needs of the situation. The truth is that, as with many other devices of management, if controls are imposed without the full participation of the people who are responsible for results and if they are applied by an authoritarian management they simply become an instrument of industrial warfare.

When we come to modern methods of stock control we move on to less emotive ground (though even in this field, there are examples of counter-measures being taken against badly designed systems[8]) and we approach self-regulating (or cybernetic) systems. Briefly, with the use of computers it has become possible to control inventories of many thousands of different items by organizing programmes to predict the future usage of any item, based on past trends; to calculate the optimum number of items for each replenishment order, offsetting the cost of procurement against the cost of holding stock; to allow for the time required to place and receive a new order; and continually to update the record of stock in hand. Once management has stated the degree of risk of stock-out that it is willing to face, the programmes will notify the need to replenish each item when it falls to a re-order point and maintain the entire stock at the most economic level. We are therefore close to a cybernetic system in which a homeostatic, or sensory, device operates on information fed back from the environment to hold a critical variable at a desirable level. The usual homely example of this process is the room thermostat which acts on a feedback of temperature readings to operate or shut off central-heating radiators and so maintain the temperature of the room within predetermined limits. Another simple example of such a system is the Watt governor on a steam engine; a more complicated one is an automatic pilot; and a vastly complex one is the natural regulation of animal populations so as to achieve ecological balance. In industry, cybernetic systems are increasingly common in such process or flow-production industries as oil-refining and flour-milling in which the many variables of heat, pressure and the constituent elements of the product are held in balance by an array of homeostatic sensors. The application of cybernetic systems in industry is still in its infancy but it is possible to visualize their spreading widely into production processes, warehouses, offices which handle routine transactions and distribution and transportation systems. There is speculation from time to time upon the ultimate feasibility of the cybernetically controlled firm, 'automatically' holding to a pre-set course of growth and profits by fine-tuning adjustments to prices, variable production costs, advertising and sales effort, investment, research and so on. Those who wish to pursue a study of cybernetics are advised to start by reading the works of the leading British exponent, Stafford Beer.[9]

So far, we have been dealing with control based on data internal to the firm: the levels of production, factory and office productivity, costs and inventory. In addition the process of budgetary control recognizes conditions external to the firm by beginning with a sales or output budget which takes account of the effects on demand of forecast changes in the firm's trading environment. With improvements in market research techniques and in the availability and reliability of national statistics it has become possible, in some industries, to measure and set standards which relate to the firm's external standing. The best example of this is share of the market. In the motor industry, for example, it is possible to set standards for market share by model and regularly to compare the actual against the standard share. With the extension of inter-firm comparisons and the greater availability of national productivity figures for different industries and more informative published company records, possibilities have opened up for greatly developing performance measurement based on criteria external to the firm and for regularly appraising its performance relative to that of its competitors.

Control systems, the first of the major developments of 'scientific' (or, more accurately, systematic) management, are still advancing on several fronts. Even in the area of their earliest development, the measurement of manual work, increasing technical sophistication is leading to data of greater reliability and objectivity. The availability of computers is permitting faster feedback, finer degrees of analysis of variances from plan and advances into cybernetic control. The growing respectability of participative management styles means that there is hope that it will become more common for worker and manager to co-operate in devising the control system appropriate to the working situation, with the aim of identifying areas where joint efforts are required to make improvements. In the context of a discussion on management by objectives (see Chapter 6) and 'self-control', Peter Drucker has written: 'To be able to control his own performance a manager needs to know more than what his goals are. He must be able to measure his performance and results against the goal. It should indeed be an invariable practice to supply managers with clear and common measurements in all key areas of business. These measurements need not be rigidly quantitative; nor need they be exact. But they have to be simple, clear and rational. They have to be relevant and direct attention and efforts where they need to go . . .'[10]

A recurring problem in this field lies in designing simple controls for complex operations and in deciding how few essential indicators of performance are required for keeping track of business performance. This is particularly important in large organizations which are decentralized into divisions or other centres of accountability each with a significant degree of operating autonomy. In many corporations the single criterion of return on investment is used to measure divisional performance, but this arrangement has been shown to be generally ineffective, misleading and unreliable.[11] The financial control system which is quoted as being at the heart of Sir Arnold Weinstock's management of the divisions of GEC Ltd is based on seven key criteria (profits on capital employed and on sales; sales as a multiple of capital employed, fixed assets and stocks; sales and profits per employee).[12]

One of the most notable and well-documented[13] attempts to establish a comprehensive system of internal and external performance criteria for large decentralized organizations was the measurement project established in 1952 at the U.S. General Electric Co. after its re-arrangement into over 100 product departments. It was decided to apply performance criteria to the eight 'key results areas' of each department's activities. These were: profitability, market share, productivity, product leadership personnel development, employee attitudes, public responsibility and the balance between short-range and long-range goals. Product leadership was established by periodic reviews of the department's record for innovation. Personnel development was measured by the qualitative assessment of programmes for recruitment, training, personal career reviews and placement; by the assessment of the department's succession plans and manpower inventories; by the rate of promotions from the staff graded as promotable and analyses of employee preformance rating. Employee attitudes were judged by statistical indicators of turnover, absenteeism etc., and by periodic attitude surveys. Public responsibility factors concerned departmental behaviour in compliance with anti-trust regulations and conflict of interest policies; in behaviour towards suppliers and dealers and in impact on the local communities as established by regular external surveys. Finally, performance in each of the preceding seven key results areas was appraised in terms of both their short-term and long-term implications.

While highly simplified measurement criteria can lead to misrepresentation of performance and the distortion of managerial effort, particularly if heavy reliance is placed on profit measurement, designing criteria to cover every dimension of performance calls for a very large information gathering and analytical effort. Regular monitoring of employee attitudes and community impact, as in the GE case, would call for the employment of a sizeable survey staff, while the use of even fairly simple work-measurement and budgetary-control systems frequently creates sizeable clerical and technical units engaged on preparing, classifying and distributing control documents. The design of management information systems calls for fine judgement on what are the key results areas for any managerial unit and how worthwhile it is to pursue the search for more refined measures of performance. Periodic *ad hoc* surveys of employee, customer, supplier and community attitudes, though a highly valuable method of viewing the impact of managerial decisions from the outside and often an eye-opener to managers otherwise aware only of their progress towards the objectives of growth and cost reduction, are expensive in specialist manpower.

Advocates of bigger and better management information systems sometimes give the impression that all organized activity is measurable if only the right formula can be found. In fact, in modern industry and government areas of virtually unmeasurable activity are becoming increasingly common: the groups of corporate staff described in Chapter 3 are an obvious example. These are areas 'where the connection between the individual job and, say, the firm's profit or rate of growth is not clear . . . Such units are typical of the headquarters of large corporations and are becoming more common as the need for specialization increases. Examples are legal, design, technical or market research and management development departments. In all of these, the quality, acceptability or effectiveness of output is what matters most and the measurement of the volume of output or of productivity is virtually meaningless. The contribution made by such units to the profit or the growth of the company may be highly significant but is extremely difficult to assess except in the long term.'[14]

As businesses have increased in size and complexity there has been a greater concentration on the analysis of information requirements. This has had a marked effect upon accounting activities: increasingly accountants are looked upon as information technologists rather than financial stewards and historians. A more analytical generation of managers is demanding to know what goes on inside the enterprises they run: they require quantitative statements of potential and performance, they realize that delegation on any scale can take place only if sufficient information exists to quantify and allocate resources and to monitor and evaluate results. They require a regular flow of data which properly serves the decision-making and accountability of different levels of management. This data can be financial (cost, revenues, expenditures compared with budget); statistical (machine and labour productivity, material waste, share of market, labour turnover) or in the form of reports and commentaries. The essential requirement is that it is comparative, sufficiently accurate, easily understood and quickly fed back from operating results.

In most firms, management information is assembled from a number of single-purpose or *ad hoc* systems. As the number of systems grows, a stage is reached where the handling of individual system records becomes a major problem and large-scale integration is required. Data-base technology aims to provide the means of integrating separate single-purpose records into a common data base, or fund of information, which allows each function or each level of management access to its requirements. From this common fund, information can be issued at the frequencies and degrees of detail which match the needs of each level of management. At top management levels the need may be for highly condensed monthly reports which provide general indications of trend while at lower levels the need is likely to be for daily, immediate or even instantaneous reports on quantities and times.

FINANCIAL CONTROL IN THE CIVIL SERVICE

The management control we have been discussing is essentially positive: it is concerned to encourage the attainment of pre-set objectives within allocated resources, to direct management attention to areas of high priority and continuously to monitor past performance. Control in public administration has usually been directed to no less essential, but negative ends; it is generally concerned to stop unauthorized things from happening by prior sanctions and post-accounting. Primarily, this kind of control is concerned to insure 'regularity' – that is, that accounts are kept correctly, that all spending is for authorized purposes and is attributable to approved estimates and that the mis-application of funds and waste and extravagance are prevented.

The machinery for exercising this control is provided by the supply procedure, an arrangement by which Parliament authorizes those cash payments by government departments which have to be voted annually. Every October, the Treasury asks departments to compile estimates of proposed expenditure for the financial year beginning in the following April. By the end of November Finance Divisions have aggregated the estimates of the branches and divisions in their departments and send these to the Treasury. Between December and January, the Treasury and the spending departments discuss the estimates, referring disputed points to Ministers. In February and March the agreed estimates are published and presented to the House of Commons. They are accompanied by a Memorandum on the Estimates by the Financial Secretary to the Treasury which compares them with the previous year's estimates, includes a functional analysis and shows them arranged according to the national accounts classification, for example current expenditure on goods and services, subsidies, capital grants, lending and investment abroad. In July or August, the Appropriation Act is passed which authorizes the expenditure of the estimated sums, now known as 'votes'. Because by this time nearly one-third of the year to which the estimates relate has already passed, a 'vote on account' is made by the House before the beginning of the financial year authorizing the next few months' expenditure. Supplementary estimates for new services to be provided by the government are presented in June or July and supplementary estimates required because of an overspend or an original under-estimate are presented in November and the following February.

Though Finance Divisions in departments and the Treasury spend a considerable time scrutinizing the estimates and challenging increases, estimating by divisions or branches is largely on an incremental basis rather than as the result of a review of the continuing purpose of the unit, its objectives, its efficiency and the effectiveness of its programmes. During the year expenditures take place on the authority of the Department's Principal Finance Officer and are recorded by his Accounts Branch. In most fields of expenditure, departments have varying degrees of authority to spend delegated to them by the Treasury, but a significant number of individual items of expenditure – even though they are in the department's vote – have still to be referred back to the Treasury for approval. In particular, Treasury approval is necessary for new items of expenditure or for any new service or for any expenditure arising from a change in policy. Thus, the Treasury controls expenditure by approving the department's annual estimate as a whole, by scrutinizing individual items of expenditure within that estimate and by requiring the submission of new projects for prior sanction. Some of the items referred to the Treasury for approval can be small. Ten years ago, the Select Committee on Estimates[15] found that the Ministry of Agriculture had recently submitted eighteen applications in respect of grants to drainage authorities, and the Foreign Office had put up, among other things, thirty-four applications for initial expenditure on domestic furniture, including soft furnishings, and five requests for permission to buy refrigerators. The Treasury justified this attention to detail on the grounds that it enabled it to gain an understanding of departmental activities (the Select Committee called this 'educative value'); that it strengthened the department's own scrutiny to the point where proposals could be justified to an informed and objective critic ('useful discipline'); and that it enabled specific economies to be made that would not otherwise be made ('specific economy'). The Select Committee thought that there was some educative value, and possibly a useful discipline, in Treasury Control by prior sanction, but at least in the civil field an examination of 213 projects had failed to substantiate the claim for specific economies. It recommended a further and more generous relaxation of control by prior sanction and more use of 'control by programmes'. Since that time, the delegation of power to spend from the Treasury to departments has been considerably extended, but the same principles still broadly apply and the Treasury does not yet control by programme.

Detailed Treasury and departmental control of expenditure depends to a large extent upon the effectiveness of the lay critic.

The Select Committee pointed out that technical officers are generally excluded from the discussion of expenditure proposals and that 'laymen may be examining proposals submitted by laymen, while the technical officers who initiated the proposals and who really understand the details, remain behind the scenes'.[16] Fulton's Management Consultancy Group made a similar criticism in its comments upon the relationships between specialists and administrators. It noted that financial responsibility lay almost exclusively with administrators, while technically qualified specialists acted purely in an advisory role: 'On the question of financial control, administrators did not have the technical competence properly to challenge the specialists except on obvious or relatively trivial points ... in industry, managers with specialist backgrounds are very often entrusted with the expenditure of funds without having their decisions under continuous scrutiny by laymen. There is no evidence that this lead to unwarranted expenditure.'[17] The control of expenditure therefore tends to take the form of pointed questions by laymen upon expenditure decisions which are increasingly taken by specialists on technical cases. Inevitably, the laymen ask questions about the peripheral matters which they can understand. Not only does this type of control give rise to massive amounts of desultory correspondence, it also leads to the maintenance of detailed records and statistics just in case a question is asked by those responsible for financial control. Regular tabulations of details of minor expense are kept at the cost of many man hours of clerical labour.

This is control orientated almost exclusively to the amount, and proper authorization, of expenditure, rather than to management efficiency or to effectiveness in achieving policy objectives. It has few of the review and evaluation features of management control, being rather a series of *ad hoc* forays in the hope of spotting extravagance. Mackenzie and Grove have put the conventional view of these procedures: 'All experience suggests that the best method of control is organized rearguard action interrupted by occasional sharp counter-attacks ... counter-attacks take the form of demands for block cuts or percentage cuts in the estimates, which throw on each department the onus of organizing cuts in its own organization or of proving its case for exemption.'[18]

At the end of each financial year, departments submit to the 'Comptroller General of the Receipt and Issue of Her Majesty's Exchequer and Auditor General of the Public Accounts', their Appropriation Accounts which show under each vote heading the amount spent and the difference between this and the amount granted, with explanation of such differences. These accounts are signed and rendered by the Accounting Officer, usually the Permanent Secretary of the department. Where departments engage in commercial activities, trading accounts are also rendered to the Comptroller and Auditor General. He then certifies the accounts as satisfactory or 'subject to the observations in my report'. The accounts he certifies and the reports that he makes on them are examined by a committee of the House of Commons, the Public Accounts Committee. This committee formally examines each Appropriation Account, but in fact concentrates its attention on those matters on which the Comptroller and Auditor General has made his personal observations. In pursuing these matters, the Public Accounts Committee may call before them the Accounting Officers of departments and their senior officials. The reports of the Committee are published and the Treasury's views on the reports are also published as a Treasury minute. Both reports and minutes are presented to the House of Commons. In the next round, the Committee can examine officials on the Treasury minute and report again.

We therefore have expenditure vetted and scrutinized at one level by a department's Finance Division, at a higher level by the Treasury and at a still higher level by an independent state auditor appointed by the Crown and reporting to the Legislature. The effectiveness of our system of state audit is discussed in Chapter 7.

In addition to the Comptroller/Public Accounts Committee system, Parliament has also until recently scrutinized expenditure by means of the Estimates Committee and its sub-committees. This committee could send for papers and records from departments and could orally examine senior civil servants. Reports and recommendations together with the Ministers' reactions to them were presented to the House of Commons for debate and published. The Sub-committees sometimes examined the estimates of a single department, or one subject of expenditure spread over several departments or a particular financial procedure.

In 1964-5 the Select Committee on Procedure considered the need to improve the sources of information available to the House in carrying out its duty of examining government expenditure and administration, observing that 'more information should be made available to members of the way government departments carry out their responsibilities, so that, when taking part in major debates on controversial issues, they may be armed with the necessary background of knowledge'. The Committee attached importance to evidence which suggested that the machinery of Parliament had failed to keep pace with the increase in the scope of departmental activity.[19] This report recommended that a number of specialist sub-committees should be established as part of a new Select Committee developed from the Estimates Committee and that these should examine how departments carried out their responsibilities and should consider estimates of expenditure and reports. This recommendation was not accepted, though four new Select Committees of the House of Commons – on Agriculture, Education and Science, Overseas Aid, Science and Technology – were later established.

Meanwhile, the House of Commons finally ended 'the procedural fiction' that it examines departmental estimates by changing 'supply days' to 'opposition days' to be used for debates, sometimes at short notice, on aspects of policy. As a result of all this, the House of Commons has found itself being able to inquire less and less into more and more public expenditure. A limited state audit organization, limited inquiry by select committee and hardly any examination of proposed expenditure by the Legislature as a whole has greatly strengthened the relative position of the Executive.

The frustration of parliamentarians with the limitations of their power over the Executive appeared again in the inquiry and report of the Select Committee on Procedure on the scrutiny of public expenditure and administration in 1968-9.[20] The Treasury disarmed some criticism by publishing the public expenditure survey for 1968-72 and parts of the medium-term economic assessment at about the time of the Committee's report. However, the Committee's recommendations went further than this. They wanted a Parliamentary mechanism for examining the management methods being adopted by departments to implement the policies and strategies reflected in public expenditure surveys. Approaching industrial concepts of management control, they also wanted to carry out retrospective scrutiny of the results and value for money obtained by departments by assessing the efficiency with which departments set and realized their objectives. The mechanism they chose was a new Select Committee on Expenditure, comprising eight sub-committees covering major 'functions' of government* – that is, not limited to one department like the Select Committee on Agriculture or to one subject like the Select Committee on Science and Technology – and assisted either by the investigatory staff of the Comptroller and Auditor General or by other experts.

In October 1970, the government issued a 'Green Paper'[21] which accepted the bulk of these proposals. It proposed a new Expenditure Committee supported by sub-committees covering every field of public expenditure and with the right to question Ministers on their policies, to scrutinize public expenditure programmes and projections and to inquire into departmental administration. The Select Committee on Nationalized Industries and the Specialist Committees on Science and Technology, Race Relations and Immigration and Scottish Affairs were to remain in existence. The Expenditure Committee and its sub-committees appeared to have the power to employ investigating and research staffs.

These reforms promise an enhancement in the power of the Legislature to examine spending by departments. However, if they are to be effective, there must also be a far greater improvement in the quality of information on expenditure. The supply procedure is quite inadequate as a source of information. H. R. N. Jamieson and the author made the following observations to the Select Committee on Procedure on the quality of present control information within departments:

'Present procedures do not provide a system of management

---

*Industry, Technology, Manpower, Employment; Housing, Health and Welfare; Power, Transport and Communications; Law, Order and Public Safety; Trade and Agriculture; Defence; Education and Science and the Arts; External Affairs.

accounting. They cannot be used to identify individual responsibility for costs, nor to show the costs of departmental functions, they do not show the true results of a period of working, they cannot be used for meaningful comparison, for the assessment of departmental priorities or for long-term planning.

'Expenditure is not subdivided in a way which corresponds to managerial responsibility. The vote heads and sub-heads usually reveal nothing of the cost of organizational units nor of particular activities. The subdivisions of the vote identify departmental salaries and the basic salary bill of divisions and branches, grants and assistance to outside bodies, and, by way of note, services provided by other departments (for example stationery and building maintenance). Though small items within the vote can be identified, it is not possible to identify the total cost of running large divisions, branches or regional or local establishments except by *ad hoc* investigation. Vote accounting also tells management nothing of the costs of operating policies or departmental functions on which expenditure is classified under different vote sub-heads (that is, expenditure on salaries, buildings, utilities, stationery, postage and printing, equipment and payments to outside bodies).

'Vote accounting is conducted on a cash basis. This involves simply recording the receipts and payments occurring during a period without regard to the timing of events or transactions to which they relate. Cash accounting cannot show the true results of a period of working: the practice in industry is to adjust cash accounts to allow for such things as the payment for services over a period of time different from the accounting period. This matter is of particular importance where the Civil Service is engaged in commercial activities.

'Control works by comparison. In the Civil Service it is not possible to draw useful conclusions during the year from comparing expenditure with estimate because, for instance, the estimate is not tabulated by months. Comparisons are meaningless when so many transactions are recorded under so few headings and the allocation of costs to sub-heads may not be entirely consistent.

'The vote accounting pattern insures that at no stage in compilation is a total picture prepared of the expected cost of any one function or unit of a department: thus cuts in estimates cannot be selectively imposed.

'Finally, the one-year vote estimates and the five-year expenditure planning estimates are classified on different bases . . . This means that it is not possible to project the future of functions or units of the department in expenditure terms.'[22]

The unsuitability for management control of the accounting routines of the supply procedure can be exemplified from a large executive organization such as Prison Department of the Home Office. Part of the costs and expenditure of that department are on the Prisons vote, part on the Home Office vote and part on the votes of other departments, mainly the Department of the Environment. It is therefore impossible to examine on a regular or comparative basis the costs of running the entire prison system or of its major organizational units in head office, its regional organizations or any of its 110 local institutions. On the Prisons vote alone, some £45m. of receipts and payments is analysed to only thirty-six headings on an input basis and then only as totals for the whole department.

The quoted evidence to the Select Committee on Procedure concluded that: 'Departmental expenditure control procedures appear to be adequate to demonstrate the stewardship of funds to Parliament but they are not supported by an analytical substructure which permits the use of modern management systems of planning and control.'[23]

The Select Committee recommended a change in the presentation of estimates and vote accounts to a form which showed the functions or objectives of departments. This recommendation was rejected by the government. Similar recommendations (and recommendations that the cash basis of the accounts be changed to an income and expenditure or accrual basis) had been made on no fewer than four previous occasions by Estimates or National Expenditure Committees of the House of Commons (1918, 1944, 1947 and 1953) with no result. Two Treasury Committees (Crick 1950, Plowden 1959) had found no reason for changing the form of accounts, arguing that they met the requirements of the 1866 Exchequer and Audit Act and that a change would be costly (this opinion was based on an experimental change in the Army Estimates in the early 1920s, long before the computer age). And so the supply procedures remain, hardly changed for over a century, serving little purpose for planning or management control, effectively concealing departmental objectives and programmes from Parliamentary scrutiny and convenient only for Treasury bookkeeping.

ESTABLISHMENTS CONTROL

As we saw from Chapter 3, every department has an establishments function, usually headed by a Principal Establishments Officer. These divisions are concerned with personnel management, efficiency studies and the control of staff numbers.

The Treasury circular of 1920 which defined the status of Principal Establishments Officer laid down that the P.E.O. of each department was to be nominated by the Treasury and approved by the Prime Minister. Though most P.E.O.s are Under Secretaries they therefore have a unique status and independence in their departments which is also derived from their close links with the central establishments authority: formerly the Treasury, now the Civil Service Department. Departmental O. & M. branches are usually under the control of Establishments Officers. In addition to undertaking O. & M. exercises, Establishments Divisions also vet and sanction requests for accommodation, equipment, typing, duplicating and reprographic services. As the Management Consultancy Group said: 'The Establishments Division is the means by which a Department checks its own growth in internal costs, which are mainly those of manpower. All requests for more staff and more equipment go to it and, in addition, it mounts O. & M. investigations into procedures and Staff Inspections into numbers and grades employed.'[24]

The control of complements (the number and grades of staff allowed) is applied by the scrutiny and vetting of annual forecasts of staff numbers, by the authorization of new posts, upgradings and promotions during the year and by *ad hoc* examination of the numbers and grades of posts. All this work is in turn under the scrutiny of the Civil Service Department and results in extreme centralization of authority in staff matters. Each year the major units of a department submit to the Establishments Division their estimates of staff requirements for the following year. The Establishments Division will have an idea of what increase the complementing side of the Civil Service Department will tolerate and will use this as a guide when vetting unit estimates. It will then enter into a debate with the Civil Service Department on its bid for staff for the whole department, having to trade off a requested increase in one section or in one class of staff against another according to the central department's view of priorities and the Cabinet's ruling on the permissible overall percentage increase in the number of civil servants. The result is the imposition of a 'manpower ceiling' on departments above which they may not recruit. During the year political or economic pressure may build up to provoke the imposition of an across-the-board cut in complements which the Civil Service Department shares out among departments. These are very rarely cuts in actual numbers because departments may have strengths (numbers actually in post) well below their complements (numbers to which they are entitled); even if they are up to strength the cut in complement will often be effected by delays in recruiting.

Apart from their annual review of complements, Establishments Divisions mount *ad hoc* investigations, by staff inspectors, of the staffing of individual posts or sections. Staff inspectors, who are H.E.O.s or S.E.O.s posted to the work in the normal course of their careers, typically investigate the need for any new post which a division applies to create and also have a regular programme of working through the department to check on the numbers of staff required to handle current work and whether the posts at each level are correctly graded. There are also teams of Civil Service Department staff inspectors who carry out central inspections.

The authority exercised by Establishments Divisions and the Civil Service Department contrasts very strongly with the weight carried by personnel departments in industry and reflects the particularly acute sensitivity of British governments to the number of civil servants they employ. This sensitivity is played upon by a vociferous Parliamentary element which can only visualize the Civil Service as employing regiments of unproductive bureaucrats. Parliamentary questions not infrequently harp on the number of civil servants and its growth from year to year, in marked contrast to Parliamentary interest in estimates of expenditure. Ministers are therefore touchy about the growth of manpower and put establishments control fairly high on their order of priorities.

The control of complements has been crudely effective in holding down numbers employed in the Civil Service. The numbers of staff employed typically lag well behind the growth in the volume of work in departments: this is reflected in growing backlogs of files and cases and periodic overtime campaigns among junior staff. Clearly, a tight grip on the growth of numbers employed is essential in the management of any organization, and some features of establishments control – annual staff estimates, the central scrutiny of bids for staff or for regrading – would be welcome innovations in many large British commercial organizations.

On the other hand, establishments control in the Civil Service has a number of weaknesses. First, it so dominates the work of establishments divisions that positive aspects of personnel work – planning, improving job content, career development – tend to be neglected (see Chapter 8). Secondly, the annual estimating routine, with its emphasis on cutting back the numbers requested, leads either to inflated bids in the first place or to arbitrary decisions on where cuts shall be made. Thirdly, a procedure which concentrates on numbers rather than cost leads to costly ways of substituting for numbers – overtime working, the employment of temporary typists and contract staff. Fourthly, the cutbacks tend to be indiscriminate and regardless of the potential value of differing types of staff – Fulton's Management Consultancy Group commented upon 'long-term diseconomies [which] may arise from a departmental decision to reduce the numbers of staff whose work could lead to increased efficiency and resultant savings',[25] and quoted training and management services as examples of this effect. Fifthly, establishments control suffers from the same negativism as financial control in the Civil Service – it is control by overall limitation of increase, by minute scrutiny of cases and by foray, rather than control by the continuing analysis of cost and benefit, fitted into 'a systematic review of the relative priorities and continuing justification of departmental activities and thus of the staff needed'.[26] Sixthly, both establishments and financial control in the Civil Service are too centralized, moving initiative and authority from the level of the individual manager, who, being close to the point where the cost is incurred, is in a far better position to do something about controlling it. Seventhly, staff inspection is inexpert and perfunctory, rarely using work-measurement techniques, usually restricted to the examination of low-level jobs and not related to studies of organization structure or of future developments. Finally, as in the case of financial and establishments planning, the financial and establishments control systems can get out of gear. For example, in one department during the cost-reduction campaign of 1969 a substantial increase in the vote for new construction was accompanied by a heavy cut in the recruitment of architects, surveyors and engineers, so that the expanded construction programme could not proceed.

THE INFORMATION REQUIREMENT

We have seen that departments operate two general financial information systems:

(i) The annual estimates, votes and appropriation accounts for Parliamentary authorization and scrutiny by the Public Accounts Committee according to the supply procedure. This system classifies data by input or line items;

(ii) For the public expenditure survey, submitted to the Public Expenditure Survey Committee and the Cabinet (see Chapter 4). This system displays planned expenditure over a five-year period, it is compiled on a somewhat different basis from the supply estimates and is aggregated into major functional categories for government as a whole.

These are underpinned by a manpower information system operated by establishments divisions and the Civil Service Department, which displays the complements and strengths of departments by grade and class and permits decisions to be taken about man-power ceilings and control of the growth of numbers employed.

In addition, departments are vitally interested in a number of economic and social indicators of political importance which enable them to keep track of the impact of policy upon the econ-omy and the community in general. Examples of these indicators are those relating to levels of unemployment, the balance of pay-ments and sterling reserves, housing starts, levels of immigration, crime statistics, traffic accident rates, statistics of homelessness, birth and death rates, hospital occupancy rates. In recent years there has been a marked improvement in the provision of these key indicators and some of them are regularly published by the Central Statistical Office. As the editorial to the first edition of the C.S.O.'s *Social Trends* pointed out, what is now needed is the attempt to fill the gaps in the statistical framework: existing statistics 'concentrate upon aspects of social conditions and problems which are already being attended to. The challenge is to illustrate those aspects, frequently involving acute social prob-lems, which are relatively poorly served by regular statistics. An example is the absence of satisfactory information about the kinds of people who fall within the purview of the available social services without benefiting from them.'[27]

Departments also keep a variety of information, on a regular or *ad hoc* basis, on their internal workloads, such as the number of cases handled, benefits claimed, stores issued, inspections carried out, but these are rarely linked to expenditure estimates in a way which would indicate the estimated cost of units of workload.

This multiplicity of systems is apparently about to be overlaid by two more:

(i) The adoption of PPB or PAR will require programme analysis which in turn will require a data system which classifies expenditure into programmes, expresses programme goals and records programme performance;

(ii) The move towards managerial accountability will require the provision of a budgetary control system – arrangements which show the resource responsibilities of managers and enable them to record the efficiency with which their resources are used. The budgetary control system will have to be supported by unit costs, activity records, work measurement statistics and in some cases accrual, rather than cash, accounts.

The risk is that departments will be required to produce or collect more and more information for all these separate purposes without any overall view being taken of the total need for information or the relationships between the different information requirements, that is, without any attention to the need for integration.

If we look at this total need, it is apparent that organizations in public administration require information in three general categories (as the New York Bureau of Municipal Research pointed out as long ago as 1907):[28]

(i) For submission to the Legislature for appropriation and for statutory audit.

(ii) For making policy and programme decisions and for evaluating the impact of policies and programmes upon the community. This category is at present provided on a very generalized level by the public expenditure survey and is in the process of being refined by PAR (see Chapter 4). It is also supported by the collection and analysis of the key economic and social indicators referred to above. Information in this category has to be organized on the basis of output or objective of expenditure (for example by programme – see page 116). Its purpose is to assist in the specification of policy objectives, to enable choices to be made between spending programmes on the basis of analyses of cost and benefit and to enable the subsequent *effectiveness* (that is, the relationship of output to objective) of the department to be measured. It is primarily designed to assist long-term decision-making by the Cabinet, by Ministers and by the top management of departments.

(iii) For budgetary control, setting staffing levels, measuring management performance and identifying managerial accountability. Information in this category has to be organized on the basis of the structure of management responsibility within a department, that is by division, branch, section and project. It is at present not provided at all in any systematic way. Its purpose is to enable the *efficiency* of the department to be measured (that is the cost/output ratio) and is primarily designed to assist short-term decision-making at middle and lower management levels in departments.

Appropriation and Audit

We have seen from an earlier discussion in this chapter that the supply procedure has become progressively detached from the reality of the policy-making and management processes of government. It is no longer the focus of attention of Parliament and it bears no relationship to the structure of departmental or interdepartmental programmes or to the structure of departmental organization. It illustrates neither effectiveness nor efficiency. It is still necessary to keep a record of inputs for internal accounting purposes and to demonstrate the stewardship of the Accounting Officer to the auditing body, but what should concern Parliament is information which demonstrates the basis of Ministerial decisions, the impact of those decisions and the effectiveness of departmental programmes. We have seen from Chapter 4 that the U.S. government now presents to Congress not only its conventional budgetary tabulations by input but an analysis of the programmes of some federal agencies. The Canadian government has gone further and since the fiscal year 1970–71 arranges its main display of estimated expenditure for submission to Parliament on the basis of programmes, supported by analyses of inputs and manpower. This arrangement can be illustrated by selections from the 1970–71 budget estimates of the Canadian Department of Agriculture:

AGRICULTURE

General Summary Vote No.		Estimates			Actual Expenditure 1968–9
		Proposed 1970–71	Approved 1969–70	Change	
A.	DEPARTMENT	Thousands of dollars			
1	Administration Program	10,764	9,052	1,712	8,247
5	Research Program	45,747	45,743	4	47,593

10, 15	Production and Marketing Program	152,512	161,175	(8,663)	176,539
20	Health of Animals Program	24,148	20,519	3,629	20,424
25	Board of Grain Commissioners Program	11,233	10,581	652	11,353
	Total	244,404	240,070	(2,666)	264,156
30	B-CANADIAN DAIRY COMMISSION	256	342	114	317
35, 40	C-CANADIAN LIVESTOCK FEED BOARD	17,957	22,883	(4,926)	18,221
45	D-FARM CREDIT CORPORATION	9,600	7,900	1,700	6,266

GENERAL EXPLANATION

The Minister of Agriculture is reponsible for the Department proper consisting of five programs and for the agencies listed below.

A-Department

The aims of the Department are:

To improve the performance of Canadian agriculture as a strong, competitive, primary industry.

To improve the level and stability of farm income.

To facilitate adjustment attendant upon economic development.

To increase unit productivity.

To improve and control product quality in the interests of both the producer and the consumer.

To increase agricultural product utilization.

To improve marketing and distribution systems.

To conserve and improve agricultural resources.

To reduce the impact of natural hazards.

The Department employs approximately 9,000 people located in about 200 separate establishments. The physical plant comprises 1.5 million acres of land and more than 2,500 laboratory, farm and office buildings. Under the authority of some thirty statutes, the Department conducts research, grades and inspects farm products, prevents and controls diseases and pests of crops and livestock and carries on a number of other activities designed to help solve production and marketing problems for the farmer. These activities are conducted under the five programs – Administration, Research, Production and Marketing, Health of Animals and Board of Grain Commissioners.

The general explanation goes on to set out the aims of the Dairy Commission, the Livestock Feed Board and the Farm Credit Corporation.

The objectives and sub-objectives of each programme are then set out and programmes are divided into activities for each of which a description is provided, together with an analysis of planned man-years of work in the coming budget period compared with last year's estimate and the previous year's actual expenditure. Programme operating expenditures are then analysed by input (salaries and wages; transport and communications; information costs; professional services; rentals; purchased repair and up-keep; utilities, materials and supplies). Programme capital expenditures are analysed by salaries and wages; utilities, materials and supplies; construction and acquisition of land and buildings; construction and acquisition of machinery and equipment. Major capital projects are described by previously estimated cost, currently estimated cost, expenditure so far, expenditure for the coming budget period and requirements in future years. Programme manpower is then analysed by type (executive, professional and scientific, administrative and foreign service, technical, operational and administrative support) and by man-years planned and authorized and number in employment for the last, the current and proposed for the next budget period. Finally, grants and contributions to outside bodies made under each programme for the current and the next budget periods are set out.

A display of information on these lines can provide the information both for appropriation and for policy and programme planning. In this way the systems for category (i) and category (ii) information can be integrated. If measures of impact and effectiveness can be attached to each programme and activity on the lines described in Chapter 4 we can construct a control system in the 'effectiveness dimension': we can state objectives, express these as programmes, track the results of the programmes and refine or re-define the objectives. The greatest benefit from integrating the two systems arises from the opportunity to open departmental decision processes to outside scrutiny and to informed debate in Parliament. No reform could do more to enable the Legislature to regain some of its lost power over the Executive.

Information for Management Control

Category (iii) information is required as a means of measuring efficiency, that is, of relating costs to output. It focuses attention on the use made by managers of the resources in their charge. To assemble this information we need to know:

(i) the total costs of a unit of organization;
and (ii) the capacity of the unit for handling work.

These two measures can then be related to establish standards of efficiency or 'performance indicators'.

We have seen that at present it is usually impossible to arrive at the total costs of even large units of government organization except by special investigation because the structure of accounting data assembled for the supply procedure does not coincide with the organization structure of departments and the costs of one unit may be borne on several vote sub-heads. In addition, some important costs are not carried on the votes of the user departments at all but are provided as an 'allied service' on the votes of service departments. For example, the costs of space and utilities are attributed to the Department of the Environment, the costs of stationery, printing, computers and other office equipment are on the vote of the Stationery Office and some training costs are paid for by the Civil Service Department. We therefore have a situation in which the departments which cause the costs of these allied services are not responsible for them and the departments which are responsible for them have little influence over them. In industry, it is a common practice to 'charge out' to users the costs of such centrally administered services as space, utilities, computing, training, printing and consultancy services. The advantages of charging-out are that it prevents the wasteful use of central resources – users are less likely to abuse a service for which they have to pay than one which is free; it offers a guide to the efficiency of the service providers – the better they are, the more their services will be sought and paid for; it helps to ensure that services are related to current needs – users will not pay for a service which they do not want or can obtain better or cheaper elsewhere; it places the accountability for expenditure on a service with the user rather than the provider. Charging-out is most effective when the service being charged for is well defined; when it is fairly easy, within a reasonable period, to establish that performance is satisfactory; and when a relatively simple or generally acceptable method can be devised for establishing the level of charge to be levied. It is least effective when the costs of the service are difficult to allocate between operating units (for instance, some research work, public relations) and recourse has to be made to allocating such costs on an arbitrary basis (for instance according to the assets of, or numbers of staff in, the user unit) or when the cost of a service is best controlled in total and centrally by specialists (such as catering costs). In the Civil Service charging-out to user departments would appear to be most easily applied in the fields of accommodation, purchasing, stationery and printing, computing, training and management servʲces.

Having established as fully as possible the costs of a unit's existence we have to try to establish some measure of its capacity and workload. Most departments include large areas of measurable work: those areas employing, for example, the 170,000 members of the clerical grades, the 24,000 tax officers, and 10,000 paper keepers and messengers, the 6,000 machine operators and so on. Very little is known about the efficiency of units employing these staff because very little clerical or manual work measurement has been carried out. The Civil Service Department's then co-ordinator of clerical work measurement, L. C. Harmer, in a paper on its application in the Civil Service,[29] refers to 'experimental studies' in a number of departments. Harmer shows that it is possible to apply a number of measurement techniques – activity sampling, PMT, short-interval scheduling – to clerical and manual activities in departments and to produce work standards which apply to a wide variety of situations. Using these yardsticks it is possible to produce regular control reports showing productivity (the workload handled compared with a standard output) and identifying sections which are under-loaded or over-loaded. Clearly, such control systems can be applied best where the work is purely routine and repetitive and least appropriately where there is a significant discretionary or considerative element. Highly routine and repetitive clerical work is particularly common in the Civil Service, where armies of clerks are engaged on, for example, keeping accounts, recording the movement of stores, issuing permits, licences and benefits, keeping personnel records, maintaining statistics, recording transactions, correspondence and applications, typing standard letters and punching computer inputs. Though discretionary or considerative work cannot be measured, the time required to carry out the simpler jobs of this kind can be estimated with a fair degree of accuracy; most people doing them are accustomed to making such estimates and to planning their time. The technique applied in industry to this type of work is called category estimating or job-slotting. This involves the supervisor in allocating one of a number of time categories to each job he distributes to his staff and in keeping a simple record of the time taken. It is widely used for maintenance work, in research establishments and in offices handling non-routine cases. Consultants in clerical work measurement have found that 'truly creative or considerative work represents a relatively small proportion of the general run of office work: mental processes are so fast that, for example, decisions can be taken during the physical process of reading written information ... An experienced clerk can read an application form with the relevant rules in mind and apply the rules automatically as he reads.'[30] For areas in which individual work measurement is not worthwhile, the unit of measurement can be based on the group or team. The technique called Group Capacity Assessment can be used in such situations and has been found practicable and useful in a recent experiment in the Ministry of Defence.[31]

These are not the only areas of the non-industrial Civil Service in which workload can be measured and productivity assessed. There are 34,000 technicians, scientific assistants and experimental officers and 12,000 draughtsmen working in sections directly supervised by most of the 10,000 scientists, engineers, architects and surveyors. The majority of those technical civil servants are engaged on closely specified projects and programmes with quantifiable outputs required by stated deadlines. In many of them it is already normal practice to monitor results by using project costing and control systems. Some of these systems are well in advance of industrial practice. Work-measurement systems are also applicable, but rarely applied, to many of them (setting up and reporting on experiments, retrieving information, simple draughting and design). At the upper administrative and professional levels of the Civil Service the work is inherently judgemental and reactive and clearly unmeasurable. Any attempt to evaluate performance must rest on purely subjective and qualitative assessments. However, many administrators and professionals are either directly in charge of, or have immediate subordinates who are in charge of, those executive/clerical and technical areas where work measurement can be applied. The conventional view has been that senior officials need not be greatly concerned with the efficiency of the units for which they are ultimately responsible and that this is a matter for their departments' Establishments and Finance Divisions. This is one reason why no great attention has been given to establishing control systems. However, if accountability is to mean anything, senior officials must be provided with information which enables them to take a view on the efficiency with which their subordinates deploy their staff and to assess the manpower effects of new demands placed upon the organization. The value of control information goes beyond simply measuring and improving efficiency: reliable performance indicators can provide the basis for planning future manpower needs and for substantiating claims for more staff, for identifying bottlenecks in the production process and directing attention to points where managerial action is needed, for enabling managers to plan and organize the flow of work and to evaluate their own performance.

In the U.S. government the development of control systems on these lines goes back to the 1930s.[32] The necessity for unit costing and work measurement (then called 'performance budgeting') was emphasized by the Hoover Commission of 1949.[33] Many agencies regularly produce comparative indices of cost per unit of output or of labour hours per unit of output as part of the annual claim for funds: that is, when submitting their budget estimates agencies also state their target levels for labour productivity. 'Requests for additional staff and even justification for current staff levels have to be supported by evidence of reasonably anticipated work loads in the light of agreed work standards . . . During the financial year reports are issued which compare total output, total input and rate of performance against the standards incorporated in the adopted budget.'[34] The value of control information was emphasized by a Presidential Order of 1949 which began the annual President's Cost Reduction (latterly Management Improvement) Programmes, the importance of which have been stressed by every President since then. Under the Management Improvement Programmes (which are dealt with in more detail in Chapter 7) every bureau has to produce for its 'priority areas' quantitative indicators for measuring perform-ance, improvement goals and evaluations of past performance. For example, the performance statements issued by the U.S. Inland Revenue Service specify the average revenue collected per dollar of cost ($234 in 1970); the average revenue collected per employee ($2.9m. in 1970 – an increase of 87 per cent during the preceding decade); the *additional* yields per *additional* dollar of cost and per *additional* employee and include comparisons with revenue-collecting agencies in other countries (though roughly the same size as the British Inland Revenue, it collects nine times as much money per employee). Similar indicators – of cheques processed and issued, the unit cost per cheque and the number of transactions per employee – are produced for the office of the Treasurer and the Bureau of Accounts. In 1964 a major project was undertaken by the U.S. Bureau of the Budget to measure the productivity of five federal agencies.[35] This exercise concentrated on the construction of simple large-scale ratios of inputs of man-power and cost to single indices of output. An output index was an aggregation of the volumes of all types of services produced by an agency weighted by their respective average man-hours work-ed, or their cost, per unit. In the case of the Division of Dis-bursements of the Treasury the volumes of issued cheques and bonds were combined into an output index with its base year at 1962. This index was then related to man-years worked, payroll cost and total budgeted cost to produce three key indicators: output per man-year, output per constant dollar of payroll cost and output per constant dollar of total cost. These indicators were tracked back to 1949 to give a picture of efficiency movements over more than a decade. Similarly in the Insurance Department of the Veterans Administration nine separate outputs (for example number of policies issued, loan applications, disablement services provided) were related to man-hours and payroll costs. In the more complex Systems Maintenance Service of the Federal Aviation Agency, where over eighty different air traffic and navigation facilities were maintained, the output index was based on a 'standard facility year' (the operation for one year of a facility requiring one man-year of maintenance effort annually). Work on these lines in Canada by the Efficiency Evaluation Division of the Treasury Board has produced five key efficiency indicators for the Unemployment Insurance Commission and twelve for the hospital service of the Department of Veterans Affairs and is being extended to twenty-two departments.

In the measurement of efficiency, the British non-industrial Civil Service is about where the U.S. Civil Service was in 1949. We know virtually nothing of the efficiency of departments, many of which include clerical and technical activities whose work is not at all difficult to measure. In the absence of any reliable information on cost, capacity and volume of work we have no basis for short-term planning, for control or for the evaluation of management performance.

BUILDING A DATA BASE

The top decision-makers and planners in departments require detailed information on the effectiveness and impact of policies and programmes and generalized information on the efficiency of departmental operations. Middle and junior management require information on the programmes or programme elements for which they are responsible and information displaying the efficiency of their units. In addition, while the supply procedure is unaltered, Parliament requires information on what is being bought. They all want to know when the money was spent.

These different requirements raise the problem of classifying a common input into three streams (by programme, for the policy makers and planners; by unit of organization, for the managers; by the items bought, for the legislators). Each stream then has to be matched with the appropriate measures of results (the policy-makers and planners want to know how effective policies are, the managers want to know how efficient their units are, the legislators want to know if the money was properly spent in the budget period). On the input side, this multiple requirement can be met by coding every item of expenditure:

1. 'Subjectively': that is by reference to the nature of the goods or services purchased or the obligations discharged. Subjective classification groups, for example, all payroll expenses, all equipment expenses, all expenses of travelling, accommodation, postage.

2. 'Objectively': that is according to the purpose for which it is incurred. Objective classification groups, for example, all construction programme costs, all training programme costs, all research programme costs.

3. By organizational unit: for example research establishment, local office, regional office, headquarters division or directorate.

4. By accounting period in which the transaction took place.

5. By vote sub-head.

Using such a coding arrangement and data-processing facilities, expenditure can rapidly be cross-analysed and summarized to meet the requirements of each function and level of management: inputs to programmes and to units can be monitored, the costs of common services can be monitored, the spend can be reviewed against the vote. Arrangements on these general lines have been a feature of management accounting in industry for decades. In public administration, however, the traditional view of the matter has been put by Mackenzie and Grove: 'Much thought has been spent on this problem, but it has not been possible to propose seriously either that more sophisticated accounting methods should replace the form hallowed by constitutional practice, or that accounts should (as a general practice) be kept twice over, in different forms for different purposes.'[36]

DEVELOPMENTS IN CONTROL

Control systems in government are undergoing rapid change at the present time. They have had to be improved in the wake of new developments in planning – PAR inevitably leads to the consideration of the measurement of programme results. In addition, the new structure of Parliamentary committees was set up in the context of a demand by Parliamentarians for a move towards control by programme. The Civil Service Department and other departments have made some progress with the design of performance indicators (see Chapter 6), though a recent article on the subject by an officer of the CSD[37] points to the problems posed in measuring total cost by the existence of the vote accounts of the supply procedure.

Perhaps more important, the growth of giant departments has inevitably led to a move towards greater delegation of authority in spending and manpower to departments, and to accountable units within them. Sir Richard Clarke, in the context of an examination of the consequences of giant departments, has said: 'The system of public expenditure control we are now approaching stands the traditional system on its head. The traditional system saw the expenditure of a department (and indeed the total expenditure of the departments) as the sum of thousands of individual items and thus the essence of the control of expenditure was the control of the items . . . The dialogue between the Treasury and the department was in terms of items, not in terms of totals. The system which is developing on the other hand, sees its focal point in the total – i.e. in the allocation . . . with the onus entirely on the department to deal with the items accordingly.'[38] He sees a similar system developing on the manpower side, with manpower allocations to departments and the Civil Service Department's role being to establish 'the centre's constraints on the department's freedom of action and above all to satisfy itself that the department's organization and system for handling its manpower problems is effective'.[39]

Having discussed the general principles on which management information could be structured for entire departments, we have to return to the problem of designing a structure of control internal to those departments. This depends upon the arrangement of accountability centres within departments which, as we shall see from the next chapter, is a field in which important new developments are currently taking place.

CHAPTER 6

Accountable Management

AN accountable manager is one to whom specific authority over
part of an organization's resources has been delegated and who is
required to answer for the results he has obtained from the deployment of those resources. Accountability implies the delegation to managers of authority over money and manpower; a
form of organization in which managers can be made responsible
for the activities of sub-units; a strategic planning framework in
which the objectives of those managers can be related to corporate objectives; an arrangement of control information so that
progress towards the attainment of those objectives can be monitored; and a procedural system for securing managerial commitment to unit objectives and for reviewing results. Accountable
management in the public service, where market forces cannot
operate, also implies the need for a powerful external audit body
capable of safeguarding the public interest in the proper, and
effective, use of expenditure (see Chapter 7).

In the three preceding chapters we have discussed the background to accountability in organization, strategic planning and
control information. In this chapter, we first discuss the scope for
delegation in departments and then turn to arrangements for
setting objectives and reviewing results.

Accountable management is said to have been developed as a
formal system in the United States in the 1920s and has since become common in large industrial and commercial organizations.
Alfred P. Sloan, who evolved a system of accountability as a
means of welding a number of separate and competing motor
companies into one General Motors in the early 1920s, described
it as decentralizing responsibility within a framework of central
control.[1] The General Motors system, which has become the
model for many accountability systems in industry has been described by Peter Drucker as 'the development of the maximum of
independent command at the lowest possible level and the

development of an objective yardstick to measure performance in these commands'.[2]

Systems of accountability in industry aim at developing in big firms the management style typical of small, thrusting ones: speed in identifying changes in the local environment and rapid reaction to new opportunities and risks; a willingness to take risks; short lines of communication, a minimum of bureaucratic rules and regulations, and tight cost control. Accountability implies the greatest possible delegation of authority to middle and junior management and the existence of a top management group who are willing to confine their activities to overall planning and overall control and supervising the supply of competent general managers.

D. Ronald David points out that too many imitators of General Motors have copied the form of its system of accountability without the substance: 'Lacking G.M.'s depth in quality manpower and G.M.'s finely tuned planning and control systems, some companies have found their divisionalized structures leading to abdication rather than delegation and to anarchy rather than accountability.'[3]

Accountability systems can also fail if it is not made clear what the manager is to be accountable for. It is essential to establish the extent to which the manager can affect his costs and results and even in industry this question is often a matter of much debate. Some cost-allocation systems attribute central overhead costs to managers who are unable to influence them in any way. It also sometimes happens that the 'accountable' manager is penalized for others' mistakes in purchasing, stockholding and transportation decisions, for example, in which he has had no say. In a complex organization in which the product passes through many different processes the assessment of managerial performance may depend on an arrangement of internal transfer prices, the calculation of which may be very often uncontrollable by the manager and sometimes unfair to him. For example, the manager of an assembly shop may be obliged to 'buy' castings and machined parts from other divisions of his company at above the market price, when it is in the interest of the company as a whole, but counter to his own interest, that he should do so.

In addition, as we saw from the last chapter, criticism has been directed at the unreliability of the control information on which management performance is judged; there are often difficulties in forecasting profits, valuing assets, attributing reasons for variance from budget, separating long-term from short-term effects. A lot depends upon the management style of the organization in which accountability is applied. In one firm it can be used as a means of coercing managers to produce bigger and better production figures; in another it can be a genuine attempt to give managers more rewarding jobs and greater freedom and scope to use their initiative.

FULTON'S PRINCIPLES OF ACCOUNTABILITY

The Fulton Committee defined accountability as 'holding individuals and units responsible for performance measured as objectively as possible' and recommended that 'the principles of accountable management should be applied to the work of departments'.[4] An accountable unit was defined as a unit of organization for which output could be measured against costs or other criteria and where individual managers could be held personally responsible for their performance. Such units would be mainly those handling a flow of regular transactions (such as supplies, stores, local offices and a wide range of other executive activities) for which measures of performance could be calculated. In areas of administrative work different considerations would have to apply. Here, output could not usually be measured because it consisted of reviewing policy and considering complicated cases, because of the unpredictable demands that arose from the Minister's responsibility to Parliament and because of the important elements of consultation, negotiation and the preparation of legislation. In these areas, the principle to be applied was management by objective: heads of branches should agree with their superiors and subordinates the tasks assigned, relative priorities and dates for completion and regularly review progress. The effectiveness of the branch and the contribution of its individual members could then be more objectively assessed.

The main evidence that the Committee received on the question of accountability was supplied by its Management Consultancy Group, which was far more tentative in its approach. It suggested that a series of research programmes should be undertaken by the Civil Service, of which some should examine the scope for delegating responsibility to individuals and measuring managerial effectiveness. Experiments in delegation would establish whether it was possible to establish 'budget centres', to which costs could be allocated and for which output could be measured, and 'responsibility centres' to which costs could be allocated but for which only deadlines and priorities could be specified.[5]

The Committee did not acknowledge that management by objectives has always been most successfully applied in areas in which output is measurable and, more important, it commended accountability as a principle without devoting any consideration to whether the constraints of public service would allow the delegation of authority over money and manpower to individual managers on the scale that enables accountability to work in industry. It made no observations on Ministerial or public accountability. The Committee's cursory treatment of the question of accountability and delegation compares badly with the proposals of the Canadian Glassco Commission of 1962.[6] Glassco proposed substantial delegation from the Treasury Board to departments which were to be given increased powers of expenditure and contract negotiation and increased flexibility in the use of their allotted moneys. The Treasury Board was separated from the Department of Finance and combined with the Civil Service Commission so that one central agency was responsible for ultimate control of both money and manpower (cf. the Fulton solution of combining efficiency services and manpower control in the Civil Service Department and leaving financial control in the Treasury). At the same time it proposed hierarchies of responsibility centres within departments and recommended substantial delegation of spending powers to centre managers: 'It is generally found that actual expenditures for various items may differ from the estimated expenditures. A regional manager within a department, for example, requires authority to deal with such variances and to offset deficiencies and surpluses on items within his budget, provided that his total budget is not exceeded and expenditures are made for approved programmes and activities for that region. Treasury Board control is to be achieved by monitoring performance instead of the earlier practice of restricting freedom to act.'[7]

PUBLIC ACCOUNTABILITY

In the preceding chapters, we have considered the framework of delegation: an organization structure which expresses managerial responsibility; a plan which specifies the objectives of the policy makers and the deployment of resources required to attain them; an information system which permits the performance of departments and managers to be compared with the plan. We now have to consider to what extent it is possible in the Civil Service to delegate authority to individual managers or whether the public accountability of the Minister and the Permanent Secretary represent such a force for centralization that the scope for delegation is negligible.

In industry, the owner-entrepreneur is a free agent within the law and even when ownership and management are separate it is rare for 'accountability to the shareholders' to have any great force. Most boards of directors like to distribute sufficient profit to maintain a healthy share price, but may not consider themselves accountable to the body of shareholders for anything more. In such a situation, the delegation of authority from the central power-group within the firm can be almost complete. The manager of an operating division can be given a wide degree of freedom over the disposition and exploitation of the resources he has been allocated and, significantly, can often manipulate, or at least influence, external factors as well. Even in a highly competitive trade, the manager can usually do something to regulate the inflow of business or can alter its characteristics so as to employ his resources most efficiently. He can use pricing, buying, advertising, promotion, manufacturing, selling and service policies to ensure an even flow of activity throughout the year or to attract profitable business or discourage unattractive business. He can use these and investment personnel and research policies to develop his business in the way which gives him the most favourable return in the long run. Even at the level of the cost centre, which may be anything from a large manufacturing plant or a national vehicle fleet to a small clerical section or a group of machine tools, the manager in industry often has wide tactical discretion to adapt his activities so as to operate at least cost or optimum efficiency.

In the Civil Service, 'the personal responsibility of each Minister to Parliament for matters within his competence is ... a basic principle of the Constitution'.[8] The Minister is responsible for the development and application of policy and for the actions of all the civil servants in his department. He may be called upon at any time to justify to Parliament not only his past and present actions but the policy he intends to pursue. His decisions are open to formal scrutiny by the Ombudsman and Parliamentary Committees. The Permanent Secretary, as the department's Accounting Officer, has to answer to the Public Accounts Committee for the proper authorization of expenditure and for the avoidance of waste and extravagance. This detailed, if somewhat random, scrutiny of the top management of a department naturally encourages the reference of cases and expenditure decisions upwards rather than delegation to lower levels of management. 'The Minister's nominal responsibility not just for strategic policy but for every executive operation of his department has meant no systematic responsibility at all. Worse still, the fear of involving Ministers in having to account for operations of which they can have no first-hand knowledge leads officials to excessive caution and secrecy, to insistence on passing decisions up to levels far higher than their merits warrant and to consequent delay. Thus the practical application of the theory of Ministerial responsibility, to the point where delegation of authority is actively opposed, has brought managerial inefficiency without any compensating benefits in the term of greater accountability.'[9]

Departments cannot fully control the demands made upon them. New tasks and activities (such as price control, selective employment tax) are given to them with the minimum of preparation. Sudden and unforeseeable demands may be made upon them not only by the Minister but by developments in the national and international environments. This turbulence is felt mostly at the top of departments: 'A senior civil servant's duty ... can often only be defined as dealing with anything which may arise within a certain sphere and sometimes no permanent overriding policy objective may have been laid down.'[10] At lower levels of responsibility, the executive civil servant is operating in a more predictable environment, often applying established legislation to a fairly well-defined client community (farmers, industrialists, claimants for benefit) but still unable to do much to influence the flow of work. Technical and specialist civil servants operating in technical fields (research and development, construction, specifying technical standards) may have a substantial degree of control over their workload but still, typically, have less than in industry.

There can also be no discrimination between customers in the interests of efficiency as there can in industry. To the outside world a department has to present a common front. The scope for delegating authority in the field of 'external relations' is therefore small. There are exceptions to this – where the possible demands made upon the civil servant by the community are so enormously wide-ranging that the rule book cannot cover sufficient eventualities and the application of the legislation has to be left to the discretion of the man in the field (the policeman, the insurance officer, the 'inspector') – but in all these cases the department is out on a possibly dangerous limb.

Some recent developments have tended to tighten central control over departments. The creation of giant departments was specifically intended to ensure the closer alignment of policies and programmes in formerly separate departments, and PAR has been designed to permit detailed evaluation by the Treasury of some, perhaps ultimately all, departmental programmes. We have seen that the creation of the Central Policy Review Staff will reinforce this process by providing an additional supra-departmental mechanism for the evaluation of priorities and the allocation of resources. This tendency may be counter-balanced by the willingness of the Treasury and the Civil Service Department to delegate the detailed control of expenditure to departments and to concentrate upon annual allocation and continuing systems supervision rather than on individual items of expenditure and bids for staff. However, some politicians and commentators argue that, whatever the degree of delegation from the centre, managers in departments will always be so constrained by public accountability and by the need to comply with service-wide financial and personnel regulations that effective managerial accountability can be achieved only by 'hiving off' some of the responsibilities of departments to autonomous public agencies or bureaux, not directly financed by the supply procedure nor accountable to Ministers except in the most general terms, or to private bodies.

The general sentiment in support of hiving-off was put by Goodnow writing over seventy years ago: 'The fact is, then, that there is a large part of administration which is unconnected with politics, which should therefore be relieved very largely, if not altogether, from the control of political bodies. It is unconnected with politics because it embraces fields of semi-scientific, quasi-judicial and quasi-business or commercial activity – work has little if any influence on the expression of the true State will.'[11]

The Fulton Committee received several submissions (from, for example, the Confederation of British Industry) supporting this point of view; it was put to the Committee that 'accountable management is most effectively introduced when an activity is separately established outside any government department, and that this solution should be adopted for many executive activities, especially the provision of services to the community. These boards or corporations would be wholly responsible in their own fields within the powers delegated to them. Although they would be outside the day-to-day control of Ministers and the scrutiny of Parliament, Ministers would retain powers to give them directions when necessary.'[12]

The problem is, of course, to reach agreement on what functions are unconnected with politics and to identify to whom, and to what extent, hived-off bodies shall be accountable if they are not to be moved out of the public sector and reconstituted under the Companies Act. No government has considered the apparently independent nationalized corporations as unconnected with politics. For example, though recent governments have made a point of disengaging from detailed interference in the nationalized industries they have at the same time pursued a policy of stoutly resisting wage increases in the public sector. No government has been able to resist tinkering with the nationalized industries' pricing policies and investment programmes in the interest of managing the economy, supporting uneconomic domestic suppliers of equipment (such as aircraft) or raw materials (such as coal) or influencing policies with pronounced social effects (such as factory location). 'Paradoxically, Whitehall's itch to drive from the back seat has increased enormously since the industries were first enjoined in 1961 to concentrate upon pursuing commercial rather than "public interest" objectives.'[13]

The recently hived-off Post Office Corporation illustrates the contradictions inherent in having public bodies outside the day-to-day control of Ministers but organized to permit Ministers to give them directions when necessary. The Minister of Post and Telecommunications heads a body which supervises the policies and spending of the Post Office and the present incumbent of that post (a member of an anti-interventionist administration) has in the recent past obliged it to fight the most lengthy industrial action in its history, has fired its chairman for failing to toe the ministerial line and has announced that he is responsible for the efficient management of the corporation.[14] The activities of the Post Office in collecting taxes, issuing benefits, banking, maintaining the nation's system of communications and its surveillance over transactions between individuals put it right at the centre of public concern and political interest. In retrospect the decision to hive it off as a commercial operation may well have given too little emphasis to the importance of the public-service nature of its activities. 'Once "profitability" is substituted for "service" as the basic motive, there seems no mechanism in the Post Office to prevent a slow, but inevitable, slide into inequitability.'[15]

At the time of writing, Ministers have been required to survey the activities of their departments for units which could be hived off as public agencies. The purpose of this exercise appears not only to create accountable units but to effect an apparent reduction in the number of civil servants. So far, the civil aviation regulating activities partly undertaken by the Department of Trade and Industry and partly by the Air Registration Board, the National Air Traffic Control Services and the Air Transport Licensing Board have been reconstituted under a new Civil Aviation Authority and it is proposed that the vocational training centres of the Department of Employment and the Industrial Training Boards will be amalgamated under a National Training Agency. It has also been suggested that the Royal Mint and the operational activities of the Social Security system should be set up as public agencies and studies are being carried out on the future status of the Royal Ordnance Factories and H.M. Dockyards.

In addition, in the last year or so we have seen the creation of the departmental agency, a departmental unit which is still under the direction of a Minister answerable to Parliament for its activities and still employs civil servants but which is headed by an accounting officer, has its own vote and has substantial freedom in personnel matters. Examples of such departmental agencies are the Defence Procurement Executive in the Ministry of Defence and apparently the Employment Services Agency in the Department of Employment, both formed in 1971. If this is to be the new pattern of organization for accountability, we might expect such arrangements to be made for many areas of executive activity in departments (for example the Passport Office, the Prison Department, the construction branches of the Department of the Environment, the Companies Registration Office, the Patent Office).

The weakness in this pragmatic approach to the creation of public and departmental agencies is that it is not taking place within the framework of any review of the scope and definition of public accountability. Contributors to a symposium held in 1969 on 'the dilemma of accountability in modern government' pointed out that there were already more than 700 'quasi-non-governmental organizations' in Britain.[16] These range from nationalized industries to the Marriage Guidance Council, the Central Midwives Board and the Charity Commission and include such substantial spenders as the University Grants Committee, the British Council, the Shipbuilding Industry Board and the new towns development corporations. Though all these bodies submit their accounts to audit, their public accountability for administrative efficiency or programme effectiveness is negligible (see Chapter 7).

MANAGERIAL ACCOUNTABILITY WITHIN DEPARTMENTS

Fulton's emphasis was upon delegation of responsibility within departments for internal costs and efficiency. The main element of internal costs is staff salaries, though expenditures on buying and running data-processing and other office equipment are becoming significant in some areas. At present, the degree of control of the Civil Service manager over the costs of his staff is minimal. He cannot hire or fire (nor often select staff), he cannot reward merit and only rarely can he even insure that the annual increment of an unsatisfactory member of his staff is withheld. He cannot vary the rate for the job according to conditions in the local labour market because salaries for each grade of staff are centrally negotiated. Crucially, there is no incentive for him to raise efficiency by evolving better working methods or replanning the work of his unit, since such matters are the concern of his department's Establishments Division and its O. & M. and staff inspection branches. He is not entitled to vary the complement of his branch or radically to re-allocate the work of the grades of staff in his unit. At present, the only area in which he can exercise some control over staff costs is overtime, but even that is often unavoidable, being due to staff shortages or absence or to the seasonal bunching of transactions and cases, for example. The incidence of such smaller items of cost as utilities and postage are usually directly related to the level of office activity, which is often determined externally. The cost of accommodation is decided centrally and often in another department.

If accountability is to mean anything the manager must be given greater influence over his manpower costs. Establishments Division must surrender part of their control over the allocation, organization and utilization of staff and instead devote more attention to the development of human resources in general (see Chapter 8): it is obviously anomalous that a senior manager can have a substantial degree of control over millions of pounds worth of contracts or construction projects and yet have very little say in personnel matters. The key reform would be to introduce a procedure in which the manager agreed with his superior his 'manpower budget' for the coming year and was then permitted to organize, staff and plan the work of his unit as he thought best. This is not to say that he could ignore general grading rules by employing people paid at less than the rate for the grade given to the job, but that he should be permitted to decide how many staff, and which grades of staff, he required to get the job done within a total manpower cost. Once he had established the form of his organization, it should be inspected by a 'job analyst' from the department's personnel division (see Chapter 8) to ensure that the jobs were correctly graded, with the analyst having the ultimate sanction of regrading in the event of a dispute. However, the initiative for setting staffing levels would rest with the manager. With his new freedom, the manager could also be given the responsibility for planning the flow of work through his unit so as to meet his objectives for efficiency.

Such a reform would amount to a substantial delegation of manpower control from present-day establishments divisions to line management. It need not be in any way inconsistent with centrally imposed rules on the number of staff employed and pay and conditions of service nor centrally established procedures for handling cases and transactions, yet it would push the responsibility for the main element of costs down the line to the operating manager. No longer could this responsibility be shrugged off as a matter for 'Establishments'.

Such a change in convention could have side effects. An important one could be to upset the balance of the present career structure. As we saw from Chapter 3, in the present-day Civil Service, career structures strongly influence organization structures. The point here is that if authority in the disposition of staff is given to line managers, then it is highly likely that the present career progression will be affected, because some managers will choose to omit some levels in organizing their work. The extent of this problem is impossible to anticipate in advance of an experiment in manpower budgeting. Another side effect is, of course, to put far greater powers over their subordinates into the hands of managers, with all the attendant risks of favouritism and victimization. It is sometimes said that the decent and civilized atmosphere of most Civil Service offices is due to the fact that advancement depends primarily upon length of service and secondly on creating a good impression with a promotion board and not upon pleasing the boss. The likelihood of this effect would be small if there was an active and informed personnel function continually reviewing the prospects and career development of all staff.

A move towards manpower budgeting could build on existing precedents. The practice of 'fluid complementing' in the scientific Civil Service incorporates an element of the proposed change and the departmental agency concept, at least in the case of the Defence Procurement Agency, appears to involve the delegation authority over a manpower budget to a large departmental unit.

There remains one important element of the costs of a department for which accountability is at present not clearly established. We saw in the last chapter that the costs of government office accommodation, furniture, maintenance, rates and rent (in total about £150 m.p.a.) is carried on the 'works' vote of the Department of the Environment, and the costs of office equipment, computers, stationery and equipment (about £50 m.p.a.) are carried on the H.M.S.O. vote under 'allied service' arrangements. There are some advantages in retaining expertise in buying standards, specifications, production and design in central service departments, but managerial accountability appears to be best served by the replacement of the allied service concept with a system of charging out in which users repay the providers of service for expenditures made on their behalf and have the right to negotiate terms with them.

At this point, we can envisage arrangements in which the accountability of managers of divisions and large operating units could be determined for, on the input side, programme expenditures, manpower, accommodation and equipment costs and on the output side, the achievement of programme objectives and target levels of operating productivity.

SETTING AND REVIEWING MANAGEMENT OBJECTIVES

It is essential that the objectives of accountable managers are congruent with those of the organization as a whole. 'Many top managements in industry and commerce have, therefore, in recent years become attracted to a managerial system based on the establishment of a hierarchy of annual objectives for managers from directorial to supervisory levels deriving from a statement of the aims of the enterprise as a whole and supported by control systems which permit the regular comparison of results and the stated objectives.'[17] These objective-setting routines are generically known as performance appraisal and review systems, and in Britain the best-known and most widely adopted of them is 'Management by Objectives' (MbO). MbO appears to be particularly suitable as a framework for accountable management in the Civil Service and its application has been enthusiastically explored by the Civil Service Department. Though MbO is generally understood to have originated with Peter Drucker's *The Practice of Management* (1955)[18] and something very much like it was tried at General Mills Inc. in 1954,[19] its development into a practical operating routine in this country has been largely due to the work of the British consultant John W. Humble [20] and to the encouragement of the British Institute of Management since the early 1960s. The result of intensive development here has been that MbO, as a 'package' of operating routines, has flourished more widely in Britain than anywhere else in the world and it has been held to be a uniquely British contribution to management practice.

One of the difficulties in getting to grips with MbO is that it can be taken to mean anything from a new philosophy of management to a tarted-up suggestion scheme and that in its short history it has been considerably expanded in scope, at one end into corporate planning and at the other into studies of management style and the behaviour of working groups. Drucker's original observations on the topic were headed 'Management by Objectives and Self-Control' and dwelt upon the prime responsibility of every manager to have his objectives clearly spelled out so that he could control his own performance and could direct his efforts towards the achievement of the objectives of the business as a whole. Early applications of MbO in the U.S.A. appear to have been orientated towards employee appraisal and salary review, while in Britain its value for management training and improving communications have received more emphasis.

The MbO process aims at getting a manager and his boss to produce a statement which sets out the purpose of the manager's job and specific objectives for the achievement of which the manager can properly be held accountable. Since most managers, and their bosses, usually find this a novel and daunting procedure, a third party, usually called an MbO officer or Management Development Adviser (MDA) acts as tutor, scribe and catalyst in the process of persuading managers to describe and think about the purpose of their jobs. The MDA carries out a series of interviews with individual managers, often working up the hierarchy by first interviewing junior managers, then their bosses and so on to the top. This method of working upwards from the bottom has been shown by experience in the Civil Service[21] to have the advantage of starting from what is actually happening rather than from what senior management thinks ought to be happening. On the other hand, it has the disadvantage of failing to set the objectives of the individual manager in the context of the objectives of the whole unit. The latest practice in the Civil Service Department is to involve top management at the outset in a discussion of overall aims and objectives and then carry out detailed investigations from the lowest levels. In the course of several interviews, the MDA and the manager together examine the latter's job and draft the 'Manager's Plan' which is a set of documents usually in three parts:

(a) *The Job Description*. This sets out the manager's title, his position in the organization, his boss and his immediate subordinates; the main purpose of the job; his main personal activities and his most frequent contacts.

(b) *The Job's Key Tasks*. That is, those activities where specific results must be obtained if the purpose of the job is to be achieved. Each of the key tasks (usually half a dozen or so) is briefly described, and tabulated against each one is the method of measuring performance in it, a statement of the standard to be achieved when the task is being properly done and the manager's suggestions for improvement.

(c) *The Job Improvement Plan.* This sets out the step-by-step action required to achieve each improvement suggested in the key tasks papers, designates the responsibility for taking this action and sets a deadline for its completion.

When the manager's plan is at a fairly advanced stage, his line superior takes over from the MDA and together superior and subordinate agree on the description of the job, the priorities to be given to the key tasks, the methods of measuring performance and the plans for improvement. The job improvement plan is then reviewed at four- or six-monthly intervals thereafter to insure that it is kept up to date and reflects any changes in the job. The MDA gradually withdraws from the scene, usually leaving behind a designated MbO officer whose task is to insure that the procedures are maintained and to apply them to any new jobs.

The compilation of managers' plans spins off a number of special studies. The key tasks analyses for a number of managers often show that two or more claim responsibility for the same task or that a task implied as very important from the statement of objectives of the whole unit is not given very high priority by any manager. Managers' guides frequently show organizational malfunctions or discontinuities – some tasks 'falling between' two managers, under-utilized or over-extended managers and staff, unnecessary levels in the hierarchy, too wide or too narrow spans of control. They also very frequently show opportunities for substantial paperwork savings: unnecessary or over-complicated returns, time-wasting reporting procedures or a badly organized flow of work. Numerous tributes have been paid to the efficacy of MbO in industry and commerce in reducing costs;[22] improving communications and sharpening financial discipline;[23] creating a clearer understanding between manager and his boss; clearly establishing line-staff relations; improving personal performance and measurement methods;[24] encouraging delegation and freeing top managers from an excessive workload;[25] revealing problems, improving morale, reducing inefficiency and establishing accountability ('How MbO Has Brought Real Accountability to Barclays DCO').[26] It has been successfully applied in a wide variety of manufacturing industries, airlines, banks and research establishments.[27]

Problems raised by MbO applications are the usual ones inherent in systems relying on control information, notably the risk of falsification or rigging of those results for which measurements are produced by the information system (for example production) and the neglect of activities in which performance is not immediately measurable or is not given great weight (for example good staff relations). This has been such a problem as to cause at least one writer on the subject to take a 'jaundiced look at MbO'.[28] There is also a tendency for 'managers to become selfish and insular when they believe that their department's performance will be the basis for their personal success'.[29] Being based on a hierarchy of objectives descending from the board's corporate plan to the operating programmes of the shop floor or office section supervisor and concentrating upon superior–subordinate relationships, MbO may also tend to emphasize the hierarchical aspects of an activity at a time when what may be needed are more effective relationships *between* the operating units and specialist groups in an organization.

It is reported[30] that the MbO systems which have failed usually petered out because top management did not back them fully, seeing them merely as exercises carried out by the personnel department or relating to middle and lower management and not to themselves, or because the MbO paperwork grew to be too complicated and time-consuming. The most serious attack on MbO has been made by Professor Levinson of the Harvard Business School.[31] He asserts that it is 'one of the greatest management illusions' and, being based on a reward–punishment psychology is ultimately self-defeating. 'The typical MbO effort perpetuates and intensifies hostility, resentment and distrust between a manager and subordinates. As currently practised, it is really just industrial engineering' (in English, work study) 'with a new name, applied to higher managerial levels, and with the same resistances.' Examination of the Levinson case shows, however, that he does not deny the value of MbO process but argues that it can be improved. The improvements he seeks are that it should pay more attention to the manager's personal goals and aspirations rather than to targets forced upon him by his boss; that it should focus upon the managerial group, rather than the individual manager, with group goal setting and task definition, group appraisal of each individual member's contribution to group effort and shared rewards based on the achievements of the group; that it should include regular appraisal of the manager by his subordinates. The cases he chooses on which to rest this argument are those in which the MbO procedure has been used in an authoritarian way and in which substantial salary bonuses have been based on those results which are quantifiable.

The latest developments in MbO aim to overcome these actual or potential disadvantages. Professor W. J. Reddin, of the University of New Brunswick,[32] has observed that 'most MbO implementations are based on a one-to-one design, where a superior speaks to each of his subordinates in turn. Virtually no MbO technique even tries to get the full team together, superior and all subordinates, to work out effectiveness areas, objectives and improvement plans as a group. 'He advocates preceding the conventional one-to-one MbO process at least by team objectives meetings in which a manager and his subordinates assemble for three days for the following purposes:

(1) To decide the team's actual role in the organization and how it might best contribute to overall effectiveness.

(2) To explore the job of each team member and to agree on the method by which his effectiveness should be judged.

(3) To decide on the best team organization.

(4) To decide how the team will make future decisions.

(5) To decide on key specific team objectives to be accomplished in the next six to twelve months.[33]

Those who commend MbO to audiences of managers are sometimes accused of dressing up some old practices in new clothes and trying to sell as a new 'technique' the kind of routine that any competent manager applies to his job as a matter of course. No doubt forms of MbO have been practised by many managers for years without being dignified with the label. In fact, any organization where there were well-organized corporate planning and budgetary control routines and where team and superior–subordinate relationships were open and participative would stand to gain relatively little from the introduction of a formal MbO programme. However, the particular promise of MbO, particularly in a Civil Service context, is that it can be used to specify exactly the extent and limits of a manager's accountability, to establish what contribution to the objectives and plans of the organization is expected from him and to integrate the objectives of the policymaker with those of the manager.

Arrangements for objective setting and performance review on the lines of MbO are essential to systems of delegation and accountability: only in this way can the personal accountability of the manager be related to the accountability of the department as a whole. 'The benefits of management by objectives go beyond providing a system of managerial control based on personal accountability. There are the benefits of conducting a regular review of the purpose of the organization in the light of its changing environment; of examining the purpose and contribution to the total task of every part of the organization and every managerial job; of establishing priorities for action and of allocating individual responsibility for seeing that action is taken; of introducing participative management in organizations that have traditionally been strongly mechanistic and hierarchical in character.'[34] The Civil Service Department sees MbO as 'one broad route towards the extension of accountable management'.[35] By May 1970, some twenty schemes were being considered or introduced in departments. Three were nearing completion: two in the Ministry of Defence (in a naval stores depot and in a naval training college), and one in the Wales Region of the Department of Employment and Productivity.

The stores depot experiment has been described and evaluated in the *O. & M. Bulletin*.[36] The scheme yielded 447 suggestions for improvement (the existing suggestions scheme had been producing about thirty ideas a year of roughly similar value). The consultants involved estimated ultimate overall operating benefits – 'largely by analogy with similar studies they have done in commercial undertakings' – of £1 million a year with once-for-all savings of £6 million. The Naval stores management doubted the validity of these claims but 'accepted that potentially there are long-term savings of some magnitude'. Other benefits reported from this scheme were that, for the first time, managers were given a clear definition of their high-priority tasks and the results they were expected to achieve; their activities 'assumed a higher quality' and the routine work was delegated; standards of performance were made explicit for the first time and control information was refined and pruned; man/boss communication was generally improved and hitherto indecisive managers were obliged to make decisions; managers' performances were generally sharpened up and morale and job satisfaction showed improvements. The greatest welcome to the scheme was given by junior managers, who were given a chance to air their views and ideas.

The MbO experiment in the Department of Employment and Productivity in Wales is a much more ambitious exercise. The procedure is being applied to 'employment work' (job-filling, job-finding, interviewing, registration, recruiting for vocational training and development work) in 147 labour exchanges and sixteen area offices. A recent report[37] has described objective-setting for managers throughout the organization for this element of their work, the establishment of each area's 'potential improvement capability' and the aggregation of office and area objectives into an Objective for Wales. The results of the scheme are still being compared with results in a control region with similar employment characteristics. 'The lack of statistical evidence as yet does not, however, alter the fact that the philosophy of MbO has been successful in influencing the attitude of staff towards employment work. There are indications that younger members of the staff now have a greater awareness of what the aims and objectives of employment work are. The ability to measure performance and give credit or guidance where due is proving valuable to managers and is satisfying to staff as well. Staff at all levels know more now about what they are supposed to be doing, how well they have been doing it in the past and that they now have the opportunity to participate in the decisions about how things could be done better in the future.'[38]

So far, the work of the Civil Service Department in MbO has corroborated the view expressed by S. D. Walker and the author at the start of attempts to apply MbO to the work of departments: 'In our view, it is no more difficult to apply management by objectives to large clerical, executive and specialist areas of the service than to similar areas in industry ... In "administrative areas", though the evaluation of output may be almost entirely a matter for subjective judgement, in our view it is still practicable to allocate programmes of work (costed where practicable), to define tasks and establish priorities and to hold an individual manager responsible for meeting those objectives over which he has control.'[39]

The question which is so far unanswered is whether departments are starting MbO applications at a high enough level. There is a very real risk that the top management of departments will consider that accountability and the MbO procedures which express it are a second-order activity: all very well for middle and junior management in executive and technical areas but of no direct concern to them. If top management is not involved, if it does not apply objective-setting and performance review to its own activities, then MbO will soon become just another bureaucratic routine, simply an exercise in which managers cursorily fill up the forms, produce a plausible explanation for what they have done since they last reported and file away the paperwork to gather dust. The short history of MbO in industry is littered with schemes which have withered away for lack of continued top-management interest and attention. Experience so far is not encouraging on this point. There is no evidence, from the reports on the MbO projects carried out so far, that the purpose and point of the organizations to which the scheme has been applied was challenged in any fundamental way: whether, for example, the need for the stores depot was critically examined or whether alternatives to existing employment policy in Wales were considered. The impression is that MbO was used simply as a means of raising efficiency and making staff feel more involved in activities for which the need was assumed. Equally important, there is no evidence that any of these experiments have seriously challenged present conventions in the delegation of authority over manpower, though the key to accountability must lie in giving line managers more say in the way they organize and reward their staff.

INFORMATION FOR ACCOUNTABILITY

The units of accountability within a department could range from the branch engaged on routine clerical processing, whose manager's performance would primarily be measured by simple efficiency criteria, to the administrative branch or project secretariat, whose managers would have to answer for the quality and timeliness of their policy advice, the efficiency of their management and the effectiveness of the programmes for which they were responsible, judged by both quantitative and qualitative standards.

At the simplest levels, we can take the hypothetical case of an office which employs thirty clerical and supervisory staff on handling applications for a grant. The costs of the operation are £75,000 a year of which £40,000 are direct staff costs. The office can handle 4,000 applications a year when working at a standard tempo as established by clerical work-measurement techniques and therefore a manpower cost of £10 per case is established as the manager's key productivity index. The performance of the office is monitored monthly by the manager and his superior and the manager is called upon to account for any significant upward variance in the index. Many such variances would be unavoidable: those that arose because of staff absences, failure of the personnel function to provide replacements for leavers, a fall in the number of applications for grants. A second key index would be the acceptable size of the backlog of unprocessed applications or an average waiting time for applications: that is, a statement of a standard of service to the client community. The standard of service to be given would be a matter for departmental policy and would be decided at a high level in headquarters, and it would be up to the office manager and his superior to decide when to make a case for bringing in more staff either on a temporary or a permanent basis so as to maintain that level of service or to reduce it.

In practice, could the manager really be expected to influence these productivity indices? Is there that much scope for attaining greater efficiency through better supervision, organization and work planning? Only experiments can show. At least the measurement of performance would direct the manager's attention towards finding better ways of organizing and staffing his unit, seeking to improve working methods and office layout, looking for opportunities for mechanization, motivating and leading his staff to meet operational standards.

In industry, the tendency would be to try to reinforce accountability with bonus payments for high levels of unit performance. As we have seen from an earlier discussion, incentive payments can do a great deal of harm to an organization which depends upon co-operation between managers and co-ordinated effort. In the Civil Service, the qualitative aspects of the work are so important as to increase the risks of counter-productive side effects from incentive payments. However, as Fulton suggested,[40] there is no reason why managers should not be given some reward for high levels of performance in the form of enhanced increments at the time of their annual salary review and why poor performers should receive any increment at all. In addition, if it was understood that performance counted significantly towards promotion this would go a long way towards putting cost consciousness at the front of management attention.

The next question is, of course, would the quality of output suffer? Even in budget centres which handle the most routine processes the quality of work may fall off if the manager and his staff are motivated only towards achieving a high volume of work so as to improve their showing against productivity indices. However, quality control should be a key area of concern for any manager. It is his job to make sure that, in addition to attaining high levels of output, the work which is produced is of a satisfactory quality. He can do this by training his staff, by spot-checking the work being produced, by personally handling complaints, by being alert to what is going on in his unit. Experience in commercial offices shows that the risk of a fall in quality is slight and worth taking. The MbO routine, with its four- or six-monthly reexamination of plans and results can provide a regular opportunity to assess the quality effects of raising or lowering the unit's performance target until a sensible balance is struck between an acceptable level of error and a reasonable cost per case.

Our small clerical office, handling a regular flow of transactions, is a good simple example of the Consultancy Group's budget centre. They exist in government departments by the hundred. Most departments have units processing applications, purchases, contracts, benefits, grants and loans; posting ledgers, issuing stores, maintaining records, collecting and issuing statistics, filing, collating and retrieving information, carrying out technical inspections. Since they have quantifiable outputs, and present no great difficulty in collecting and arranging control information, they are the obvious places in which to start experiments with accountable management. An example of such an experiment is provided by a recent performance-measurement exercise in the Vehicle Inspection Division of the Department of the Environment.[41] This division has ninety-four local stations where goods vehicles are subjected to tests of roadworthiness. Using methods described in the last chapter, a single weighted output index was produced for a range of tests on different vehicles. Costs and manpower were related to this index to produce three performance indicators: man-hours per unit of output (reported monthly) variable costs (quarterly) and total costs (annually) per unit of output. The variable-cost indicator was based on those costs over which a station manager had some control (payroll and personal expenses, utilities, maintenance, post and stationery) and which therefore could provide the basis of his accountability.

At higher levels of complexity, we are faced with applying accountability to the management of scientific and technical projects. Though we can measure the input in man-hours and the external contract and equipment costs of these projects, their outcomes are often uncertain. In these cases the practice can be to assign costs to time periods punctuated by 'landmarks' at which the project manager accounts for the resources he has consumed so far and for the results he has achieved, makes a bid for funds for the period until the next landmark and states, or assigns levels of probability to, what he proposes to have accomplished when that point is reached.

At the highest level of complexity we are faced with the problem of applying accountability to purely administrative work: primarily concerned with overseeing the management of departmental programmes, drafting and adapting policy, dealing with Ministerial matters, reacting to political pressures, but also ultimately responsible for the efficient management of the department. For the bulk of the work of this small group of administrators it is almost always impossible to set quantifiable objectives, or to measure performance, or to specify accountability for results. However, the branches and divisions which they manage attract costs and must produce benefits in exchange. Clearly, it would help to assess just what proportion of this work has a quantifiable element and to assess for the rest what scope there is for establishing priorities between the variable load of casework and such *ad hoc* projects as a review of the operation of a particular policy or an inquiry into its effects: for such projects, the setting of objectives in the form of deadlines or target dates for completion is the nearest one can get to objective performance standards. Inevitably we are obliged, for this small part of the range of Civil Service activities, to rely on subjective assessment of achievement based on some qualitative description of the situation which will exist when the job is being done well.

In all of these areas, whether simple budget centres or responsibility centres where the work is highly complex and intangible, the three-, six- or twelve-month cycle of objective-setting and feedback may be too short a time over which to measure performance. We have seen from the discussion on planning that one year would in many areas be too short to establish any measure of programme effectiveness. In this case, the annual cycle must be supplemented by periodic post-audits of results in which some attempt is made to assess the effects of departmental action against a reconstruction of the conditions at the time.

LINKING PLANNING TO ACCOUNTABILITY

Finally, there is the question of whether the long-term planning process of PESC and PAR can be linked to the control and accountability process of MbO so as to create an integrated managerial system. Departments are not yet at the stage in either process at which they have to bother about this problem, but it will arise at some time and some recent American experiments may help to provide a solution.

These experiments, under the sponsorship of the Bureau of Management and Budget, are based on the concept of the department as a structure of managerial entities, or 'building blocks'. A building block is a unit of activity which consumes resources, produces results and is under the control of an accountable manager. It is an entity in respect of strategic planning (it represents a programme or a self-contained programme element) and management (it is a section, branch or division) and of appropriation (it has a vote or vote sub-head). Its manager can be made accountable for his total costs, for the efficiency of his unit and for the effectiveness of the programme he manages and his performance can be evaluated in all three dimensions.

We can thus envisage a structure of departmental accountability as a hierarchy of blocks in which planned objectives, delegated authority, specified responsibility and information all coincide. Top management would specify and monitor its accountability in terms of 'macro-indicators' comparable to the profitability, return on investment, growth and market share criteria used in industry. These macro-indicators would enable Ministers and top management to track the results of major programmes or programme categories; the results of large projects or contracts; the result of cost reduction programmes and improvements in manpower efficiency in the labour-intensive areas of the department. Managers of sub-departments, large divisions and directorates would specify and monitor their accountability in terms of indicators of the effectiveness of individual programmes and the efficiency of the processing activities directly managed by them. Managers of divisions and branches would be concerned with programme elements or projects and accountable for the performance of budget centres. The entire edifice would be held together by the departmental planning cycle and by an MbO routine which enabled each manager to view his performance in the context of the plans and objectives of the whole department.

An example of how this concept can work is given by the U.S. office of Management and Budget from the field of rural housing:

National Goal*   Provide every American with a decent home.

Department of Agriculture
  Department goal*   Provide every rural American with a decent home.
  Department objective   Provide x units of adequate housing to rural families and individuals in . . . (time).

Farmers Home Administration

         Low income Housing Program
         Moderate Income Housing Program
         Rural Renting Housing Program
         Farm Labor Program: Families
         HUD Guaranteed Loan Program
         Above Moderate Income Housing Program

Building Block (LOW INCOME HOUSING PROGRAM)

Objectives: Provide x units of adequate housing for low income residents who need an interest credit in . . . (time)
Expected   Make \$ worth of loans providing x housing units in Financial Year 19 . . .

*In British terminology, 'Aim'.

This structure defines the line of responsibility from the National Goal for Housing to the specific objectives of the manager responsible for the Farmers Home Administration's Low Income Housing Program. It enables that manager to contribute his operating experience to the planning routines of the FHA and the Department of Agriculture. The building-block objective establishes measures of output and effectiveness and to these he can attach measures of efficiency (manpower and total cost per loan compared with standard, speed of response compared with standard, level of backlog compared with standard): together these summarize his accountability and form – as the Office of Management and Budget like to say – 'his contract with the President'. On the face of it, the building-block approach could be applied to any direct management activity of a department if the information were properly organized. It appears to be a most promising area of research and development for those concerned with the design of accountability systems in government.

These last four chapters have dealt with organization, planning, control and accountability: together these form the heart of the new managerial style which Fulton proposed, or at least apparently meant to propose, for the Civil Service. The reforms discussed in these chapters in each of these areas of management are inter-related and inter-dependent and none can properly be implemented without considering the others. Experiments that have so far been carried out show that the adoption of this new management style carries the promise of improved efficiency and effectiveness and the better utilization and commitment of the people employed in departments. Of all these linked reforms, the one whose feasibility, effects and side-effects we know least about is managerial accountability. The promise of great benefits is there, but the effects on the control of staff numbers, relations with staff associations and on the responsibilities of Permanent Secretaries and Ministers to the Legislature and the community can only be assessed by genuine attempts to apply accountability systems at all levels in departments.

The concept of applying managerial accountability has, after all, a long tradition in some areas of British public administration. In the memorable words of Sir Frederick Hooper: 'The solution of the fullest decentralization in creative combination with the essential minimum of central control, is simply the application in business of the principle which built the British Empire. It is one wholly in line with the British genius in the social leadership of men.'[42]

CHAPTER 7

Management Services and Efficiency Audit

As we saw from Chapter 3, growth and increasing complexity in industry leads to the creation of staff groups instituted to provide a service to line management or to formulate and enforce organization-wide standards and procedures. Among the earliest of such staff groups to appear is usually one which represents expertise in those management techniques which are particularly relevant to the operations of the organization. Thus in a manufacturing plant of any size there is almost always a work-study unit, carrying out analyses of labour productivity and prescribing efficient working methods, production control and materials handling systems and shop layouts. In large offices there is often a O. & M. unit concerned with clerical work measurement and method study, carrying out assignments to improve the flow of paper work and studies on the feasibility of installing or developing the use of office machines and computers. As efficiency techniques have improved, work-study departments have developed their activities from simple time-and-motion studies into quality-control routines using statistical analysis and sampling, statistical methods of production and stock control and the application of mathematical models to the flow of products through the stages of production, assembly, dispatch and distribution. O. & M. units have also become involved in systems analysis: evaluating and improving the flow of information through the business and developing procedures for so organizing and displaying data as to facilitate better managerial decision-making. From the growth of the personnel function in industry have sprung specialists in organization and job evaluation and behavioural scientists who examine and provide advice on organization structures, grading and payment systems and industrial and human relations. Much of this advice is bought from management consultants, whose numbers in this country have virtually doubled in the past ten years, but most large companies feel the need to set up management services, systems analysis or internal consultancy units of their own to insure that in the management techniques relevant to their work they are abreast of outside developments. These management services units are not only widening the technical range of their activities but are increasingly called upon to deal with major problems of structure and operations and to act as corporate 'change agents'. Whereas only a few years ago they would have been primarily engaged in factory and office efficiency studies, today they are often engaged on studies of company organization, on company-wide operating systems and on designing and maintaining programmes for increasing managerial effectiveness. The larger management services units also include a research activity, providing access to developments in the business schools, universities and management consultancy firms.

These units can be seen as developing a triple role: providing a service to line management, carrying out audits of efficiency and effectiveness on behalf of top management and providing a 'centre of excellence' in management studies for the company as a whole. The terms of reference of the consultancy group of one large international company are to:

(a) carry out studies of efficiency in head-office departments and subsidiaries identified by the board as requiring attention;

(b) carry out studies at the request of the management of departments and subsidiaries;

(c) advise the board and departments on the employment of outside consultants where internal resources require to be supplemented;

(d) advise the board, departments and subsidiaries on the development of management techniques both inside and outside the Group;

(e) carry out special studies for the development of new information and accountability systems.

The work of the Management Services Division of the British Oxygen Company (which, unusually, includes that company's central sales accounting and computing units) has been described as providing those services devoted to change: 'The responsibility for action is that of the decentralized profit centre: but the detailed preparatory and staff work required to facilitate that profit centre's change is available from Management Services.'[1]

In order to establish the accountability of both the management services group and its client companies and departments, there are often arrangements whereby clients are charged fees for consultancy assignments comparable to those of commercial management consultants.

The basic skills and qualifications of management services staff are typically in accounting, engineering, statistics or mathematics and the behavioural sciences, followed by some years of management experience. One problem with such staffs, as with the specialists in other staff groups, is that they usually have closer links with an external technical community than with the organization for which they work. This means that they tend to have relatively little loyalty to their employers and to stand outside the attitudes and values of the firm. As they are usually young and technically qualified they also often have difficulties in their relationships with senior line managers, and the differences in age, experience and attitudes makes for the same kind of difficulties which frequently exist between line managers and corporate planners. Coupled with this is the problem of what has been called 'technical arrogance' – 'the tendency of the highly numerate computer people to have relatively undeveloped inter-personal skills, but yet be acutely sensitive to poor handling by their chiefs in such matters. Unfortunately, it seems to be a widely distributed phenomenon that numeracy goes with a convergent mind and the inter-personal skill goes more with a divergent mind; and therefore in places where we need numeracy and logic we often have inter-personal problems.'[2]

One argument which is advanced against management services groups is that, since they are in the career employment of their client organizations, they cannot be as objective as external commercial consultants are, or ought to be. They might not, for example, feel able to challenge fundamental corporate assumptions or policies or reveal unpleasant home truths because of the effect these might have on their future relationships with the board or their colleagues in the firm. Another is that being 'tame consultants' they are less credible and their recommendations carry less weight than professional and expensive outsiders. These objections can be overcome to some extent by recognizing the standing and detachment of the management services group by having it report directly to the main board or to its chairman, by staffing it with career professionals rather than trainees or passed-over managers and by either topping it up occasionally by external recruitment or by running major assignments as joint projects with management consultancy firms. At least two large companies (Rio Tinto, British Petroleum) actually own autonomous management consultancy businesses who work not only for their owners but compete in the consultancy market.

The typical management services unit is engaged on *ad hoc* assignments or appraisals organized on a project basis with a team of consultants of different specialisms led by a project leader. These assignments usually arise from the reference of a particular problem to the head of the management services group by a client manager or director. The group head and the client agree upon a definition of the problem, draw up the terms of reference for the assignment, the date of its completion, the arrangements for reporting progress and the fee (if any) for the work to be carried out. On the completion of the assignment, the report and recommendations of the management services team are the property of the client to implement as he wishes. If part or all of the report is accepted, the management services team are often retained to assist the client's staff in implementing them. The management services group does not usually have authority to mount assignments in areas which it thinks need attention without the permission of the line management concerned, but it is not uncommon for them to be used for audits of efficiency and management performance on the authority of the board.

In addition to carrying out *ad hoc* assignments, management services units are often engaged on sponsoring MbO schemes and providing MDAs and on mounting cost-reduction or management-improvement programmes on a regular or cyclical basis, taking each unit of the organization in turn. Management-improvement programmes are aimed at producing specific results in terms of lower costs or better service in a particular unit. The concept is that significant improvements in service or savings in cost can be made in any activity if it is subjected to a detailed and thorough scrutiny by a project team specially constituted for the purpose and led by an experienced consultant. The client for the programme is a senior manager of the sector of the company which includes that unit. He appoints two or three team members from that sector but not from the unit itself and secures as team leader a specialist consultant from the management services group. The manager of the unit under scrutiny advises the team on the feasibility of their ideas for improvement and on problems likely to arise in implementing them. At the end of the programme, which rarely lasts more than two or three months, the team members return to their former jobs. Substantial cost reductions and improvements in output or service are claimed for such programmes. Involvement in them is also good training for junior managers, who are taught to look for methods of improving the way in which their own unit is managed. The involvement of consultants and managers in teams also helps to familiarize line managers with the personnel and the working methods of the management services group.

To be effective, management services groups have to employ high-calibre, technically qualified and independent-minded staff who can make themselves credible and acceptable to all levels of management and staff in the organization. In particular, they have to have the confidence of the board sufficient to be trusted with audits of efficiency and major studies of organization and corporate systems. If they are restricted to assignments concerned with labour productivity or systems design, they can neither recruit nor retain highly qualified professionals nor are they likely to be taken seriously by line management.

In large and technically advanced companies there can be problems at the boundaries between the management services group and other functional departments. For example, both management services and the personnel department may be engaged on programmes to apply the behavioural sciences or in studying communication problems; both management services and computer units may be carrying out systems analysis; some aspects of the work of internal auditors (who check the 'regularity' of accounting methods) are virtually indistinguishable from consultancy assignments. So long as there is no evidence of serious overlap, duplication and conflict between these activities no harm is done, but the line of demarcation should be that management services assignments are concerned with specific problems with defined time and cost limits and that the other activities in similar fields are concerned with the development of operating procedures on a regular or continuous basis.

Another problem arises in the relationship between management services units and line management. When a technique has been in use in a company for a sufficiently long time it should be incorporated in the normal operating routines of management (this is typically the case in work study and frequently true of statistical stock-control methods and clerical work measurement). In these cases, line managers expect to have their own technical specialist in the field, concerned with up-dating and improving the use of the technique, rather than to have to call on management services for special assignments. The management services staff are therefore faced with the possible threat of competing centres of expertise in techniques which have hitherto been their province. In such cases, it should be recognized that, when a technique has been developed to maturity, responsibility for applying it should pass to line management and the management services unit should be concerned only with general research into its future development and the co-ordination of operating experience.

MANAGEMENT SERVICES IN U.S. AND CANADIAN GOVERNMENT

Most U.S. government departments have management services and audit units which carry out *ad hoc* assignments to examine administrative efficiency. The central Bureau of the Budget (now the Office of Management and Budget) has had such a unit since 1939. In the Treasury Department, for example, the Office of Management and Organization provides these services for all the bureaux of the U.S. Treasury. Its Management Analysis Division performs the following tasks:

(a) provides advisory services on organization, cost reduction, management improvement and systems of control and appraisal;

(b) formulates policies and plans for efficient and effective administrative management and organization;

(c) conducts reviews, surveys and inspections of missions, organization, functions, activities, procedures and systems of control and appraisal;

(d) reviews and makes recommendations on plans, requests and requirements for outside consulting and advisory services;

(e) develops and installs reporting systems on programme and management performance and accomplishments;

(f) conducts projects to resolve special problems or provide required information in the area of administrative management;

(g) evaluates overall progress of organization, management improvement and systems development;

(h) conducts research and inquiries into new and unusual developments or problems and serves as a focal point for the co-ordination and exchange of information relating to these activities.

It provides these services on request, but it has been directly ordered by the Secretary of the Treasury to investigate the management of bureaux. Its assignments on organization, efficiency and effectiveness have ranged from small offices engaged on the highest flights of policy work (such as the Office of International Finance, with seventy staff, nearly half of them Ph.D.s) to very large executive organizations (such as the Mint, Customs).

The President's management-improvement programmes have been referred to in Chapter 6. They begin with the proposition that 'it is vital that the ability exist to establish objectives, measure performance and evaluate results in all areas of governmental activity'.[3] The instruction from the Office of Management and Budget specifies the action required from departments to establish management-effectiveness programmes, cost-reduction programmes and programme incentives and rewards and makes arrangements for the interchange of ideas on management improvement. It also recognizes the need for periodic government-wide studies of common operations (such as records management, travel and transportation, communications, printing) and sets out arrangements for the establishment of interagency steering groups under the leadership of the Office of Management and Budget to supervise studies by agency managements of these operational areas. 'Agency management . . . will submit a report on accomplishments which will include resulting dollar savings, management improvement actions taken and plans for future improvements and controls in the area.'[4]

In addition to departmental organization and methods groups and a central Treasury Board management services group, the Canadian government also has a Bureau of Management Consulting, organized as a commercial consulting practice within the central department of Supply and Services and charging fees to departments. The Bureau has divisions for finance and accounting, planning and research, personnel consulting, operational research and data processing and organization analysis. The Organizational Analysis Division carries out studies of the machinery of government and of the organization of departments, agencies and public authorities and makes recommendations on the management and staffing of these organizations. Canadian departments are also required to carry out 'operational audits' of their activities, defined as 'an independent periodic review and appraisal of the effectiveness of the entire operations of an organization and of their management controls designed to guide and circumscribe departmental activities',[5] in addition to their regular work-improvement programmes.

MANAGEMENT SERVICES IN THE CIVIL SERVICE

The Civil Service was a pioneer in the development of management services in this country. Soon after its creation in 1919 the Treasury's Establishments Division set up an Investigation Section staffed with investigation officers concerned to give expert attention to clerical methods, office machines, forms, records and procedures. In 1941 the Investigation Division became Treasury Organization and Methods (O. & M.) Division. This Division was transferred with the rest of the Pay and Management side of the Treasury to the Civil Service Department in 1969. Since the end of the war most departments have set up their own O. &. M. units, some of which are now called Management Services units, usually within Establishments Divisions. There are now about 600 staff engaged on O. & M. work, 700 on work study (mostly in Defence), some 2,000 on computers (excluding computer operators) and 600 on operational research or similar work.[6] The Ministry of Defence and the Department of the Environment and Trade and Industry each have operational research groups. In addition, there are about 350 staff inspectors concerned with seeing that posts are properly graded and evaluating claims for more staff.

Prior to the Fulton Report, the work of O. & M. units was largely concerned with studies of clerical efficiency. Typical assignments were to review and make recommendations on the organization of small executive/clerical units, on clerical methods, the flow of paper through clerical or technical sections, manual filing systems, recording and reporting procedures. They were usually carried out by an officer at the H.E.O. or S.E.O. level. The narrowness of Civil Service O. & M. work, its concentration on methods rather than organization, had been criticized by Parliamentary committees long before the Fulton Committee reported. The Select Committee on National Expenditure of 1941 observed that since the establishment of the Investigation Division there had been a failure 'to foster the systematic study of organization as applied to government departments', and it recommended that officers engaged on this work should examine the distribution of functions in departments as well as routine business.[7] The Estimates Committee in 1946-7 made the same point: 'The part played by O. & M. techniques and knowledge must be that of planning the structure and machinery of government rather than that of attending to its plumbing and maintenance.'[8]

In spite of these observations, O. & M. work was never generally seen as having any contribution to make to the higher management and organization of departments. The activity was a preserve of the Executive Class and administrators and specialists were rarely engaged on it. It was seen as a low-level 'housekeeping' activity rather than as a positive force for change. In the words of Mackenzie and Grove: 'These [O. & M.] officers come largely from the Executive Class and their main work is at that level, in improving the smooth flow of business in routine operations. It is rarely possible for organization officers to do useful work on the higher organization of the Department: that is a matter for the Establishment Officer himself, and his contribution depends largely on his personality and experience.'[9] Traditionally the management of O. & M. work was given not to promising administrators but either to senior executives or to men promoted from the executive into the administrative grades who were at, or near, their career ceiling. The posting of a Principal to an O. & M. branch would have been considered by him as a mark of his unsuitability for policy work and therefore for the highest positions in the Service.

FULTON ON MANAGEMENT SERVICES

The Fulton Committee made several recommendations on departmental management services units. Its Consultancy Group had found that the Executives who staffed O. & M. sections usually spent about five years in them and that the Assistant Secretaries to whom these sections ultimately reported served for even shorter periods in this area and had little or no training and no first-hand experience of the work. As others had done before them, they commented on the concentration of O. & M. units upon clerical methods and procedures: 'We saw no evidence that top-level organization and procedures were ever scrutinized by departmental O. & M.'[10] They criticized O. & M. work in the Service on the grounds of the lack of qualification of O. & M. officers – contrasting the generalist H.E.O. with a few weeks' training with the typical management consultant who would normally have a degree or professional qualification at degree level (for instance in accountancy or engineering) and six months' formal training. They saw O. & M. and the staff-inspection activities of establishment divisions as separated aspects of a common task: the analysis of procedures and the examination of the number and grades of staff required to carry them out. They thought that departmental management services units should be 'empowered, under the direction of top management, to examine any part of the organization of a department', and should be involved in the implementation of their recommendations; that career specialization in the consultancy function should be encouraged and that its direction should be in the hands of officers who had specialized in the work. They thought that there should also be a central management consultancy unit in the Civil Service, responsible for consultancy training, research into the development of new techniques, inter-departmental and high-level assignments and reviews of the efficiency of the management of departments as a whole.[11]

The Fulton Committee accepted these proposals and recommended that each department should contain a management services unit with wider responsibilities and functions than had been given to O. &. M. divisions in the past. There should be the following operational changes:

(a) there should be efficiency audits involving all aspects of the department's work at all levels, with special attention to studies designed to improve organizational efficiency;

(b) the management services unit should be made responsible for promoting the use of the best management techniques;

(c) O. & M. should be combined with staff inspection;

(d) management services staff should be drawn from administrators and appropriate specialists, including accountants, and many should have a relevant degree or professional qualification and experience of management in an operating division.

DEVELOPMENTS IN MANAGEMENT SERVICES

Since Fulton reported, there has been a marked change in the status and scope of management services units in the Civil Service. This has been due not only to the Committee's strictures, but also to the growth in automatic data processing. Most of the old O. & M. units have been enlarged and rechristened Management

Services Divisions and in six departments they are now headed by Under Secretaries. The biggest changes, however, have taken place at the centre. With the weight of Sir William Armstrong behind it, the old Treasury O. & M. Division has blossomed into the Management Services Division of the Civil Service Department, and has taken on the commercial management consultants at their own games of management by objectives, cost accounting and operational research.

The Department has started to undertake studies of the organization and management of large government organizations. This activity is called 'management review'. J. N. Archer, Under Secretary in charge of Management Services in the Department, has written that management reviews began because there was 'a feeling that too much of our work was concerned with the minutiae of day-to-day operations rather than with fundamentals ... Usually, we were asked to deal with problems identified by others and were not given a free hand to diagnose what was wrong and suggest how it could best be put right.'[12] He describes how developments in government efficiency audit in the U.S.A. and Canada had led to speculation on its applicability in Whitehall. It was decided not use the term 'audit' because it is an emotive word 'apt to put the recipient on the defensive'. The term 'management review' was decided upon and as the Treasury was considering how to get a review launched in mid-1967 the opportunity presented itself at the Prison Department of the Home Office. This Department was under severe pressure from an expanding workload and recurrent crises, and the Treasury was invited to join with the Home Office O. & M. unit to consider how a comprehensive study of the problems of the Department might be mounted. It was decided to organize a team of O. & M. officers from the Treasury and the Home Office and outside management consultants under Treasury leadership to carry out a study to review the functions, organizational structure, management and administrative practices of the Prison Department and to recommend any changes considered necessary to improve efficiency.

The work of this review team and its supporting groups has been described in the *O. & M. Bulletin*.[13] It began with a series of investigations 'aimed at establishing the relevance of the organization structure and its supporting systems to the present and prospective aims and objectives of the organization'.[14] These investigations took the form of studies of organizational sub-units (Building and Works, Industries and Stores, Research and Development, etc.) and of operating systems (prisoner allocation, the handling of appeals and petitions, management information, financial control, etc.). After these had been completed, new headquarters and regional organizations were proposed, and new systems were designed for planning, management information, management accounting, building construction and maintenance and prison industries. The conclusion on the exercise as a whole was that 'it demonstrated the value of mounting an investigation by specialist consultants and internal management services staff on the working of a large unit of government, from policy making levels to first-line management'.[15]

In May 1969 a second management review was started, this time of the operations of management services units themselves. The Civil Service Department decided to mount a study of all such units in departments, their function and their organization, in the light of the recommendations made in the Fulton Report and the needs of management.[16] The review team considered the resources available to management services units and the use made of these units by line managements in departments. By February 1970, the work had progressed to the point where the aims of management services could be drafted. These were:

To provide a focus for innovation and a service for the improvement of efficiency in management.

To assist in securing responsible, participative and effective management at all levels.

To assist in developing the means by which top management can monitor, control and improve the efficiency of an undertaking.[17]

The last aim was said to involve consideration of Fulton's recommendations on efficiency audits and on combining O. & M. and staff inspection into one auditing body. These questions were at that time unresolved, but it was considered 'desirable to devise a system of advisory and monitoring services which, to a greater extent than in the past, would ensure that those who seek advice will get the best possible service available and that those who rarely seek it, but need it, will be under pressure to do so'.[18] The results of this review[19] included recommendations that departmental management services units needed staff with a wider range of expertise and qualifications (accountants, scientists, statisticians) than in the past; that the lone assignment officer should be replaced by teams of executive and professional civil servants and outside consultants; that 'the standing of project teams will be raised so that the leaders may deal, where necessary, direct with top departmental officials. It may be necessary to have Under Secretaries in charge of projects so that ... they can discuss recommendations at board level.'[20]

The tasks of the Civil Service Department in the field of management services were defined as:

(a) providing a focus for the development throughout the Civil Service of management services disciplines and technical skill, management systems and techniques and expertise in special subjects;

(b) supplementing departmental management services where necessary including providing a service to smaller Departments without their own management services units and advising on the use of management consultants;

(c) carrying out work crossing departmental boundaries;

(d) acting as a centre for communication on management services matters within and with bodies outside the Civil Service.[21]

In December 1970 the management services divisions in the Department were reorganized 'in order to make resources available for carrying out high-level organization and management reviews, to improve the quality of specialist advice and to improve the management of assignments and staff resources'.[22] A special asssignments branch, including three Assistant Secretaries and several management consultants seconded from commercial consultancies, was formed to carry out high-level consulting projects. Examples of these in 1971 were a review of the future status, organization and management of the Patent Office and reviews of the Central Office of Information and the Ordnance Survey.

As a result of all these developments, the management services activity in departments is no longer the backwater that O. & M. used to be. Staff engaged on the work are being given a higher status and more important and challenging assignments. It still suffers, however, from some of the weakness to which the Fulton Committee drew attention. Staff inspection and O. & M. are still separate activities, so that the control of numbers and grades is separated from studies of administrative efficiency, though they should be elements of a common task. Management services groups are not used in an independent auditing role but provide a service on demand, so that those areas which most require the application of modern management techniques usually do not get them. There are no mandatory cost-reduction or value-improvement programmes which require line management to examine critically all their activities on a regular basis and to enter into a commitment to improve efficiency. There are still relatively few specialists – engineers, statisticians, economists, particularly accountants – and yet these are the type of staff needed to tackle the problems of designing the management information systems which will be required to support programme planning, control and accountable management. The design of these systems should be the major task of management services staffs in the future. There are also very few qualified psychologists and sociologists in management services groups, yet these are the kind of staff most needed if these groups are to be effective agents of organizational change.

STATE AUDIT

Public accountability implies 'a statutory obligation to provide, for independent and impartial observers holding the right of reporting their findings at the highest levels in the state, any available information about financial administration which they may request',[23] that is, a public or state audit. Most Western countries have a state audit body, reporting directly to the legislature or a committee appointed by the legislature, and charged with inquiring into, and reporting on, the justification for public expenditure.

The Exchequer and Audit Department

As we saw in Chapter 5, the Public Accounts Committee is charged with examining the regularity of expenditure and with seeing that full value is obtained from the expenditure of public money. It is served with reports by the Comptroller and Auditor General, who since 1866 has had two functions: as Comptroller he controls receipts and issues of public money to and from the Exchequer Account and the National Loans Fund, and as Auditor General he audits departmental accounts and submits his reports to the Public Accounts Committee and to Parliament. Originally he was concerned to see that expenditure was properly authorized and backed by statutory authority and Treasury sanction. Since 1887 he has also been encouraged by the Public Accounts Committee to examine departmental expenditure for evidence of waste and extravagance. In recent years, for example, he has reported on unsatisfactory procurement and contracting procedures for aerospace equipment (the 'Ferranti affair') and national health service drugs. The Exchequer and Audit Department he heads employs about 450 officials.

A comparative study by E. L. Normanton[24] has pointed to the differences between the authority, scope and effectiveness of the Exchequer and Audit Department and those of other state audit bodies. The following observations draw upon this excellent study. In the first place, other state audit organizations are far more independent of the Treasury or Finance Ministry than is the Exchequer and Audit Department and cover a far wider field of expenditure. The Comptroller General, heading the General Accounting Office in the U.S. government, is an agent of Congress and of the President. He has statutory powers to direct principles, standards, forms and systems of accounting and has been concerned to advise on financial management, management accounting, data-processing and planning systems in U.S. departments and agencies. No public authorities are exempted from his investigations, which have reached into the White House, Congress, the Treasury, government departments, agencies and corporations and into those sectors of industry where public money is spent. Recent legislation has charged the G.A.O. with inquiring into the efficiency of the agency administering it (for example the Office of Economic Opportunity's War on Poverty). In France, the Central Committee of Inquiry into the Cost and Efficiency of the Public Services, an arm of the Cour des Comptes founded by Napoleon, comprises high officials of the public services, M.P.s and representatives of Civil Service trade unions. The Committee's investigators range through government organizations and private companies which benefit from subsidies or other payments of public funds. The Central Committee has been instrumental in introducing management-accounting systems in public administration and has devoted attention to the problem of designing performance and efficiency indicators for government departments. In West Germany, the President of the State Audit is a consultant on administrative efficiency to the government, to departments and to public and local authorities. The State Audit Office is independent of all institutions and is subject only to the law. Ministers are bound to consult the President of the State Audit, who also has a separate capacity as Federal Commissioner for Efficiency, on major organizational or financial changes and on the preparation of budgetary estimates. In contrast, the Comptroller and Auditor General, though a servant of the Legislature and appointed by the Crown, is under more direction from the Executive than any other state auditor: 'At least in legal form, powers of executive direction could scarcely be more complete, and they are incomparably more so than in any other Western country.'[25] Whereas in other countries there is legislation to protect and insure the independence of the state auditor from the intervention of the Finance and other ministries, in Britain the Treasury decides on the form of the accounts and on who shall prepare and render them; the Civil Service Department decides upon the number and status of the auditors and it regulates their recruitment and pay and the Comptroller and Auditor General is nominated from the higher ranks of the Administration Group.

The field and the scope of the Comptroller is also more narrowly confined than those of other state auditors. While state auditors in the U.S.A., France and Germany, for example, can investigate all spenders of government money, the Comptroller covers only about half of public expenditure. The nationalized industries are not accountable to a public audit (Herbert Morrison thought the prospect would be unnerving for the managements of public enterprises and the Comptroller and Auditor General of the day was not in favour of undertaking the work)[26] and neither are the new state corporations; university expenditure is not subject to public audit, and since the Local Government Act of 1958 local authorities receive a general grant rather than grants for specific functions and that element of public expenditure disappeared from the Comptroller's detailed scrutiny altogether. The new Post Office Corporation now also escapes consitutional audit. 'More types of expenditure escape from constitutional audit in the United Kingdom than in any of the other powers of the West.'[27] Furthermore, unlike other state auditors, he does not examine organizational effectiveness and administrative efficiency. The U.S. General Accounting Office makes its main interest the organization, methods and systems of the higher levels of public administration and has carried out many assignments leading to major re-organizations of departments, agencies and Congressional legislative functions. The French Central Committee makes recommendations on administrative structure, operating methods, the rationalization of government activities and the promotion of efficiency. It has examined the organization and procedures of the state tobacco monopoly, the banks, the universities, state intervention in industry and the immigration service. The German Federal Commissioner for Efficiency aims at simplifying administration, diminishing costs and raising efficiency and has carried out high-level organization and methods studies throughout public administration, often on his own initiative.

The status and scope of these state audit bodies is reflected in the training and qualifications of their staffs. The Exchequer and

Audit Department (apart from the Comptroller) is staffed from executive ranks: 'It fixed the status and careers of the state audit staff at a level in the public service which is unquestionably and demonstrably the lowest of any major country in the Western world.'[28] Ours is the only state audit in which the auditors are of a standing inferior to those whose decisions are being audited. The department does not usually employ accountants, but is almost entirely staffed by men who entered the Service directly from school at O-level or A-level: their average age of entry is eighteen. In contrast, the U.S. General Accounting Office has over 4,000 staff of whom 2,500 have professional qualifications, mostly in accounting but including business-school graduates, engineers, statisticians and economists: their average age of entry is twenty-two. State auditors in France have to be qualified at post-graduate level in public finance (average age of entry, twenty-seven). The investigating staff of the Federal Commissioner in Germany are graduates, and often post-graduates, with an average age at entry of thirty.

The traditional British view of the role of the state auditor has been put by Chubb in a standard text on the control of public expenditure. He describes the Comptroller and Auditor General as 'an amateur head of a department of professionals, which is a feature of British administration'.[29] Describing the activities of the Comptroller as first and foremost an expert audit, he considers that 'to change its composition and procedure would be to destroy an old and tried machine and to substitute a new and unknown one'[30] ... 'to modify it would be to destroy its established position in the system and to endanger its ability to do its primary job of checking'[31] and concludes that 'whatever the nature of efficiency checks, it is generally agreed that they ought to be organized internally by the administration itself'.[32]

As Normanton points out, there have been no statutory innovations in the field of public accountability in Britain since 1866: 'In America, France and Western Germany the principle of high-level audits of administrative efficiency has been admitted, put into practice and encouraged. In the United Kingdom it has not.'[33] His 'idealized solution' to the problem, proposed in the course of a recent symposium on public accountability,[34] would be created out of existing institutions and familiar relationships and by borrowing selectively from the experience of state audit in other countries. He proposes the creation of a collegiate Council for Administrative Efficiency under the chairmanship of the Comptroller and Auditor General.[35] On this council there would be official representatives from the Prime Minister's Office, the Treasury and/or the Civil Service Department, the body being audited, the appropriate specialist Ministry and a research body for public expenditure studies (concerned with studying problems of, for example, pricing, budgeting and accounting, the control of capital investment, measuring profitability and contracting). There would also be audit and efficiency counsellors concerned with government departments and their agencies, nationalized industries and local authorities, backed by a body of professionally qualified state auditors and specialist consultants. The Council would consider audit and efficiency reports for transmission by the Comptroller to Parliamentary Committees. Departmental representatives on the Council could make requests for reports and so could Ministers, M.P.s, Parliamentary Committees and the House of Commons. The Comptroller could also detach expert staff from the force of auditors to assist Parliamentary Committees and could provide expert advice on management to all public bodies. The Council would have full control of its own working methods, its operating budget and its staffing and recruitment policies. Normanton observes that the nineteenth-century idea of public accountability was a negative one . . . 'that of keeping officials in their place by means of a meticulous financial discipline', while the need of the present is 'a positive form of public accountability, aiming to assess and improve the working of the manifold organizations which now depend upon national and local revenues'.[36]

Large bureaucracies have many strengths, but they are not good at generating ideas for change and improvement. They are not good at the critical evaluation of the continuing relevance of their own purposes and activities. They are not the best judge of their own efficiency and prefer not to have to demonstrate it. They stifle the searching examination, the pointed question, the assessment of efficiency. They prefer stability, secrecy and orderly growth. There are few incentives for improving efficiency in a rigidly hierarchical arrangement of status and seniority, particularly one in which managerial expertise is not the most highly prized attribute. Top management prefer to keep their own efficiency services staff in a subservient position and well away from the upper administrative levels. These staff are heavily dependent upon the goodwill of their clients for their work and for their career prospects, and they take care to stress the 'service' nature of their activity. If there is ever to be any dynamic behind the drive for efficiency in government, then the bureaucracy must be subjected to efficiency audits, backed by the highest authority and by explicit sanctions, and carried out by experts.

Management services units should report directly to the highest level of authority in departments and should carry that authority with them. They should continue to provide a service on request, but they should also supervise and lead management improvement programmes and should carry out audits of the efficiency of departmental units when directed to do so by top officials and Ministers. The central Civil Service management services unit should provide more specialized services, should maintain and supervise government-wide management improvement programmes and should be capable of mounting studies of the efficiency of major units of government on the direction of Ministers. Beyond this, experience over many years in other countries must lead to the conclusion that a powerful and independent state auditor, with the authority to examine and report publicly on the financial management, administrative efficiency, procedures and organization of government, public bodies and 'quasi-nongovernmental' bodies, even of all recipients of substantial public funds, would give public accountability a force and meaning which it does not have today. The status, authority and fields of activity of the Comptroller and Auditor General raise constitutional issues beyond the scope of this book, but they are clearly ripe for re-appraisal.

CHAPTER 8

Personnel Management

IN industry and in the Civil Service, personnel management is undergoing exceptionally rapid development at the present time. We shall see that personnel management in the Civil Service had entirely different origins from personnel management in industry but that they are now converging on a common course of experiment, research and development.

CHANGE IN THE PERSONNEL FUNCTION

No management function in industry has undergone greater changes in recent years than personnel management. Fifteen years ago Peter Drucker asked 'Is Personnel Management Bankrupt?' and answered, 'No, it is not bankrupt. Its liabilities do not exceed its assets. But it is certainly insolvent, certainly unable to honour, with the ready cash of performance, the promises of managing worker and work it so liberally makes.'[1] In this country, that same answer could have been given up to ten years ago. The typical personnel manager had a bundle of jobs but no purpose. He had housekeeping jobs; did a bit of amateur welfare work; was a soft touch for a loan; kept the accident book and visited the sick; did a lot of interviewing, usually badly; tried to soften the impact of the most authoritarian managers; often did the firm's dirty work (like firing people); exhorted everybody to be punctual, wear protective clothing and mind they didn't drop things on their toes; ran the suggestion scheme, charity collections and the children's Christmas party; tried to get people to go on courses; listened attentively to those who complained that they couldn't get on with their bosses and tried to convince shop stewards and union officials that he could see their point of view. He was frequently a retired military man who thought he was rather good with chaps. His repeated refrain was that nobody

234

would listen to him and that there ought to be a personnel man on the board.

Then in the last decade three great changes took place which have tended to make personnel management a much more important function in the firm, to 'professionalize' it and to take it into entirely new fields of activity.

First, there have been changes in national policy: governments have introduced a mass of legislation affecting the worker and his job, his pay and his working conditions. The Factory Act of 1961 was followed by the Office and Shops Act (1963); the Contracts of Employment Act (1963); the Industrial Training Act (1964); the Redundancy Payments Act (1965); the Race Relations Acts (1965 and 1968); the Prices and Incomes Acts (1966, 1967, 1968); the Equal Pay Act (1970); and the Industrial Relations Act (1971). In addition to all this new legislation, instructions and advice – on, for example, the criteria for wage increases and on productivity bargaining – have poured out of Whitehall and numerous government reports have obliged companies to consider changes in their personnel policies: the report of the Donovan Commission on Trade Unions, the Albemarle Report on youth employment services, *In Place of Strife*. Prospective entry into the Common Market has also had legislative implications for the personnel function: worker representation on supervisory boards, labour mobility.

Secondly, there have been changes in the power structure in industrial relations. Power has swung from union headquarters to the shop floor. The growth of plant and company bargaining and the rejection of the established processes of centralized industry-wide negotiations by increasingly powerful shop stewards has brought more emphasis on the negotiation of important issues of pay, working conditions, benefits and productivity at the level of line and personnel management in the factory and office.

Thirdly, the technical complexity of personnel work has shown a marked increase. Wage and salary administration has become much more systematic and has spawned such specialisms as job evaluation and schemes for sharing profits and the benefits of improved productivity. Recruitment, selection and training activities have involved the application of new techniques for testing aptitudes, assessing performance, programming instruction. Manpower planning has appeared as a new specialism, involving the analysis of the pattern of skills required now and in the future, forecasting future manpower demands and future output from the education system. Most recently, and perhaps in the long run most important, 'a growing number of companies have been looking to the behavioural sciences for insights and understandings about people and their motivations in relation to increased productivity'.[2] Large companies, at least, have been concerned to study the attitudes, motivation, aspirations and needs of their staff partly as a result of a generally more enlightened attitude towards employees and partly because shortages of skilled labour have given a new emphasis to the importance of the utilization of all the talent available to the enterprise.

All these changes have taken place in the context of rapid technological, social and economic change: the growth of a more highly educated work force; the growth of new career specialisms; a questioning of the validity of traditional values and of the 'rights' of management; an increase in the rate of obsolescence of skills and techniques. These developments have given personnel management a new time dimension: whereas it has usually had a short focus (dealing with crises, hiring, firing, making sure that there were sufficient able bodies on the strength to cope with next week's production schedule) it now has to consider manpower needs in the context of long-term changes in the enterprise and in its social and economic environment and has had to become concerned with questions of organization, planning and control.

The transformation of the personnel function is still largely confined to the inner circle of 'progressives' – the managers of very large companies, the academics and the management consultants – who are quick to seize on, and to promote, every new development in management. However, the indications are that these changes are beginning to be felt even in small organizations and that almost everywhere the personnel manager is no longer a slightly embarrassing do-gooder hanging about on the outskirts of decision-making but is being recognized as having an important role in the management of the enterprise. The personnel function is becoming a centre of expertise in the development of the human resources of the organization and in the applied social sciences equal in weight to the centres of expertise in accounting or research or production.

THE ACTIVITIES OF THE PERSONNEL FUNCTION

Personnel management in industry has grown from two distinct kinds of activity: welfare work and record-keeping. It began at the end of the nineteenth century with the establishment of women factory inspectors in 1893 and with the appointment by paternalistic employers of welfare workers (such as Rowntree, 1896). Many firms also established, often as an offshoot from their wages offices, small units concerned with recruiting manual workers and with keeping records of employment and of union agreements. The clerks in charge of these units gradually attained the status of 'Labour Officers' or 'Industrial Relations Officers'. Anne Crichton[3] has pointed to the problems raised in the 1920s by efforts to integrate the social workers in the welfare activity and the record clerks into a single personnel function.

The 1939–45 war gave a new impetus to personnel work and most factories acquired a training or labour-relations specialist. After the war, labour shortages persisted and the then Ministry of Labour continued to advise on good practice in the fields of employment, training and terms and conditions of service. In the 1950s the Ministry was allowed to run down, and without much government support personnel work went into something of a decline outside the most progressive employers. In the early 1960s, the government rediscovered the importance of the Ministry of Labour as a means of tackling the deterioration in management-worker relations in the motor, shipbuilding and public-service industries and started the wave of legislation and regulation to which reference has already been made. The 1970 government, though dedicated to the reduction of government intervention in industry, has been more active than any other in the field of labour relations and has not only put collective bargaining within a highly defined legal framework but has issued a code of practice for the guidance of managers in this field.

In a typical large company, the personnel function has the following basic activities:

1. Employment. Recruitment (or at least screening applicants for selection by line managers); induction; the application of company employment regulations (hours of work, breaks, overtime); employee transfers; employee records and statistics; the application of national employment legislation; liaison with other employers.

2. Wages. The development and application of employee grading and pay rates; calculations and payment of wages, bonuses and other benefits; maintenance of a wages structure.

3. Consultation and negotiation. Advising line management on negotiations with unions, maintaining grievance procedures; maintaining and developing the machinery for joint consultation.

4. Health and welfare. The application of the provisions of the Factory and other Acts relating to working conditions; accident prevention, medical and dental services; investigations and claims; sickness payments; canteen administration; the provision of recreation facilities; grants and loans; assistance with housing, legal, transport and personal problems; suggestion schemes; social activities; house journals.

5. The development of the individual. The formulation and application of training policy, arranging courses, liaison with educational institutions. Staff assessment and appraisal, career and succession planning, studies of manpower utilization, attitudes and morale.

Some large companies support these activities with a substantial personnel research, analysis and planning activity for which the main topics of attention in recent years have been management development, organization, 'compensation' (that is, the total range of wages, salaries and benefits), staff-assessment systems and motivation.[4]

In organizational terms, personnel is usually both a functional and a service staff group: that is to say that in some areas personnel managers have functional authority over line management whereas in others they offer a service which managers can take or leave. Thus in most companies the personnel department has mandatory authority in such matters as hours of work, leave, overtime payments, job grading and union relations and any action a manager takes must comply with the procedures laid down by the department. In such areas as career development and joint consultation the department is available to give advice and help if requested to do so, but the option is often left to management. Not surprisingly, the functional authority of personnel departments often gives rise to conflict with line management. Though line managers are charged with organizing and controlling people in pursuit of company objectives, the personnel department is vested with ultimate authority in many matters which greatly affect these activities. The greater the authority of the personnel function, the more managerial accountability is weakened. A manager may want to pay his staff more (or less) than the company rate in order to reach his cost and performance standards; he may want to give a particularly valuable or high-performing member of his staff a higher pay grade than the job-evaluation system says it is worth; he may want to introduce an incentive scheme of his own invention; he may want to reduce (or increase) the cost of amenities or recreational facilities; he may not want to release a particularly valuable member of his staff for a long training course, nor to be bothered with a staff appraisal scheme. In each of these areas there is likely to be a conflict between the line manager who deploys manpower in pursuit of the short-term budgets and plans of his unit and the personnel manager who considers the long-term development of manpower as a company resource, often in the context of a multi-plant operation. The conflict is made more likely by the professionalization of personnel management. The personnel manager today belongs not only to his company but to the wider community of personnel specialists and academics in the social sciences. A large company may have a personnel career stream whose members have little experience of the problems of actually managing a work force and very little in common with those who do. In addition there is a long anti-management tradition in personnel work. The welfare side of personnel work has from its beginning tended to side with the worker against the boss: the welfare worker tried to protect the employee from the worst excesses of exploitation and inhumanity of the manager or owner and tried to represent the voice of the worker in the councils of management. We shall see that the present emphasis in personnel work on the applied social sciences also frequently takes the personnel function on a collision course with line management. The conscientious personnel man therefore finds himself continually having to face in different directions: managers expect him to provide them with staff in the right numbers and quality at the right time: employees look to him for advice on their problems and prospects and often for protection from line management; his professionalism obliges him to be concerned with the maintenance and development of the stock of human resources available to the organization. These three different considerations sometimes bear on a single case: a promotion or transfer, for example, and call for the highest standards of judgement and sensitivity.

The technical content of personnel work is now so great and is increasing so quickly that it would be impossible to do justice to it in a general text of this kind. There are, however, three technical areas in which current developments are of great consequence to the Civil Service, because of the reforms proposed by the Fulton Committee, because of changes in the human relations environment and because the personnel function in departments is generally not equipped to handle them. These are job evaluation, man-power planning and the application of the social (in the occupational area more specifically called 'behavioural') sciences.

JOB EVALUATION

Job evaluation is the operation of determining the value of an individual job in an organization in relation to all the other jobs in it. It provides a rational basis for a wage and salary structure. It is concerned with the worth of the job and not the abilities or performance of the job holder. It usually involves a written description of the tasks, duties and responsibilities attaching to each job or group of similar jobs, the ranking of jobs in order of worth and the 'banding' of jobs into grades. A pay scale is then constructed which assigns a range of payment to each grade. The job holder frequently participates in the preparation of the job description, and unions and staff associations are often involved in the ranking procedure and the assignment of pay ranges. There are several job-evaluation systems,[5] which differ from each other in the degree of quantitative analysis involved in ranking jobs. A widely used system for evaluating supervisory and managerial jobs is the points rating method, which is designed to lessen the degree of subjective judgement inherent in the ranking process. It has been successfully used in large organizations in industry and public administration, employing a very wide range of managerial and professional staff.

The points rating method involves the selection of factors which differentiate jobs in terms of their 'value' to the organization (for example the responsibility of the job holder for expenditure and manpower, his contribution to policy, the complexity of the task), the assignment of relative weights to those factors and the definition of degrees or levels within them. Typically between five and ten factors are selected for rating, though the fewer there are the easier it is to insure that each is discrete. One scheme for managers in a large public corporation recognizes five groups of factors; 'background' (levels of education and experience required to do the job); 'decisions' (authority to commit the corporation's resources); 'judgement' (the extent to which the holder is involved in the analysis and appraisal of alternatives); 'leadership' (related to the size and diversity of the group of staff reporting to the job holder); 'contacts' (the representational content of the job). A more elaborate scheme for a large international company involves the analysis of supervisory and managerial jobs under eight factors, most of which are further analysed into sub-factors; education; training; general and specific experience; scope of activity (reflecting the scale and complexity of responsibilities); accountability (for decisions, man-management, cash handling, work planning, the development of procedures); supervision received; relationships within the company; relationships with outside bodies (customers, competitors, official bodies).

The next step is to assign weights to each of the chosen factors: to specify the relative importance of, say, the education required to do the job compared with the number of staff directly reporting to the job holder. Increasingly, the effort is being made to system-atize this process by the use of statistical techniques. One such technique is the 'Direct Consensus Method' which involves a panel of 'judges' who, acting individually, state their preference between many pairs of jobs. For each pair the judges are asked to state to which one they would give greater weight in respect of each factor. A computer programme then calculates the resulting rank order for all the jobs which have been considered and rank orders for each individual factor. A second programme, using multiple-regression analysis, determines such weights for each factor as will explain the preferred overall rank order of jobs. The result is a set of factor weights which represents the consensus view of the judges. In the case of the public corporation which has been quoted this view was that the relative weights of factors were best represented by giving 40 points to 'judgement'; 25 to 'decisions'; 17 to 'background'; and 9 each to 'leadership' and 'contacts' – making 100 points available in total.

Next comes the problem of deciding upon degrees within the weighted factors. Thus there are degrees of responsibility, of complexity and of significance of decisions. In the case of the public corporation 'decisions' were distinguished at eight levels, ranging from those closely prescribed by rule or precedent to those which commit corporation resources and have funda-mental consequences for its future. In the case of the international company the 'specific experience' factor was distinguished in seven degrees from three to six months' experience to fifteen years'.

Next, certain jobs are selected as 'benchmarks' and are des-cribed, analysed by factor and awarded points under each factor. These serve as reference points for all the other jobs under re-view, for each of which a points score has to be produced. Once each job is scored, jobs are grouped into grades and each grade is allocated a pay range. Thus all jobs scoring up to 20 points might be grouped as grade 1, those between 20 and 30 grade 2 and so on. Grade 1 jobs might then be given a pay range of £700–£1,500 p.a., grade 2 £1,250–£2,000 p.a. and so on. The practice usually is to have overlapping pay ranges and to increase the width of each range towards the upper levels. Frequently it is necessary to have more than one factor system in a large enterprise to which job

evaluation is applied to all jobs, from manual worker to directorial levels. In manual jobs, working conditions, hazards, physical
effort may be the most important factors to take into account; in
clerical jobs accuracy and speed of working may be appropriate;
and in managerial jobs, discretion, the effect of decisions, creativity and innovation, and responsibility for assets will be more
important.

Job evaluation is concerned to establish the relative values of
different jobs inside an organization. However, salaries also have
to be related to rates in the external labour market. In most cases
job-evaluated pay scales are fixed in relation to market values at
the bottom of the scale where the rates for lower grades are determined by union-negotiated manual or clerical rates and at the top
where there is a publicly known 'going rate' for company chair-
men (or in government departments and nationalized industries, a
Cabinet decision on the appropriate rate for top jobs in the public service). The bench mark jobs are also usually examined for
consistency with external pay rates. It sometimes happens, however, that market shortages in special categories of skill may
oblige an organization to pay more for a particular group of staff
than would be warranted simply on the basis of comparative
worth. Examples of such skill categories in recent years have been
computer programmers, systems analysts and accountants. In
such cases the organization has to recognize market values, for as
long as the shortage lasts, by paying a special supplement or by
starting a man with the required skill at a high point within the
grade for his job.

A job-evaluation scheme, if properly conducted, has the advantage of introducing a logical, factual and systematic method of
arriving at an equitable pay structure: a question of great dispute
and dissatisfaction in many organizations. There is still a substantial element of subjectivity in job-evaluation schemes, for
example in deciding the factor weights, or the responsibilities
carried by a particular job holder, but this subjective element can
be clearly identified and openly discussed. These schemes have the
advantage of being based on a written description of what actually happens in a job; on the comparison of jobs against common
criteria and on a careful examination of the importance or diffi-

culty of a job. They can be used to create a payment system the cost of which is acceptable to management and which is seen to be fair by employees and unions.

MANPOWER PLANNING

Manpower planning is a series of activities concerned to insure that:

(1) an organization is provided with staff of the skills required to match the demands likely to be placed upon it by internal and environmental change;

(2) the best use is made of the developing abilities of individual members of the organization;

(3) the manpower implications of prospective policies and operational developments can be identified.

Manpower planning rests on an information base. A body of personnel records is required relating to the age, job history, qualifications and skills of the population so organized as to permit comparisons between different groups and the evaluation of trends in recruitment, retirement, wastage, wage and salary movements, occupational and skill changes, developments in training needs. External data is also required to enable relevant movements in the labour market as a whole to be detected: trends in labour supply, wage and salary trends, trends in education and outputs at different levels of the educational system, trends in retirement policy, hours of work and overtime, the impact of national training policies.

Manpower planning has to be closely linked to the corporate planning process of the enterprise, so that the implications of the assumptions and objectives of the corporate plan are read into the objectives and programmes of the manpower plan and so that, in return, corporate planners are aware of manpower constraints. Once corporate objectives are promulgated the manpower planners usually begin with an assessment of the present labour resources of the enterprise and the prospective effects of present trends in wastage and in the employment of different skills. Age-distribution profiles are produced showing retirement rates over the forecast period and likely surpluses or shortfalls in different age brackets; occupation profiles are produced showing the forecast movements of population in different skill groups; forecast patterns of promotion and transfer are constructed. At this stage external limitations on the supply of different skill groups can be assessed. In parallel with the supply forecast, studies of the total demand for manpower can be constructed using forecasting techniques which relate manpower trends to the movement of the major indicators (such as sales, investment) of the corporate plan. In a company which has had reliable systems of productivity measurement for a long enough period it is possible to break down future production and sales forecasts into their labour and skill content and to calculate from these what the demand for manpower, by category, is likely to be. The gap, if any, between demand and supply forecasts can then be analysed to discern any serious shortages or surpluses of different types of manpower which warrant anticipatory action by management: training or retraining programmes, recruitment drives; early retirement programmes; overtime arrangements or work sharing; internal transfers; premium payments; further research. The planning cycle is 'closed' by annual audits of the performance of personnel activities and by the restatement of corporate and personnel function objectives. In recent years there has been rapid development in the mathematical modelling of manpower processes for analysing the interactions of, for example, various rates of wastage and changes in organization.[6]

Planning in the personnel function is developing not only at this broad demographic level. Large businesses attempt to provide for management succession by compiling management inventories: analyses of their stock of present and future managers and the likely promotion paths of individuals with management potential. Staff, particularly graduate staff, also expect to be informed of the view that is taken on their future prospects and expect to be able to discuss some scheme of career development which sets out the mix of formal training, job rotation and assignments which will enable them to make the best use of their abilities. One of the problems of employing large numbers of graduate staff, made much worse by the advent of business-school graduates in quantity, is that they tend to have inflated aspirations and place a particularly optimistic valuation on the possession of academic qualifications as the price of admission to top management. However, a side benefit of employing members of this highly articulate and volatile group is that they are obliging the personnel function to assess the value of a degree, to explore the relationship of job demands and academic qualifications and to specify the future pattern of recruitment and placement. Unfortunately the concentration of effort in some large businesses upon how to employ, and where to put, graduates tends to divert too much attention from the needs and legitimate claims of non-graduate staff.

The basic data for any career planning system must derive from regular (usually annual) personal assessment interviews. The personnel policy of one large corporation states: 'Every individual has the right to be considered an integrated member of an organization and know how he stands within it. Staff usually want to be sure that their work performance is acceptable to management and that the effort put into a job will serve as an investment for the future. They want to be sure that their careers will be determined fairly and not left to the haphazard whim of their immediate managers.'

The statement goes on to say that this requirement can be met by the corporation's staff assessment scheme, which is based on an annual interview between the employee and his manager at which are discussed the employee's performance in this job, his need for wider experience or further training, his personal problems, attitudes and morale. The manager rates the performance of the employee (in five degrees from outstanding to unsatisfactory) and indicates his potential for promotion in terms of the fields of work for which he appears suited, the grade range which he might expect ultimately to reach and the time in which he is likely to reach it. The employee is entitled to read the assessment, which provides essential data for salary administration, the internal transfer and placement system, the training function, management succession planning, career development and overall manpower planning.

THE BEHAVIOURAL SCIENCES

Industry was first made aware of the behavioural sciences by the publication of the results of the Hawthorne experiments by Elton Mayo and his colleagues in the late 1920s (see Chapter 3). Since then a very great volume of academic study has been carried out on the behaviour and motivation of people at work; on human relationships within working groups and between groups; on relationships between superiors and subordinates; and generally on what Douglas McGregor called 'the human side of enterprise'. Some large employers have become interested in securing greater productivity or a more peaceful life or a better reputation through improving the social climate of the organization and have become attracted to the promise of behavioural science programmes flourished by some academics and consultants. Such programmes are often concerned with understanding the attitudes and pre-occupations of staff; improving communications between managers and managed; improving the cohesion of working groups and encouraging their identification with corporate objectives; encouraging the participation of workers in the planning and decision-making processes which affect them; improving superior –subordinate relationships; improving morale; making more interesting and worthwhile jobs; and assisting in organizational change.

Most of the ideas behind these programmes have been derived from the work of half a dozen American behavioural scientists, of whom the leading place is usually accorded to the late Douglas McGregor, whose major work was published in 1960.[7] McGregor saw that managers were concerned to influence human behaviour in the attainment of organizational objectives and yet rarely had any grasp of what was known about behaviour from research in the social sciences. His contribution was to explain to the managerial community the insights that behavioural science could offer them in the course of their work as managers. He made his observations about human motivation in two simple theoretical constructs illustrative of managerial attitudes: these he called

'Theory X' and 'Theory Y'. The assumptions of Theory X were that the average human being dislikes work and will avoid it if he can; he must therefore be coerced, directed and threatened if he is to work towards organizational goals; that he prefers to be directed, wishes to avoid responsibility, has little ambition and wants security above all. Traditionally many managers felt that in order to meet their production, sales and profit goals they had to adopt the assumptions of Theory X and ignored the question of whether these assumptions adequately explained human motivation. Theory Y embodied a contrasting set of assumptions. These were that the expenditure of effort in work was as natural as play or rest; that self-direction by people who are committed to an objective can be an alternative to external control and the threat of punishment; that people learn, under proper conditions, to accept and seek responsibility; that most people's intellectual potentialities, their ingenuity and creativity in solving problems, for example, are only partly used. McGregor saw the negative behaviour of Theory X as being created by the managers who adopted its assumptions. The emphasis of Theory Y on self-direction and on the need to recognize human needs and aspirations offered an alternative way of harnessing effort to meet organizational goals. It was not long before Theory Y was taken as a prescription for the 'right' way to manage and became, for some managers, as rigid a dogma as Theory X had been for their predecessors. McGregor, however, always made it clear that the value of Theory Y lay primarily in opening managers' minds to the possibilities for finding new ways of organizing and utilizing human effort and ability.

Chris Argyris, another pioneer of modern human-resource management, has pointed to the tendency of organizations to thwart the social and personality needs of those who work in them. The hierarchical arrangements of authority and responsibility, rigidly defined jobs and channels of communication, the rigorous division of labour, highly defined work schedules and quotas, ignore the personal needs of the worker, deny him self-esteem and the opportunity to make his contribution to the enterprise. He concluded that 'organizations can be modified so that they offer increasingly meaningful challenges and opportunity for responsibility'.[8] The modifications he suggested were the general encouragement of openness and candour in personal relationships by, for example, 'group laboratory' training situations in which people can discuss the obstacles to greater cohesion in the working group. He also advocated the formation of *ad hoc* project groups or task forces to tackle particular problems and laid emphasis upon 'job enlargement' (see below).

In the early 1950s Abraham Maslow developed a concept of personality and motivation based on a 'hierarchy of human needs'[9] each of which is a motivator of human behaviour. At the lowest level are physiological needs (for food, shelter, warmth etc.); next, safety needs (for assurance of safety from physical and emotional injury); next, the need for social belongingness and affiliation; then the need for esteem and a feeling of personal worth; finally, at the apex of the hierarchy, the need for 'self-actualization'– that is, the need to express one's personality 'by becoming what one is capable of becoming'. Any need does not become dominant until the lower order needs are satisfied: 'a satisfied need is no longer a motivator of behaviour.' A personality which has reached the self-actualization stage has fulfilled all the preceding 'deficit needs' and has a drive to fulfil its intellectual potentialities and to see new goals and means of expression.

This emphasis upon the 'higher' needs of the individual and the complex motivation of relatively affluent people in an industrial society is also a feature of the work of Frederick Herzberg, which has had a marked impact on personnel management in some large institutions in this country. An attitude survey of accountants and engineers carried out by Herzberg and his colleagues revealed that most respondents felt personal satisfaction about the content of their jobs but felt most dissatisfaction with the context, or external rules and procedures, within which they had to do their jobs. Herzberg listed the job *content* factors or '*satisfiers*' as achievement (completing a job, solving a problem); recognition (of personal accomplishment); the nature of the work itself; responsibility; advancement and growth (for example learning new skills, taking on wider responsibilities). The job *context* factors or '*dissatisfiers*' were company policy and administration (such as unclear organization); the quality of supervision; physical working conditions; interpersonal relations (with the boss, with subordinates and equals); salary, security and personal life (that is, the effect of the job on home life). Herzberg calls the dissatisfiers 'hygiene' factors and the satisfiers 'motivators'. He contends that satisfiers and dissatisfiers were quite distinct and separate; they were not opposite ends of one range of factors. For example, high salary or good working conditions rarely contributed to job satisfaction but low salaries and bad working conditions were invariably sources of dissatisfaction. Herzberg points out that management typically emphasized the hygiene factors (wages, benefits, accommodation, security) but ignored the motivators. He calls for a focus on efforts to improve and enrich the content of jobs so as to motivate workers to achievement and self-actualization. Herzberg's early studies were published in 1959[10] and have been repeated in widely varying work situations and in a number of different countries with what are claimed to be similar results.[11]

Herzberg's work has led to numerous experiments in 'job enrichment' in industry. Enrichment, like job enlargement and job rotation, aims at making jobs less monotonous, less predictable and less fragmented, so that the individual worker can find greater meaning in his job.[12]

Job enlargement involves increasing the number of tasks that a worker has to do; for example, lengthening the cycle time of his job by giving him a complete product to assemble instead of putting together one sub-assembly. Job rotation involves switching a worker from one job to another; for example working on different sub-assemblies at different times. Job enrichment attempts to do more than either of these schemes. It involves giving the worker greater responsibility: for example giving him responsibility for maintaining the stock of parts he uses in assembly work, for inspecting the quality of his own work, for choosing his own methods and working tempo.

One of the most extensive experiments in job enlargement is currently under discussion in the Italian Fiat motor company. There the trade unions 'maintain that the repetition of one brief, simple operation *ad infinitum* is soul-destroying. They want each man to be given three or four successive operations to carry out.

They say that this would give the men greater feeling of fulfillment.'[13] The management has agreed that in a new assembly plant which is at present being built a joint management–union commission will supervise experiments in job enlargement.

The most widely quoted early example of Herzberg's job enrichment is the apparently successful work which was carried out at American Telephone and Telegraph in a large department employing girls who write letters in response to shareholders' complaints or requests for information. Supervision was reduced to a minimum and the girls were made responsible for the accuracy of their own letters. They were encouraged to use their own initiative in seeking answers to queries. They were urged to write in their own language rather than use the standard form, and they were allowed to sign their own names.[14] As a result of this scheme, to which the girls responded with enthusiasm, productivity is said to have increased and there have been fewer mistakes. There are other examples of successful job-enrichment programmes. One of the longest-running and best-validated is the use of self-managing groups of workers at Philips, the Dutch electrical manufacturer. Beginning in 1965, nearly 300 women assembly workers engaged on short-cycle repetitive work who had formerly been on an individual-performance bonus scheme were re-formed into fourteen working groups. Each working group was made responsible for the allocation of jobs, the supply of materials and quality inspection and each group negotiated a six–twelve-month wages contract with the head of the department. Generally, worker satisfaction and efficiency have increased and absenteeism and labour turnover have declined.[15]

In 1969 Herzberg and two British colleagues reported on five job-enrichment studies which were being carried out in Imperial Chemical Industries Ltd, and other British companies.[16] These studies covered laboratory technicians, sales representatives, design engineers, production and engineering foremen. The experimental design included changes in the technical, financial and managerial content of the work of these groups. For example, the technicians ('experimental officers', also a class in the Civil Service) were encouraged to write and sign reports, to plan projects and set targets, to follow up their own ideas; they were authorized to requisition materials and equipment, to request analysis and to order services, such as maintenance; they were made responsible for training junior staff, interviewing candidates for laboratory assistant jobs and for staff assessment. The report indicates substantial improvement in the performance and motivation of the groups of staff whose jobs were enriched compared with control groups whose jobs content was unchanged.

Another development in the general movement towards treating workers as people rather than as machines is in the field of communications and the encouragement of participation in the affairs of the enterprise. There have, of course, been numerous experiments in 'industrial democracy', mostly half-hearted, and as often as not opposed by unions as well as management. The history of works councils shows how such experiments can be nullified by the opposition or indifference of these two power groups. A more modest and rewarding approach to improved communications is contained in the idea of 'briefing groups', which is now appearing in industry. 'The system involves bringing people together with their immediate boss in groups of between four and eighteen on a regular basis. Such meetings should take place at least once a month at all levels of management down to the supervisor and at least once every thirteen weeks for every employee. The object of these briefing sessions is to explain and discuss what is happening that affects the work group.'[17] The benefits claimed for the use of briefing groups in Guardian Royal Exchange Assurance are 'savings in cash through improved policy and decision-making, a higher level of staff commitment, improved relations between teams and their leaders and a rapid feed back on policies and decisions. Supervisors gain greater confidence and increased respect from the staff. The staff themselves get increased job satisfaction higher morale and improved relations with their superiors.'[18]

Another development in the application of the behavioural sciences in industry concerns group or training 'laboratories' and sensitivity training. These processes involve training in awareness of one's own behaviour, attitudes and personality characteristics and in awareness of the perception of one's behaviour by other people. The point of sensitivity training is that it encourages the trainee to drop the façade he usually lives behind and to behave according to his inherent nature. This takes place in the T- (for training) group, which is isolated from outside distractions, usually for some weeks, and for which there are no rules or agenda or organization. The result is a series of intimate interactions or confrontations between participants, at the end of which they gain increased insight into the way in which others see them. Many people return from sensitivity training feeling that they have had a valuable experience and know how to become more effective managers, although they may have experienced a degree of emotional stress. Variants of group laboratories are the 'managerial grid' seminar, developed by Blake and Mouton,[19] and the '3D Theory' managerial effectiveness seminar developed by Professor Reddin,[20] which are concerned to explore the management styles of the participants as evidenced by the way they handle case studies and problems and as evaluated by other participants.

The behavioural sciences are far from winning general acceptance in industry or even in personnel departments. They cover a field of rapid change, with one package of techniques succeeding another with bewildering rapidity, and some of their exponents use a jargon that frequently has a phony ring. Behavioural scientists may also confront management, particularly untrained management, with some awkward and unwelcome truths and may challenge the intuitive beliefs about how to motivate people which have hitherto reigned in an organization. With their emphasis upon the social needs of the worker they can be construed by the traditionalist as anti-management and trouble-making.

In addition, behavioural scientists frequently claim too much for their prescriptions. In particular, as a recent article by James A. Lee[21] (based on American experience) has pointed out, they tend to assume that a particular management style (for example greater autonomy for the individual, wider participation, more widespread recognition of the potential power of the non-manager, more self-evaluation, more organic organization structures) which suits their own small sub-culture suits everybody else as well. 'The vast majority of the behavioural theorists today are professors, whose strong autonomy needs and anti-authoritarian bias govern much of their research approach and ideal model-building. They bounce their ideas off other faculty members and students, who are well known to have similar needs and biases; they use students for subjects for some of their studies and they arrive at a recommended work environment in the image of the ideal university.'[22]

On the other hand, the behavioural science movement mirrors a substantial change in our culture: the appearance of the articulate, powerfully represented, better-educated worker whose demands will increase for greater respect for the individual, for a say in matters that affect him, for a more meaningful job. American experience[23] shows that the selective use of behavioural science methods has helped many companies to adjust to change, to improve their effectiveness and to create a better environment for their workers and that behavioural scientists can provide a valuable measure of the mental health of the organization.

ESTABLISHMENTS WORK

Personnel work in the Civil Service has had quite different origins and history from personnel work in industry. It has been part of a much wider establishments function and has acquired the attitudes and overtones associated with that powerful arm of financial control.

After the First World War, one of the periodic campaigns against the numbers employed in the Civil Service and the need to redeploy wartime civil servants led the government of the day to examine controls over the population of the Civil Service. A Select Committee on National Expenditure considered financial control in the Civil Service and led to the Haldane Committee on the Machinery of Government of 1918 and the Bradbury Committee on the Organization and Staffing of Government Offices of 1919. Their reports led to the creation of an Establishments Division in the Treasury in February 1919 (which had become five divisions by September of that year) concerned with all questions of staff, pay, recruitment, grading and the use of office machinery and other labour-saving appliances. They also led to the institution of Principal Establishments Officers and establishments divisions in departments. This remarkably swift series of moves consolidated and defined Treasury control over manpower and organization in a model of bureaucratic centralism which hardly changed over the next fifty years. The first appointments of Establishments Officers were made about the time that the 'anti-waste campaign' was at its height, and soon after, in 1921, the Geddes Committee was constituted to make recommendations 'for effecting forthwith all possible reductions in the National Expenditure on Supply Services'. In this environment, there began the tradition of Establishments work as an instrument for the limitation of staff numbers.

The Fulton Committee's Management Consultancy Group described the responsibilities of establishments divisions as threefold:

(1) Work concerned with personnel, including:

(i) A highly developed form of control over the complement of the department (that is, over the numbers and grades of staff employed).

(ii) the co-ordination of departmental requirements for manpower, recruitment, postings, promotions, pay and conditions of service, welfare and training.

(2) Provision of accommodation, equipment, typing, duplicating and reprographic services.

(3) The encouragement of efficiency by Organization and Methods studies including, in some cases, the installation and operation of automatic data processing.[24]

These functions are exercised within strict control by the Civil Service Department (formerly the 'manpower side' of the Treasury). This central department lays down recruitment policy, it decides on whether to give established status to staff recruited by departments and formulates policy on pay, conditions, promotion, transport, postings, retirements and welfare matters. These policies and rules are all set out in a manual, *Estacode*. Within this framework, departmental establishments divisions have a little latitude to modify terms and conditions of service to meet the needs of their working situation. In Chapter 5 we saw that central control makes itself strongly felt in the matter of numbers and grades employed by the scrutiny of manpower estimates, by the imposition of manpower ceilings and by occasional across-the-board cuts in complements.

In some respects, the personnel function in the Civil Service is in advance of general industrial practice. It is powerfully represented in the councils of top management, with clear functional authority. It is highly effective in keeping the increase of staff on a tight rein: British industry, which is notoriously over-staffed, could learn some valuable lessons from the independent inspection of bids for staff, the imposition of manpower ceilings, a central review body for employment. Only the best British employers have a system of annual staff-appraisal interviews, now becoming a regular routine in the Civil Service. Promotion procedures are generally fairer in the Civil Service than in industry. After a specified number of years of service in a grade, an officer becomes eligible for promotion to the next higher grade and is usually summoned before a board, where he is examined by an array of senior officials. In some departments an officer can request to appear before a board once he is in the promotion 'field' and if he fails to gain a recommendation he can appeal against the board's decision. In some areas, the Civil Service is also an example to industry in the field of training, particularly for junior staff, and it is a model employer of women, with very few obviously discriminatory practices in training, promotion or grading.

Industrial relations are generally well handled by the Whitley machinery for negotiation and consultation, which has now existed for over fifty years. The start of Whitleyism is a good example of the way in which a bureaucratic machine handles a powerful external demand for change. The first Whitley report of 1917 proposed the creation for every industry of a National Joint Standing Industrial Council constituted of representatives of employers and workers. The Civil Service staff associations then requested that this arrangement be extended to cover Civil Servants. This was refused by the Permanent Secretary of the Ministry of Labour. A further representation to the Treasury was also rebuffed: the Chancellor denied that the Civil Service could be regarded as an industry and therefore within the scope of Mr Whitley's recommendations. The Whitley Committee then produced a second report which extended its recommendations to state and municipal authorities.

One inter-departmental committee recommended the acceptance of the Whitley proposals for the industrial civil service (to which the Treasury now gave whole-hearted support),[25] while another concluded that the executive functions of Whitley councils could not be extended to the non-industrial Civil Service and that councils in this field should have only advisory and consultative functions. The staff associations pressed for full Whitleyism for non-industrial civil servants and at a conference between them and Treasury officials in early 1919 the Chancellor of the Exchequer, Austen Chamberlain, presented a most dramatic change in Treasury policy. He welcomed the proposals for full Whitley councils ... 'it will make the task of the Treasury much lighter. I venture to think when you know us better you will think us more reasonable than you have thought us in the past ... the new machinery will remove any grievances, real or fancied.'[26] Agreement between the two sides led to the formation of a National Whitley Council, a number (now seventy) of departmental Whitley councils and many hundreds of district, office and works Whitley committees on each of which there are an equal number of 'official' and 'staff side' representatives. Sir William Armstrong has described the lessons of this story: 'Everything is there; the initial instinctive negative reaction of officialdom to anything new; the equally instinctive catching on by the Staff Associations to a new opportunity; the laborious working out by the officials side in isolation of something that was not quite good enough; the necessary confrontation with the hint of possible disaster; and the eventual coming together with each side seeing far more in the other's position than they had thought possible; and arising out of the experience, successful collaboration in the carrying out of some much needed reforms.'[27]

The following fifty years of Whitleyism in the Civil Service have seen the evolution of mutual confidence and respect between Official and the Staff sides and the development of a system of collective bargaining and joint negotiation largely based on infor-

mal contacts as a means of avoiding direct and public confrontations. The National Staff side of the Whitley Council now represents half a million civil servants in membership of Civil Service
Staff associations. These staff associations are independent trade
unions representing over 80 per cent of all civil servants and having full-time headquarters staffs; two thirds of the total membership is affiliated to the Trades Union Congress. The main policy
committee of the National Whitley Council Staff side includes the
general secretaries of the six largest unions. Negotiations with the
official side are handled by a system of sub-committees and by
staff side officials while the National Staff side negotiates on
issues which are of wider application than to the members of any
one union. Recent examples of such issues are·London 'weighting' allowances, overtime arrangements and disturbance allowances, and a special committee set up to consider the implications
of the Fulton Report.

The main objections to the establishments view of personnel
work are that it is impersonal, remote, dehumanizing. It is the
bureaucrat's bureaucracy, regulating the behaviour of management and staff by a set of rules and precedents backed by highly
centralized authority. Its focus is primarily upon systems for preserving order, discipline, regularity and economy through the
application of impersonal rules. Changes in the environment and
activities of departments are dealt with by the elaboration of rules
which regulate the future actions of all departments in these
fields. The need to review the rules is all too rarely considered.
Thus the simple three-class career structure of the late nineteenth
century became the 1,400 class structure of the late twentieth
century because each new skill requirement usually led to the
automatic establishment of a new class.

The central aim of Establishments Divisions has been to preserve good order and equity; to preserve the existing relationships between classes and grades, existing task definitions and
arrangements and to dampen the effects of internal and external
change. The enforcement of these rules by a centralized authority
does make for equitable treatment and predictability; it avoids the
excesses of upheaval and uncertainty which arise from rapid
organizational change; it gives many staff a sense of assurance

and an expectation of fairness; it serves the public interest in controlling the growth numbers and keeping the shop open while ministers indulge in one reorganization after another. The establishment style, however, often has a leaden impersonality and the appearance of a greater concern with rules than with people.

Establishments Officers are concerned to fill vacancies in the organization with any available member of the appropriate class and grade, and to resist the inflation of staff numbers. They have paid very little attention to career planning and development for staff outside the Administrative Class; to the application of job-enrichment or enlargement programmes in organizations which usually have thousands of tedious manual and clerical jobs; to participative or consultative styles of management; to improving communications with junior staff in highly hierarchical organizations and to the line manager's role in personnel management.

In a recent lecture Sir William Armstrong described 'Establishments Man', the variety of personnel administrator found in the Civil Service and now gradually giving way to the personnel manager, as exercising 'basically a negative function – the old personnel administrator saw his job in terms of recruiting people to fill vacancies, paying them, applying the rules to them and dealing *ad hoc* with any problems which arose'.[28] He also commented on 'the tendency for the line manager to be less involved in personnel management than his counterpart elsewhere, and for him often not to recognize so clearly his responsibilities for personnel management problems'.[29]

FULTON ON ESTABLISHMENT WORK

The Fulton Committee had more to say on personnel work in the Civil Service than on any other management function. Its Consultancy Group observed that 'the unification in the Civil Service of these somewhat disparate functions within one division rests on the present concept of cost control . . . The Establishments Division is the means by which a department checks its own growth in internal costs, which are mainly those of manpower . . . It also illustrates the fundamental and unifying fact that Establishments work, with its emphasis on the regulation of manpower costs, is an aspect of financial control and thus gives initiative and ultimate sanction in these matters to the Treasury.'[30]

The Consultancy Group criticized the Treasury's custom of making swinging across-the-board cuts in staff complements, which it saw as counter-productive. It was also critical of the operations of staff inspectors, considering them to be inadequately trained and to be guided by superficial experience rather than analysis. It criticized the annual staff-appraisal routine for concentrating upon such subjective factors as initiative, leadership and zeal and for failing to assess in any objective terms an individual's performance in his job. These appraisals were often conducted, or countersigned, by officials who had little idea of what their subordinate's job entailed (that is, administrators who had little first-hand knowledge of the work of the executives on whom they reported). Career planning was largely non-existent – 'we found that much of the movement of staff from job to job arranged by Establishments Officers masqueraded as career planning'.[31] Though this movement was sometimes an inevitable result of the turbulence created by the imposition of new tasks upon the Civil Service, establishments divisions tried to make a virtue of it by seeing all movement as 'broadening' and all specialization as 'narrowing'.

The Consultancy Group also criticized features of the promotion arrangements. Many competent officers regularly failed promotion boards because they could not create a good impression in these unnatural circumstances: the Group observed that boards place emphasis upon 'articulateness in a stress situation'.[32] It also questioned whether the brief conversation on broad topical issues which is the content of many board interviews adequately tested the managerial abilities of interviewees; whether the administrators on boards fully understood the qualities required to do executive and specialist jobs; and whether board members were adequately trained. The Group considered that there should be a change of emphasis in promotion procedures so that more weight was given to an officer's performance in his job as assessed by his superiors and rather less to seniority and to the impression he made on a promotion board. The Group also questioned the effectiveness of the procedures after an officer passes a board: the practice was to list them in the order of the seniority they held in their existing grade and then usually to promote them in seniority order as each vacancy arose, regardless of their suitability for that particular vacancy.

Other reforms in the personnel field suggested by the Consultancy Group were that annual increments in pay should be based on a review of the officer's performance in the past year: unsatisfactory performance should be marked by the withholding or reduction of an increment while exceptional merit might be recognized by a double increment. Officers who obtained qualifications while in the Service should also be eligible for merit awards. The impersonality of the personnel activities of Establishments Divisions was criticized by the Consultancy Group. This work appeared to be untouched by developments in personnel work outside the Service: 'In the Establishment area of activity the isolation of the Service was most marked.'[33]

'Establishments Officers . . . apparently prefer to remain remote from the men whose careers they are handling. This cultivation of detachment reflects the emphasis upon equity and impartiality in promotion arrangements; as a result discussion between Establishments Officers and individuals is not only rare but is regarded as inappropriate. This detachment of Establishments Divisions is particularly daunting to new young entrants to the Service'[34] . . . 'It would be difficult to say from what we saw that "Establishments" is generally held in high regard in the Service, either as an area in which to work or as a service to the staff.'[35]

As we have seen from Chapter 2, the Fulton Committee accepted the Consultancy Group's proposal that all Civil Service career classes should be merged into one unified grading structure, using job-evaluation techniques to assess the relative worth of every job. That is to say that every Civil Service *job* would be classified into one of a number of pay grades running from the top limit of the Deputy Secretary (around £9,000 p.a.) scale to the bottom of the clerical assistant scale (around £500 p.a.). The Group thought that there might be seven or so such grades. For example, there might be one grade which included the Senior Scientific Officer, Basic Grade Engineer or Architect, Tech 1 Senior Draughtsman and H.E.O. grades and grades in other classes with comparable pay scales and a grade which included the Senior Principal Scientific Officer, Superintending Grade Architect or Engineer, Assistant Secretary, Principal Executive Officer and comparable grades in other classes. 'A number of pay grades would be required to provide a ladder in which each rung corresponds to a level of responsibility and job content. It therefore follows that a system is required which would permit across the service comparison and ranking of the content of jobs: i.e. a system in which a scientific job in a research establishment, a high-level casework job in an administrative division, an engineering job and a line management job in an executive/clerical establishment can all be analysed and ranked in the same terms. This system can be provided by job-evaluation techniques.'[36] The Fulton Committee accepted these proposals and went on to embody them in its own recommendations. It added a number of other recommendations in the personnel field. Its report said that the Treasury had lost the confidence of civil servants as the centre of Civil Service management. Central management required more expertise and professionalism than the Treasury could muster and it should not be carried out by officers whose main experience had been in government finance and expenditure control. Central management required a separate institution (a Civil Service Department) 'in a position to fight, and to be seen fighting, the Treasury on behalf of the Service'.[37] The Committee recommended the adoption of a unified structure for the Service by the use of job evaluation, but added the idea that the job-evaluation system should 'define and measure the "end result" required of each post'.[38]

The Committee thought that the professionalism required of administrators and executives called for new principles to be applied to their selection, training and deployment. In particular, it thought that they should specialize in their early years in one of the various areas of administration. This specialization should be organized on the basis of the subject-matter of their work rather than on the basis of the particular department in which the work was done. The Committee could immediately identify two subject-matter categories. The first was economic and financial; the second social. Each administrator should specialize for his early years in the Service in one or other of these major categories of work (or in any other category that later investigation proved necessary). They should have qualifications appropriate to their specialization. Some would have sub-specialisms – in the economics and finance category, for example, there might be officers who specialized in the financial appraisal and control of scientific and technological projects. Some social administrators might specialize in personnel or O. & M. work. These categories of specialization would run across departments, so that social administrators might move from one department to another during their careers, assigned to progressively higher levels of personnel, O. & M. or 'social administration' work. There would continue to be professional specialists in accounting, scientific research, economics, technical administration and so on.

The Committee recommended the introduction of a training grade for the graduate entry and for those of the non-graduates who had shown the highest ability: on leaving this grade these trainees should go straight to the level justified by their performance, without regard to the claims of seniority. While in the training grade they should be given a responsible job. By a majority of eight members to four (who included the two Permanent Secretaries) the Committee expressed its controversial 'preference for relevance'. This meant that the relevance of the subject-matter of their university or other pre-Service studies should be an important qualification for the appointment of new entrants. 'Today, when the tasks of government have changed, the Service should seek to recruit those equipped for the new tasks. First degree courses based on the study of modern subjects especially attract young people with a positive and practical interest in contemporary problems, political, social, economic, scientific and technological. These problems will yield their solutions only to the most concentrated assaults of minds equipped through rigorous and sustained intellectual discipline with the necessary apparatus of relevant ideas, knowledge, methods and techniques. We therefore wish the Civil Service to attract its full share of young people motivated in this way . . .'[39]

The Committee's recommendations in the personnel field can be criticized on a number of counts.

First, it examined the detail, but not the context, of personnel work in the Service. It did not challenge the basic philosophy, the orientation, of establishments work. In fact, in recommending the creation of the Civil Service Department concerned not only with pay and conditions, recruitment, training and promotion, but also with complementing and control of manpower and with the provision of efficiency and data-processing services it endorsed the conventions of establishments work. A number of Fulton's other recommendations and developments since Fulton – management by objectives, delegation to accountable managers, the application of social sciences – challenge the conventions, the staffing and the style of establishments divisions.

Secondly, the Committee's idea of cross-departmental career specialization by subject category would be vastly difficult to apply. It would be extremely difficult to categorize either jobs or men into such categories as 'economic and financial' or 'social'. In many departments a large number of upper-level jobs fall into both categories (monitoring the expenditure on social programmes; examining the social effects of economic programmes). Clearly, there will be those who by training and interest should spend their careers in such specialisms as programme planning, accounting, consultancy, training and research and it should be open to them to move from one department to another. Existing procedures for internal recruitment and transfer could well be adapted to deal with these cases. For the bulk of administrators and specialists, however, the only comprehensible career field for the greater part of their service is the department or the group of small departments. If the greater professionalism of departmental management is the aim then the confinement of managers to economic or social or other streams (assuming that they could be defined) would make very little contribution to it. The aim is more likely to be achieved by a system in which future top managers are given managerial reponsibilities (in jobs in which they are held accountable for the use they make of money and manpower) as early as possible in their careers; in which they spend long enough in a division to understand its procedures of management and policy formulation; in which they progress through related postings into the top management cadre of the department passing on the way into a Civil Service-wide promotion field. Such a system requires a highly developed, and expensive, information system which can enable departmental personnel managers to describe the skills and characteristics of individuals, to forecast future jobs, to plan careers, to match skills to job requirements, to determine training needs and to appraise the progress of the individual. The construction of such a system and its information base is a task which will take many years.

Thirdly, the Committee confused job evaluation for the purpose of creating a pay structure with the appraisal and review of the performance of individuals. We have seen that a job-evaluation system is not concerned with 'end results' but with establishing the relative worth of one job compared with another. Measuring end results is a feature of management by objectives or similar systems of accountability reporting: it focuses upon the performance of the manager. We shall see below that Fulton's confusion in this matter is persisting.

Since the Fulton Report, there have been some suggestions that the construction of a unified grading system based on job evaluation would conflict with existing procedures for determining salaries. The principle underlying these procedures is 'fair comparison' with outside salaries as laid down by the Priestley Commission of 1955. It is maintained by the Pay Research Unit, which undertakes a programme of comparisons of the pay of certain classes or posts with analogous posts outside the Service. The Fulton Committee recommended that the principle of fair comparison should be retained, and its Consultancy Group even said that classless service might facilitate rather than complicate the work of the Pay Research Unit.[40] The Prices and Incomes Board, in a study of job evaluation, found some conflict between unified grading structure and fair comparison, concluding that because of the size and diversity of the Civil Service, there was likely to be a 'number of jobs whose pay, because of external market conditions, will not fit into the uniform grade structure developed from job evaluation results'.[41] However, all large organizations with systematic grading systems occasionally have the problem of grading staff for whom market forces have inflated the going salary rate. The Civil Service had this problem under the existing arrangements: the Higher Executive Officer grade, for example, represents a fair pay rate for the manager of a clerical branch but may not for a systems analyst in a computer branch; in recent years the main grade of the Works Group has been a fair pay level for a junior engineer but not for a junior architect. We have seen that job evaluation systems can be arranged to cope with external market pressures, which are usually temporary anyway. Numerous large international companies apply a unified grading structure to a staff as diverse as that of the Civil Service without suffering unduly from the effects of external market conditions.

Implementation policy for a unified grading structure was laid to a Joint Committee of the National Whitley Council, which decided to tackle the problem in a series of steps.[42] First, it proposed to create a unified grading structure to include all posts at and above the level of Under Secretary (about 650 staff, of which 400 were in the Administrative Class). Concurrently, it would make a series of moves towards the unification of classes at lower levels by merging the larger classes – for example Executive and Administrative (merged on 1 January 1971); the Works Group and its subordinate technical classes; the Scientific Officer Class and its supporting experimental classes – into larger interim structures within each of which class barriers would be removed to give a continuous series of grades from bottom to top. It would then go on to merge departmental classes into these interim structures. It would establish procedures to facilitate the free movement of individuals between the new groupings. The next steps would be to expand the unified top structure to include all staff at the level of the Assistant Secretary (5,700 staff in all) and then at the level of the Principal (11,000). Preliminary studies of the feasibility of merging the classes at these two lower levels 'suggest that a sound system of job evaluation can be devised for comparing jobs of different kinds at these levels ... on the evidence so far there are grounds for believing that an advance below the level of Under Secretary towards the unified grading structure recommended by Fulton is technically feasible'.[43] The National Whitley Council hoped that a decision could be taken on the unification at Assistant Secretary level early in 1971 and, if such a merger is feasible, that a decision could be taken on the Principal level early in 1972.

However, it must be counted unlikely that Fulton's single unified grading structure will ever be achieved. The cost of a Service-wide job-evaluation programme (easily postponed in an economy drive) and the special interests of a number of powerful pressure groups will probably combine to insure that unification will never reach very far down into the structure as a whole. The concern of the members of the former Administrative Class will be to restrict horizontal unification to the level of the Under Secretary and above (as the Treasury originally proposed) where they predominate. If specialists are not considered for policy or administrative jobs before they have reached a high level in their own specialist group they are unlikely to be able to obtain wide enough experience to fit themselves for those jobs. The prophecy that specialists are too 'narrow' for general management will become self-justifying. Similarly, as unification creeps down the scale the Executive Class will begin to feel the competition from the specialist classes; for example, professional accountants might start to want to get into the executive grade jobs in Finance Divisions, Computer Divisions and O. & M. branches. Even the recent merger of the Administrative and Executive Classes, so strongly advocated by the executives, may lose some of its attraction for them when administrators secure some of the senior line-management jobs which had always been the prizes of the Executive Class. The rigid pecking order of the old arrangements protected as many people as it frustrated. In addition, the staff associations, each with a bureaucracy of its own, face abolition if the classless structure is carried very far. They may not be all that sorry to lose their few top-level members to a unified higher Civil Service, but if unification reaches down into the big battalions of the Society of Civil Servants, the Institute of Professional Civil Servants, the Inland Revenue Staff Federation and the Customs and Excise Group of Associations they face merger or abolition. In the face of such an alliance of interests the chances of survival of Fulton's scheme are fairly slight.

The result in the long run is likely to be a merged top structure, at Under Secretary level and above, supported by a number of vertical groups (such as the 'Administration Group' and 'The General Professional Category'). In this situation, Fulton's objective of free movement could be approached only by widespread cross-posting between the groups and the most careful attention to staff appraisal, career management, training and the assessment of potential by the personnel function.

THE DEVELOPMENT OF PERSONNEL MANAGEMENT IN THE CIVIL SERVICE

However far office automation proceeds in the future, the Civil Service (or the public bodies that replace parts of it) will continue to be a very large employer of manpower. In addition, it is increasingly a very large employer of highly skilled and specialized staff. The manpower history of the Civil Service shows the progressive accretion of specialist cadres on to the original categories of administrators, managers of clerical operations and clerks. If the developments foreshadowed in earlier chapters of this book take place, then we may expect the planning, accounting and personnel cadres to grow to the size of many of today's Treasury classes. The need to manage large construction, aerospace and data-processing projects in the context of greater delegation of authority over money and manpower is also likely to lead to the creation of a technical project-management cadre of engineer–scientist–executive/accountants.

The need to develop these new skills will place new demands upon the personnel function and few establishments divisions are constituted, staffed or funded to cope with them. The Civil Service can no longer run its personnel management on the cheap: this function will have to be far larger and more expensive than in the past (but should produce equivalent benefits – for instance in the reduction of labour turnover, in the more effective use of talent). We can exemplify the weight of new demands upon the personnel function by considering the areas in which most rapid change is taking place in the outside world: job evaluation, manpower planning and the application of the behavioural sciences.

Even if the unification of the classes never goes as far as Fulton envisaged, the work which has already been started: the unification of the classes down to Assistant Secretary level, and the combination of hundreds of small classes into a few large ones, will engage all the effort that the Civil Service Department can put to the task for some years. When this task is completed, departments will have to maintain the job-evaluated structures and employ trained job analysts who can describe, analyse and evaluate new and changing jobs, review gradings and defend the structure from erosion by 'grade drift'. These analysts will replace the existing staff inspectors, but there will have to be more of them and some of them will have to be of senior rank.

There will have to be a substantial investment in manpower planning. While the Civil Service Department will need to plan the development and career progression of members of senior grades, departments will require forecasts and models of their own populations. In addition, the personnel function will require to prepare succession plans and career development paths for individuals, identify potential managers and arrange training, promotion and transfer patterns. This new activity requires far better information than can be provided by the present personnel records, which consist of innumerable fragmented, inaccurate, overlapping, single-purpose and manually prepared documents. In particular, it requires information about the jobs a man has done, his performance in those jobs and the potential he shows for promotion devised from a standard form of appraisal interview.

The most exciting new area of development for the personnel function lies in the application of the more practical concepts of the behavioural sciences. Fulton's Consultancy Group nodded in the direction of job enrichment and enlargement, the 'unfreezing' of bureaucratic structures, a more participative management style and so on, but the Committee did not refer to these questions. It hardly acknowledged the existence of the junior civil servant, let alone considered what might be done to make his job more interesting and meaningful, or what might be done to give him a sense of accomplishment, or involvement, or individuality.

As we have seen from earlier chapters, the Civil Service is always likely to be highly 'bureaucratic', since this is the most efficient form of organization yet evolved for handling most of the routine tasks of public administration. However, the bureaucratic style often carries with it severe human penalties and it is incumbent upon the personnel function to find ways of alleviating those bureaucratic tendencies which stifle human needs and aspirations. The behavioural sciences, however fad-ridden and specious some of their propositions may be, offer some hope of reconciling the needs of the human being and those of the organization. Much Civil Service activity rests, and will continue to rest, on a foundation of clerical drudgery, but this does not mean that clerical civil servants have to be treated as drudges. The Fulton and other committees, commissions, working parties and study groups have never done much for the junior clerical or technical civil servant: the man or woman at the bottom of the pile, often burrowing away at a job of great tedium in drab working conditions. In addition, the attitudes of potential recruits are changing. Young clerical and executive officers will no longer obediently troop from their grammar or comprehensive schools bearing their General Certificates of Education into boring routine jobs, grateful for the security and ultimate promise of steady advancement. Even less will arts graduates, engineers and sociologists be willing to sit quietly and wait their turn at the bottom of a hierarchy which is held together by values and attitudes they have learned to question, if not reject. A behavioural science group in every department's personnel function should be concerned to understand and communicate with the staff in their care, to explore their attitudes and their social and working needs, to design new and more demanding patterns of working, to create an environment of openness and concern and to liberate under-used talent. This is a territory which has never yet been explored, or even acknowledged to exist, by establishments divisions.

The result of Whitleyism has been the construction of a model system of orderly and peaceful collective bargaining. However, recent developments may subject this system to increasing strain, perhaps to the point where a fundamental review may again be necessary. First, the rise of aggressive white-collar trade unionism in the outside world cannot go unrecognized by those unions which represent the lower-paid civil servants, particularly since governments like to use their power as employers to set an example in the freezing or restraint of wage demands. Several unions in recent years have announced the adoption of a strike policy and the annual conference of others have declared their intention to take militant action if necessary. Union officials will increasingly find themselves caught between the orderly deliberations of the Whitley machinery and the frustration of their members. Secondly, the Industrial Relations Bill of late 1970, which was to apply to the Civil Service as to business organizations, introduced a system of legal provisions which could well disturb the informal harmony of Whitleyism. A letter of November 1970 from Mr Leslie Williams (Secretary General of the National Whitley Council Staff Side) to Sir William Armstrong pointed out that the Staff side had never broken the agreements into which they had entered and saw no justification for the imposition of a legal framework. However governments, as employers of civil servants, had been guilty of breaking agreements (during periods of pay restraint in 1961 and 1968, for example). If legally binding agreements were introduced by the proposed Act then the Staff side would 'not hesitate to sue the government as employer for any breach of an agreement even though this would inevitably harm the normal working relationship which has been developed over many years between the Official and Staff sides'.[44] Mr Williams also went on to point out that the Bill allowed any 'substantial' group of employees to have a claim examined by the Commission of Industrial Relations and that this might lead disgruntled groups to upset the bargaining structure. Thirdly, the Whitley system of central negotiation on major personnel issues with the Civil Service Department is likely to be affected by the adoption of accountable management, particularly in its extreme form of 'hiving off'. If there is greater devolution of authority to major units of government and greater delegation to accountable managers, then, as we have seen in Chapter 6, this must mean greater control by individual managers over the organization and grading of their staffs. Fourthly, the creation of the Civil Service Department, ostensibly to 'fight the Treasury on behalf of the Service' in fact put an intermediary between the union negotiators and the authority for expenditure. Previously, dealings been directly with the Chancellor, who ultimately made decisions on pay. Though the Civil Service Department reports to the Prime Minister its operations are run by a fairly junior Minister and if in the future he and his officials are outgunned by more powerful Ministers then the bargaining position of Civil Service Staff could be considerably weakened.

There is no doubt that under the leadership of Sir William Armstrong and under the eye of the Staff side of the National Whitley Council the Civil Service Department has put much effort into the improvement of personnel management in the Civil Service. Gradually, this effort is being felt in the larger departments: the Department of Health and Social Security now has a Principal Establishments Officer and Director of Personnel; the Department of the Environment has a personnel management branch within its Establishments Division. In the absence of a unified structure at middle and junior management levels new arrangements have been made for 'lateral movement', that is, the permanent or temporary posting of a member of one career category into a post designated as belonging to another category as a means of broadening experience and providing new career opportunities (such as the movement of a scientist into an administrative branch) and 'opportunity posting', that is the identification of posts for which members of more than one group are automatically considered. The Staff side of the National Whitley Council sees these arrangements as an important further step towards 'an open road to the top'.[45]

New arrangements have been developed for career management ('to provide for more specialization for the administrator and less for the specialist'[46]): the Civil Service Department is working towards a system of planned postings to jobs in the Administration Group which are related by subject-matter and functional skills, and for the specialist classes development panels are being set up so that those specialists who show particular promise will be given the experience and training in administrative work to enable them to compete for the top posts in the Service.[47]

The Civil Service has also acted on the Fulton recommendation that appraisal interviews should concentrate more on a man's performance and less on his personal characteristics by introducing the job appraisal review system (JAR) for all staff up to Assistant Secretary level.[48] The JAR system involves an annual interview between the man and a line manager (not the man's boss) at which the man's job and his performance are discussed and at which he has an opportunity to discuss his future and his need for training and experience. Though an improvement on the previous arrangement, JAR appears to confuse performance appraisal with man appraisal. Experience in industry has shown that these two activities are best kept separate: that target-setting and performance review (as in management by objectives) should not be confused with personal career counselling. The first activity is obviously a matter for a man and his line superior, the second may well best be handled by a personnel officer who has all the information on job and training opportunities in the department. Unfortunately, a feature of the JAR system appears to be that the interviewers 'praise jobs well done, mention failures frankly' and 'agrees goals for the future'.[49]

In the field of manpower planning, there is now an interdepartmental steering group concerned with the application of statistical models to the manpower effects of policy decisions and with research into labour-demand forecasting techniques.[50] The construction of a data base for manpower planning has begun with the design by the Civil Service Department of a computerized Central Management Staff Record (CMSR)[51]: a file of the personal history, experience and qualifications of 6,500 senior staff and an information-retrieval programme designed to assist establishments divisions in filling vacancies, manpower planning and statistical analysis. CMSR became operational in June 1970 and is being extended to cover staff at the new Senior Principal and Principal levels. Work is also going on to create the much larger PRISM (Personnel Record Information System for Management) system which will cover the entire non-industrial Civil Service by 1974–5 and will be held on ten departmental computers linked to a central computer in the Civil Service Department.

The Civil Service Department now has a small Behavioural Sciences Unit: its published report on morale and attitudes among the 1,500 clerks at the office of the Inspector of Taxes, Centre 1, East Kilbride[52] ('an efficient organization with a hard working and tolerably happy staff') illustrated the conflicting pressures on junior management, the isolation of trainers from the actual need for training, the impact of computers upon the older clerks and the effects of the size of working groups. Further assignments include studies of the reasons for high staff turnover in the Estate Duty Office of the Inland Revenue; of the reactions of staff to working in an experimental open office and the evaluation of management by objectives schemes. Work has been started in the field of job enrichment as a means of reducing the wastage of Executive Officers and equivalent grades in their early years of service.[53]

The personnel function in the Civil Service will, for the rest of this decade and beyond, be at the centre of enormous pressures for change: new tasks, new techniques, new demands will all focus on establishments divisions. As we have seen from Chapter 3, professional personnel management does not sit well with the functions of management services and efficiency audit. Establishments officers may be hard pressed in future simultaneously to play the roles of the demon king of manpower control and the fairy queen of personnel management.

Finally, though much good work has been done in a very short time by the Civil Service Department in taking up many techniques of modern personnel management some fundamental questions have yet to be answered. Will the system allow technically trained managers to reach top administrative positions? What is the role of the line manager in personnel management? How much authority can be delegated to him in the manpower field?

CONCLUSION

Much of the discussion on management in the Civil Service tends to wander off into such areas as the characteristics of education and attitude of the former Administrative Class and the value of the techniques of business management in public administration.

The first is an area of controversy which will inevitably diminish in time as the effects of the reforms initiated by the Fulton Committee are gradually felt at the higher levels of the Service; the second derives from a misunderstanding of the nature of public administration and perhaps of business as well. Though Chapters 3 to 8 of this book each begin with a description of the present state of technical development in industrial management it should soon be obvious to the reader that the Civil Service environment is so different that industrial techniques of organization, planning, control, accountability, efficiency audit and personnel management will have to undergo substantial adaptation before they can serve management in government. At present, we do not know whether any of these techniques or their derivatives will prove to be of lasting value in departments or whether experience will show that the apparent promise of some of them is likely to be unattainable. In order to evaluate their prospective benefits and their effects and implications it is important that programmes of management research are supported by departments.

The assumption is freely made in industry and in political circles that the Civil Service must be inefficient, overstaffed, sluggish. Anyone who has worked in both industry and the Civil Service will know how grossly untrue this stereotype is. The Civil Service handles its many production processes with exemplary efficiency and copes with unforeseeable change as effectively as any industry has done. It has pioneered a number of management practices which are still not general outside the largest industrial firms: O. & M. reviews, staff inspection, manpower control systems, staff appraisal, long-term expenditure planning. The Civil Service Department, at least under its present management, represents a locus and authority for development and change of a kind possessed by few industrial giants. The Civil Service has management resources to a depth and of a calibre that are rarely equalled in industry. Nevertheless, in two areas at least the Civil Service has tended to lag in the development of management practice and substantial investment is now required to make up for lost time.

The most important area where this investment is needed is in personnel management. We have seen that the establishments function is not well suited to provide departments with the benefits of modern procedures of personnel management and is not constituted or funded to act as a centre of excellence in the applied social sciences. This is an area where, contrary to appearances, increased expenditure would represent a very worthwhile investment rather than an addition to unremunerative overheads.

The second area which requires investment and research is that of management information. We have seen that departments have extremely complex information needs: they have to monitor their spend against budget, their internal efficiency and their external effectiveness in activities where outputs, and even some inputs, are frequently intangible and unmeasurable. The risk is that several single-purpose management information systems will be allowed to develop in isolation at an enormous cost in duplicated and wasted effort. On the other hand, all experience so far shows that no complex institution can fully integrate all its information requirements into the 'supersystem', the 'Total Management Information System' which nowadays is the Holy Grail of so many computer experts and information analysts in industry.[1] The suggestions in this book for an advance towards the rationalization of the information flows in departments via the integration of planning and control and management by objectives are no more than possible lines of approach to this enormous problem.

The management of government is a field of rapidly changing technology. In the three years since this book was started, there have been many important advances in it, partly as a result of political initiatives and partly as a result of the efforts of the Civil Service Department. By the time it is published more will have taken place. Those who are concerned about the introduction of the best in management procedures into Britain's central administration are entitled to show guarded optimism.

REFERENCES

1: The Managers and Their Environment

1. Committee on the Civil Service, Report, June 1968, Cmnd. 3638, Vol. II, para. 303.
2. ibid., para. 305.
3. ibid., para. 305.
4. *Report on the Organization of the Permanent Civil Service* (Northcote–Trevelyan Report). Reprinted in Report of the Committee on the Civil Service, Vol. I, Appendix B.
5. Civil Service National Whitley Council, *Report of the Joint Committee on the Organization of the Civil Service*, 1920.
6. Committee on the Civil Service, Vol. II, para. 98.
7. ibid., Vol. V(1), Memorandum No. 15, para. 3.
8. ibid., Vol. I, Appendix D, para. 7.
9. Civil Service Commission, *Careers for Graduates*, 1969, p. 8.
10. Sisson, C. H., *The Spirit of British Administration*, Faber & Faber, 1959, p. 13.
11. Committee on the Civil Service, Vol. I, para. 18.
12. Jenkins, Roy, 'The Reality of Political Power', *Sunday Times*, 17 January 1971.
13. Sisson, op. cit., p. 8.
14. Bray, Jeremy, *Decision in Government*, Gollancz, 1970, p. 66.
15. Fry, G. R., *Statesmen in Disguise*, Macmillan, 1969.
16. Bray, op. cit., p. 66.
17. Mackenzie, W. J. M., and Grove, J. W., *Central Administration in Britain*, Longmans, Green, 1957, p. 72.
18. Brown, R. G. S., *The Administrative Process in Britain*, Methuen, 1970, p. 261.
19. Dunsire, A., ed.; *The Making of an Administrator*, Manchester University Press, 1956, p. 9.
20. Sisson, op. cit., p. 136.
21. Dunsire, op. cit., p. 91.
22. Bridges, Sir Edward, *Portrait of a Profession*, Cambridge University Press, 1950, p. 25.

23. Committee on the Civil Service, Vol. II, para. 73.
24. Bridges, op. cit., p. 22.
25. Dunsire, op. cit., p. 119.
26. Sisson, op. cit., pp. 37 and 28.
27. Dunsire, op. cit., p. xii.
28. Mackenzie and Grove, op. cit., p. 207.
29. Fry, op. cit., p. 7.
30. Barnett, Malcolm Joel, *The Politics of Legislation*, Weidenfeld & Nicolson, 1969, p. 51.
31. *Financial Times*, 15 May 1971.
32. Levin, Bernard, 'The Unthinkable Thoughts of Herman Kahn', *The Times*, 29 December 1970.

2: Fulton: The Establishment, the System and the Amateur

1. Mallalieu, J. P. W., *Passed to You Please*, Introduction by H. J. Laski, Gollancz, 1942.
2. ibid., p. 7.
3. ibid., p. 8.
4. ibid., pp. 10–11.
5. ibid., p. 82.
6. ibid., p. 152.
7. Thomas, Hugh, ed., *The Establishment*, Anthony Blond, 1959.
8. ibid., p. 83 ff.
9. Granick, David, *The European Executive*, Weidenfeld & Nicolson, 1962, p. 242.
10. ibid., p. 243.
11. Chapman, Brian, *British Government Observed*, Allen & Unwin, 1963, p. 31.
12. *Whitehall and Beyond*, B.B.C. Publications, 1964.
13. ibid., p. 52.
14. *The Administrators*, Fabian Tract No. 335, Fabian Society, 1964.
15. Foot, Paul, *The Politics of Harold Wilson*, Penguin Books, 1968, p. 149.
16. Estimates Committee, Sixth Report, *Recruitment to the Civil Service*, August 1965.
17. Nicholson, Max, *The System*, Hodder & Stoughton, 1967.

18. ibid., p. 54.
19. ibid., p. 476.
20. Caves, Richard E., and Associates, *Britain's Economic Prospects*, Allen & Unwin, 1968.
21. ibid., p. 303.
22. Committee on the Civil Service, Vol. 5, Memorandum No. 1, May 1966.
23. ibid., Vol. 5, Memorandum No. 15, September 1966.
24. ibid., Vol. 5, Memoranda Nos. 36–9.
25. Seers, D., ibid., Vol. 5, Memorandum No. 145.
26. Group of Members of the Economic Planning Staff, O.D.M., ibid., Vol. 5, Memorandum No. 124.
27. Munby, D. L., ibid., Vol. 5, Memorandum No. 136.
28. ibid., Vol. 5, Memoranda Nos. 47, 48.
29. ibid., Vol. 5, Memorandum No. 80.
30. ibid., Vol. 5, Memorandum No. 97.
31. ibid., Vol. 2, *Report of a Management Consultancy Group*, 1968, p. 101.
32. Committee on the Civil Service, Vol. 1, Report, Cmnd. 3638, H.M.S.O., 1968.
33. ibid., para. 15.
34. ibid., para. 25.
35. *New Statesman*, 28 June 1968.
36. *Daily Telegraph*, 27 June 1968.
37. *Guardian*, 27 June 1968.
38. *Evening Standard*, 26 June 1968.
39. *Sunday Times*, 29 August 1968.
40. Dunnett, Sir James, *The Fulton Report*, Institute of Public Administration, 1969, p. 31.
41. Robson, William A., 'The Fulton Report', *Political Quarterly*, Vol. 39, No. 4, 1968, p. 400.
42. Helsby ,Lord, 'The Fulton Report', *Listener*, 18 July 1968, p. 66.
43. Hobsbawm, Eric, 'The Fulton Report – a Further View', *Listener*, 18 July 1968, p. 67.
44. Bishop, F. A., 'Fulton – The Cart Before the Horse', *Spectator*, 28 June 1968, p. 883.
45. Redcliffe-Maud, Lord, *Daily Telegraph*, 27 June 1968.

46. Sendall, Wilfred, *Daily Express*, 1 July 1968.
47. House of Lords Debates, 24 July 1968, Vol. 295, No. 122, Cols. 1049–1194.
48. House of Commons Debates, 21 November 1968, Vol. 773, No. 17, Cols. 1542–1681.
49. Committee on the Civil Service, Vol. 3 (1), *Social Survey of the Civil Service*.
50. ibid., p. 400.
51. Dean, Malcolm, 'Whitehall Elite Holds Its Own', *Guardian*, 25 September 1969.
52. Report of a Committee of Enquiry, *The Method II System of Selection*, Cmnd. 4156, September 1969.
53. Evans, Richard, '"No Oxbridge Bias" in Top Grade Appointments', *Financial Times*, 25 September 1969.
54. Balogh, Thomas, *Labour and Inflation*, Tract 403, Fabian Society, October 1970, p. 58.
55. Committee on the Civil Service, Vol. 1, para. 7.
56. 'Civil Service Fears over Tory Policy', *Financial Times*, 17 July 1970.

3: Organization

1. Weber, Max, *The Theory of Social and Economic Organization*, Free Press, Glencoe, Ill., 1947.
2. Weber, op. cit., p. 337.
3. Weber, op. cit., p. 337
4. Weber, op. cit., pp. 329–36.
5. Blau, Peter, and Scott, W. Richard, *Formal Organizations*, Routledge & Kegan Paul, 1963, pp. 33–6.
6. Fayol, Henri. *General and Industrial Management*, Pitman, 1949.
7. Taylor, F. W., *Principles and Methods of Scientific Management*, Harper, New York, 1911.
8. Graicunas, V. A., *Relationships in Organization*, Papers on the Science of Administration, Institute of Public Administration, Columbia University, New York, 1937.
9. Mooney, J. D., and Reiley, A. C., *The Principles of Organization*, Harper, New York, 1939.
10. Robinson, Webster, *Fundamentals of Business Organization*, McGraw-Hill, New York, 1925.

11. Gulick, L., and Urwick, L. F., eds., *Papers on the Science of Administration*, Institute of Public Administration, Columbia University, New York, 1937.

12. Urwick, L. F., *Elements of Administration*, Pitman, 1947.

13. Urwick, op. cit., p. 89.

14. Simon, H. A., *Administrative Behaviour*. Macmillan, New York, 1945, p. 44.

15. Fayol, op. cit., p. 37.

16. Stephenson, T. E., 'The Longevity of Classical Theory', *Management International Review*, No. 6, 1968, p. 77.

17. Roethlisberger, F. J., and Dickson, W. J., *Management and the Worker*, Harvard University Press, Cambridge, Mass., 1939.

18. Mayo, Elton, *The Human Problems of an Industrial Civilization*, Routledge & Kegan Paul, 1949.

19. Whyte, W. F., *Human Relations in the Restaurant Industry*, McGraw-Hill, New York, 1948.

20. Walker, C. R., and Guest, R. H., *The Man on the Assembly Line*, Harvard University Press, Cambridge, Mass., 1952.

21. Seashore, S. E., *Group Cohesiveness in the Industrial Work Group*, Michigan University Press, 1954.

22. Argyris, Chris, *Personality and Organization*, Harper & Row, New York, 1957.

23. Likert, Rensis, *New Patterns of Management*, McGraw-Hill, New York, 1961.

24. Von Bertalanffy, L., 'The Theory of Open Systems in Physics and Biology', *Science*, Vol. III, 1950, pp. 23–9.

25. Simon, op. cit.

26. March, J. G., and Simon, H. A., *Organisations*, Wiley, New York, 1958.

27. Trist, E. L., and Bamforth, K. W., 'Some Social and Psychological Consequences of the Long Wall Method of Coal Getting', *Human Relations*, 1951, Vol. 14, pp. 1–38.

28. Rice, A. K., *Productivity and Social Organization*, Tavistock Publications, 1958.

29. Rice, A. K., *The Enterprise and Its Environment*, Tavistock Publications, 1963.

30. Emery, F. E., and Trist, E. G., 'Socio-Technical Systems',

reprinted in Emery, F. E., ed., *Systems Thinking*, Penguin Books, 1969.

31. Katz, D., and Kahn, R. L., *Social Psychology of Organizations*, Wiley, New York, 1966.

32. Burns, Tom, *Management in the Electronics Industry*, Social Science Research Centre, University of Edinburgh, 1958.

33. Burns, Tom, and Stalker, G. M. *The Management of Innovation*, Tavistock Publications, 1961.

34. Woodward, Joan, *Industrial Organization: Theory and Practice*, Oxford University Press, 1965.

35. Hickson, D., Pugh, D., Pheysey, D., 'Organization – Is Technology the Key?', *Personnel Management*, February 1970.

36. Katz and Kahn, op. cit.

37. Lawrence, P. R., and Lorsch, Jay W., *Organization and Environment*, Harvard, 1967.

38. Morse, John J., and Lorsch, Jay W., 'Beyond Theory Y', *Harvard Business Review*, May–June 1970.

39. Middleton, C. J., 'How to Set Up a Project Organization', *Harvard Business Review*, March–April 1967.

40. Schon, Donald, 'Evolution of the Business Firm', Third Reith Lecture, *Listener*, 3 December 1970.

41. Argyris, Chris, 'Today's Problems with Tomorrow's Organizations', *Journal of Management Studies*, February 1967.

42. ibid., p. 49.

43. Clarke, Sir Richard, 'The Shape of the New MinTech', *Financial Times*, 17 November 1969.

44. Committee on the Civil Service, Report, Vol. 2, Appendix IV, p. 107.

45. ibid., p. 108.

46. ibid., para. 190.

47. ibid., para. 331.

48. op. cit., Vol. 1, para. 165.

49. ibid., para. 185.

50 ibid., para. 150.

51. op. cit., Vol. 2, paras. 360–73.

52. See Blau, D. M., and Scott, W. R., *Formal Organizations*, Routledge, 1963. Etzioni, A., *A Comparative Study of Complex Organizations*, Free Press, Glencoe, Ill., 1961.

53. Rhenman, Eric, *Industrial Democracy and Industrial Management*, Tavistock Publications, 1968, p. 9.
54. Merton, Robert, 'Bureaucratic Structure and Personality', *Social Forces*, XVIII (1940), pp. 560–68.
55. Thompson, Victor A., in *The Study of Policy Formation*, ed. R. A. Baver and K. J. Green, Collier-Macmillan, 1968, p. 129.
56. Crozier, Michel, *The Bureaucratic Phenomenon*, Tavistock Publications, 1964, p. 194.
57. ibid., p. 198.
58. Perrow, Charles, *Organizational Analysis*, Tavistock Publications, 1970, p. 60.
59. *Computers in Central Government Ten Years Ahead*, Civil Service Department, 1971, p. 70.
60. ibid., p. 33.
61. ibid., p. 32.
62. ibid., p. 78.
63. ibid., p. 81.
64. Mumford, Enid, and Banks, Olive, *The Computer and the Clerk*, Routledge & Kegan Paul, 1967, p. 174.
65. Clarke, Sir Richard, *New Trends in Government*, H.M.S.O., 1971, p. 10.
66. Jay, Peter, 'The Tools of the Treasury', *The Times*, 19 February 1971.
67. Clarke, op. cit., p. 66.
68. Howell, David, *A New Style of Government*, Conservative Political Centre, 1970, p. 13.
69. Clarke, op. cit., p. 6.
70. Garrett, John, and Walker, S. D., 'Management Review – A Case Study from the Prison Department of the Home Office', *O. & M. Bulletin*, August 1970, p. 132.
71. *Hansard*, 15 July 1969, cols. 338–90.
72. 'Line Managers in the Ministry of Agriculture', *Financial Times*, 22 May 1970.
73. Speigelberg, Richard, 'Whitehall Tries the Fulton Line', *The Times*, 4 January 1971.
74. *Government Organization for Defence Procurement and Civil Aerospace*, Cmnd. 4641, H.M.S.O., April 1971.
75. ibid., p. 14.

76. 'Managing Mr Carr's Job Shops', *Financial Times*, 15 December 1971.
77. *The Re-organization of Central Government*, Cmnd. 4506, H.M.S.O., October, 1970.
78. Klein, Rudolf, 'Mismanaging the NHS', *Management Today*, December 1971, p. 73.

4: Planning

1. Ansoff, H. Igor, *Corporate Strategy*, McGraw-Hill, 1965, Penguin Books, 1971.
2. *Model Forecast*, Arthur D. Little Inc., Industrial Bulletin No. 478, Cambridge, Mass., November 1969.
3. Von Allmen, Erwin, 'Setting Up Corporate Planning', *Long Range Planning*, September 1969, p. 3.
4. Select Committee on Estimates, Sixth Report, Session 1957–8, *Treasury Control of Expenditure*, House of Commons Paper 254, July 1958.
5. ibid., para. 18.
6. ibid., para. 22.
7. ibid., para. 23.
8. ibid., para. 29.
9. *Report on the Committee on the the Control of Public Expenditure*, Cmnd. 1432, July 1961 (The Plowden Report).
10. ibid., para. 7.
11. ibid., para. 12.
12. ibid., para. 12.
13. *Public Expenditure: Planning and Control*, Cmnd. 2915, H.M.S.O., 1966.
14. Select Committee on Procedure, Session 1968–9, H.C. 410, *The Planning and Control of Public Expenditure*, Memorandum by H.M. Treasury, p. 19.
15. ibid., p. 20.
16. *Public Expenditure: A New Presentation*, Cmnd. 4017, April 1969.
17. *Public Expenditure: 1968–9 to 1973*, Cmnd. 4234, H.M.S.O., December 1969.
18. *The Task Ahead, Economic Assessment to 1972*, H.M.S.O., 1969.

19. Marquand, David, 'The Treasury Lifts Its Veil at Last', *Sunday Times*, 7 December 1969.

20. Noyes, Hugh, 'M.P.s' Apathy on Historic Debate', *The Times*, 23 January 1970.

21. Committee on the Machinery of Government, 1918, Cmnd. 9230, para. 12.

22. Garrett, John, 'Planning Government Action', *Management Decision*, Autumn 1969, p. 50.

23. Grey, Alexander, and Simon, Andrew, 'People, Structure and Civil Service Reform', *Journal of Management Studies*, October 1970, p. 302.

24. Committee on the Civil Service, Vol. II, para. 146.

25. Garrett, op. cit., p. 51.

26. *The Re-organization of Central Government*, Cmnd. 4506, October 1970.

27. Seers, D., Committee on the Civil Service, Vol. V, p. 1095, paras. 38, 39.

28. Caves, R. E., ed., *Britain's Economic Prospects*, The Brookings Institution, Allen & Unwin, 1966, pp. 386 and 444.

29. Committee on the Civil Service, Vol. I, para. 173.

30. ibid., Vol. II, para. 364.

31. Gross and Spring, *Annals of the American Academy of Political and Social Science*, May 1967, quoted by David Novick, in 'The Origin and History of Program Budgeting', *California Management Review*, Fall, 1968, p. 8.

32. Select Committee on Procedure 1968–9, Memorandum by the Ministry of Defence, p. 61.

33. *Program Review and Estimates Manual*, Treasury Board, Ottawa, 1967, p. 2.14.

34. *Planning Programming Budgeting for City, State and County Objectives*, PPB Note No. 5, State-Local Finances Project, George Washington University, Washington D.C., 1969.

35. Carlson, Jack W., *The Status and Next Steps for Planning, Programming and Budgeting, The Analysis and Evaluation of Public Expenditures: the PPB System*. Papers submitted to the Sub-Committee on Economy in Government of the Joint Economic Committee, Congress of the United States, Vol. 2, 1969, p. 618.

36. ibid., attachment 6, p. 656.
37. Atkinson, A. B., *Poverty in Britain and the Reform of Social Security*, Cambridge University Press, 1970.
38. Fisher, G. H., 'The World of Program Budgeting', *Long Range Planning*, September 1969, p. 59.
39. Williams, Professor Allan, *The Economics of Public Expenditure*, Memorandum to the Select Committee on Procedure, 1968–9, p. 141.
40. Hall, Peter, 'Roskill's Felicific Calculus', *New Society*, 19 February 1970.
41. Fisher, op. cit., p. 57.
42. Select Committee on Procedure, 1968–9, Q. 183.
43. McNamara, Robert S., *The Essence of Security*, Hodder & Stoughton, 1968, p. 67.
44. Novick, D., ed., *Program Budgeting*, Harvard University Press, 1965, p. 85.
45. McNamara, op. cit., p. 88.
46. Carlson, op. cit., p. 624.
47. Frankel, Marvin, 'Federal Health Expenditures in a Program Budget', in *Program Budgeting*, ed. D. Novick, Holt Reinhart & Winston, New York, 2nd edition 1969, p. 216.
48. Meyer, John R., 'Transportation in the Program Budget', in Novick, op. cit., p. 147.
49. Hirsch, Werner Z., 'Education in the Program Budget', in Novick, op. cit. pp. 178–9.
50. Quoted in *Hearings before the Sub-Committee on National Security and International Operations of the Committee on Government Operations of the U.S. Senate. Ninety-First Congress*, Part 5, U.S. Government Printing Office, December 1969, p. 328.
51. ibid., p. 328.
52. Schlesinger, Dr James R., in *Hearings before the Sub-Committee on National Security*, op. cit., p. 309.
53. *Los Angeles Times*, 13 September 1970.
54. Carlson, op. cit., p. 626.
55. ibid., p. 620.
56. ibid., p. 622.
57. Schlesinger, op. cit., p. 328.

58. ibid., p. 323.
59. ibid., p. 322.
60. Carlson, op. cit., p. 627.
61. Schultze, Charles L., *The Politics and Economics of Public Spending*, Brookings Institution, Washington, D.C., 1968, p. 95.
62. Carlson, op. cit., p. 632.
63. *The Royal Commission on Government Organization*, Vol. 1, Queen's Printer, Ottawa, 1962.
64. Owen, David, 'Why Service Boards Should Lose Their Power', *The Times*, 27 July 1970.
65. *Output Budgeting for the Department of Education and Science*, H.M.S.O., 1970.
66. ibid., p. 19.
67. 'What's School For?', *Economist*, 25 April 1970.
68. Burgess, Tyrell, 'Try Again DES', *New Society*, 23 April 1970.
69. Wasserman, G. J., 'Planning, Programming, Budgeting in the Police Service in England and Wales', *O. & M. Bulletin*, November 1970, p. 197.
70. ibid., p. 201.
71. Garrett, John, and Walker, S. D., 'Management Review – A Case Study from Prison Department', *O. & M. Bulletin*, September 1970, p. 133.
72. *The Re-organization of Central Government*, Cmnd. 4506, October 1970.
73. Jay, Peter, 'PESC, PAR and Politics', *The Times*, 31 January 1971.
74. Jay, Peter, 'CPRS: Magic Circle or Fifth Wheel?', *The Times*, 21 January 1972.
75. Rothschild, Lord, *A Framework for Government Research and Development*, Cmnd. 4814, November 1971.
76. See Schultze, op. cit., p. 36.
77. Quoted in Rose, K. E., *Towards Multi-Purpose Budgeting in Local Government*, Institute of Municipal Treasurers and Accountants, 1969, p. 34.
78. *Close Circuit Television in Small Secondary Schools, Cost Benefit Analysis in Local Government*, Institute of Municipal Treasurers and Accountants, 1969.

79. Novick, D., 'Long Range Planning Through Program Budgeting', *Business Horizons*, February 1969.

5: Control

1. Taylor, F. W., *Principles and Methods of Scientific Management*, Harper, New York, 1911.
2. Gilbreth, F. B. and L. M., *Applied Motion Study*, Sturgis & Walton, New York, 1917.
3. Harmer, L. C., *Clerical Work Measurement*, C. A. S. Paper No. 9, H.M.S.O., 1968.
4. Leffingwell, W. H., *Scientific Office Management*, A. W. Shaw, Chicago, 1917.
5. McKinsey, James O., *Budgetary Control*, Ronald Press, New York, 1922.
6. Argyris, Chris, *Impact of Budgets on People, in Organization, Structure and Behaviour*, ed. Joseph Litterer, John Wiley, New York, 1963.
7. Jones, R. S. 'The Control of Complex Organizations,' *Management Decision*, Autumn 1969, pp. 6–11.
8. Jones, ibid, p. 9.
9. Beer, Stafford, *Cybernetics and Management*, E.U.P., 1959.
10. Drucker, Peter F., *The Practice of Management*, Heinemann, 1955, Pan Books edition, 1968, p. 162.
11. Dearden, John, 'The Case Against ROI Control', *Harvard Business Review*, May–June 1969, p. 125.
12. Vice, Anthony, 'The Weinstock Yardsticks of Efficiency', *The Times*, 29 November 1968.
13. Lewis, Robert W., in *Planning, Managing and Measuring the Business*, Controllership Foundation, New York, 1955.
14. Garrett, John, and Walker, S. D., *Management by Objectives in the Civil Service*, C.A.S. Paper No. 10, H.M.S.O., 1969.
15. Select Committee on Estimates, Sixth Report, Session 1957–8, *Treasury Control of Expenditure*, July 1958.
16. ibid., para. 48.
17. Committee on the Civil Service, Vol. II, *Report of a Management Consultancy Group*, 1968, para. 202.

18. Mackenzie, W. J. M., and Grove, J. W., *Central Administration in Britain*, Longmans, Green, 1957, p. 218.

19. Select Committee on Procedure, Session 1964–5, House of Commons Paper 303, 1965, paras 3–4.

20. Select Committee on Procedure, Session 1968–9, House of Commons Paper 410, 1969.

21. Select Committees of the House of Commons, Cmnd. 4507, H.M.S.O., 1970.

22. Jamieson, H. R. N., and Garrett, John, *Control of Public Expenditure: The Need for New Management Systems*, Select Committee on Procedure, Session 1968–9, pp. 169–70.

23. ibid., p. 170.

24. Committee on the Civil Service, Vol. II, para. 210.

25. ibid., Vol. II, para. 217.

26. ibid., Vol. II, para. 218.

27. Nissel, Muriel, *Social Trends No. 1, 1970*, Central Statistical Office, H.M.S.O., p. 4.

28. Schultze, Charles L., *The Politics and Economics of Public Spending*, Brookings Institution, Washington, D.C., 1968, p. 9.

29. Harmer, op. cit.

30. *Office Staffing Standards*, Associated Industrial Consultants Ltd, 1969.

31. Pearce, B. C. G., 'Group Capacity Assessment', *O. & M. Bulletin*, February 1970, p. 39.

32. Bowden, W., *Technological Changes and Employment in the United States Post Office*, U.S. Department of Labor, Bureau of Labor Statistics Bulletin No. 574, U.S. Government Printing Office, 1932.

33. *Budgeting and Accounting*, A Report to the Congress by the Commission on Organization of the Executive Branch of the Government, Washington, D.C., February 1949.

34. Rose, K. E., *Towards Multi-Purpose Budgeting in Local Government*, Institute of Municipal Treasurers and Accountants, 1969, p. 51.

35. *Measuring Productivity of Federal Government Organization*, Bureau of the Budget, Washington, 1964.

36. Mackenzie and Grove, op. cit., p. 330.

37. Holbrow, J., 'Progress with Performance Measurement', *O. & M. Bulletin*, December 1971.

38. Clarke, Sir Richard, *New Trends in Government*, H.M.S.O., 1971, p. 53.

39. ibid., p. 54.

6: *Accountable Management*

1. Sloan, Alfred P., *My Years with General Motors*, Sidgwick & Jackson, 1965.

2. Drucker, Peter F., *The Concept of the Corporation*, Beacon Press, Boston, 1960, p. 32.

3. Daniel, D. Ronald, 'Re-organizing for Results' in *The Arts of Top Management*, McGraw-Hill, 1970, p. 69.

4. Committee on the Civil Service, Report, Vol. I, para. 150.

5. ibid., Vol. II, paras. 372 and 373.

6. *Royal Commission on Government Organization*, Queen's Printer, Ottawa, 1962.

7. Strick, J. C., 'Recent Developments in Canadian Financial Administration', *Public Administration*, Spring 1970, p. 79.

8. Ennis, R. W., *Accountability*, Lyon, Grant & Green, 1967, p. 15.

9. Howell, David, in Smith, Bruce L. R., and Hague, D. C., eds., *The Dilemma of Accountability in Modern Government*, Macmillan, 1971, p. 237.

10. Baker, R. J. S., 'Organization Theory and the Public Sector', *Journal of Management Studies*, February 1969, p. 21.

11. Goodnow, F. J., *Politics and Administration*, Macmillan, New York, 1900, quoted in Simon, H. A., *Administrative Behaviour*, Macmillan, New York, 1945, p. 55.

12. Committee on the Civil Service, Report, Vol. I, para. 188.

13. Jones, Colin, 'State Boards; Why There Is Plenty of Room at the Top', *Financial Times*, 27 November 1970.

14. 'I Did It in the Public Interest – Chataway', *Financial Times*, 26 November 1970.

15. Laurie, Peter, 'The Power of the Post Office', *Sunday Times Magazine*, 20 June 1971.

16. Smith and Hague, op. cit. p. 71.

17. Garrett, John, and Walker, S. D., *Management by Objectives in the Civil Service*, C.A.S. Paper No. 10, H.M.S.O., 1969, p. 3.

18. Drucker, Peter F., *The Practice of Management*, Heinemann, 1955, pp. 150–56.

19. Wikstrom, Walter S., *Managing by – and with – Objectives*, Personnel Policy Study No. 212, National Industrial Conference Board, New York, 1970, p. 27.

20. Humble, John W., *Improving Management Performance*, British Institute of Management, 1965.

21. Pascoe, B. J., 'The Introduction of MbO into the Royal Navy Supply and Transport Service of the Ministry of Defence', *O. & M. Bulletin*, August 1969, p. 139.

22. Humble, John W., 'Management by Objectives', *The Director*, November 1969, p. 275.

23. Jones, Robert, 'Case Book', *Financial Times*, 21 July 1969.

24. De Soet, Jan, 'MbO in Practice', *Financial Times*, 25 June 1969.

25. 'What is Management by Objectives?', *Economist*, 25 April 1970, p. 61.

26. Morison, Ian, 'How MbO has Brought Real Accountability to Barclays DCO', *The Times*, 2 March 1970.

27. Eastman, Neville, 'MbO in R. & D.', *Business Management*, February 1970, p. 28.

28. McGivering, Ian, 'A Jaundiced Look at MbO', *Financial Times*, 15 April 1969.

29. Thorncroft, Anthony, 'People: The Vital Factor', *Financial Times*, 11 March 1970.

30. *Economist*, op. cit., p. 61.

31. Levinson, Harry, 'Management by Whose Objectives?', *Harvard Business Review*, July–August 1970, p. 125.

32. Reddin, W. J., *Effective MbO*, Management Publications, B.I.M., 1971, p. 186.

33. ibid., p. 190.

34. Garrett and Walker, op. cit., p. 14.

35. Walker, S. D., and Charkham, J., *Accountable Management and Management by Objectives*, Seminar on Management Developments in Central Government, 4 May 1970.

36. Pascoe, op. cit.
37. Hill, D. W. G., and Bostock, R. E., 'An Approach to MbO in DEP', *O. & M. Bulletin*, November 1970, p. 223.
38. ibid., p. 230.
39. Garrett and Walker, op. cit., p. 14.
40. Committee on the Civil Service, Report, Vol. I, para. 229.
41. Holbrow, J., and Sprigg, J., 'Performance Measurement – A Case Study', *O. & M. Bulletin*, May 1970.
42. Hooper, Sir Frederick, *Management Survey*, Pitman, 1961 p. 167.

7: Management Services and Efficiency Audit

1. Williams, J. M., 'The Application of the Concept of Productivity Services in BOC', *Work Study*, January 1971, p. 29.
2. ibid., p. 35.
3. Circular No. A-44 (Revised) Bureau of the Budget, Washington, February 1970, p. 1.
4. ibid., p. 7.
5. Archer, J. N., 'Some New Approaches to Efficiency in Government Departments', *O. & M. Bulletin*, August 1969, p. 121.
6. Woolston, Trevor, 'The Future of Management Services', *Civil Service Opinion*, August 1970, p. 236.
7. Select Committee on National Expenditure, 1940–41, Sixteenth Report, *Organization and Control of the Civil Service*, H.C. 120, para. 81.
8. Select Committee on Estimates, 1946–7, Fifth Report, *Organization and Methods and Its effect on the Staffing of Government Departments*, H.C. 143, para. 49.
9. Mackenzie, W. J. M., and Grove, J. W., *Central Administration in Britain*, Longmans, Green, 1957, p. 190.
10. Committee on the Civil Service, Vol. II, para. 286.
11. ibid., para. 292.
12. Archer, J. N., 'Management Review', *O. & M. Bulletin*, August 1970, p. 122.
13. Garrett, John, and Walker, S. D., 'Management Review – A Case Study from Prison Department of the Home Office', *O. & M. Bulletin*, August 1970, p. 124.

14. ibid., p. 126.
15. ibid., p. 135.
16. Archer, J. N., 'Planning Government Management Services for the Seventies', *O. & M. Bulletin*, February 1970, p. 8.
17. ibid., p. 10.
18. ibid., p. 11.
19. Woolston, op. cit., p. 236.
20. ibid., p. 236.
21. Archer, J. N., 'A New Look for CSD Management Services', *O. & M. Bulletin*, February 1971, p. 12.
22. *CSD Report 1970–71*, H.M.S.O., 1971, p. 8.
23. Normanton, E. L., *The Accountability and Audit of Governments*, Manchester University Press, 1966, p. 2.
24. Normanton, op. cit.
25. ibid., p. 373.
26. ibid., p. 325.
27. ibid., p. 373.
28. ibid., p. 272.
29. Chubb, Basil, *The Control of Public Expenditure*, Oxford, 1952, p. 173.
30. ibid., p. 194
31. ibid., p. 195.
32. ibid., p. 252.
33. Normanton, op. cit., p. 414.
34. Smith, Bruce L. R., and Hague, D. C., *The Dilemma of Accountability in Modern Government*, Macmillan, 1971.
35. ibid., p. 337.
36. ibid., p. 341.

8: Personnel Management

1. Drucker, Peter, *The Practice of Management*, Heinemann, 1955, p. 345.
2. Rush, Harold M.F., *Behavioural Science, Concepts and Management Application*, Personnel Policy Study No. 216, National Industrial Conference Board, New York, 1969, p. 179.
3. Crichton, Anne, *Personnel Management in Context*, Batsford, 1968, p. 23.

4. Janger, Allen R., *Personnel Administration – Changing Scope and Organization*, Personnel Policy Study No. 203, National Industrial Conference Board, New York, 1966.

5. *Job Evaluation*, Management Publications Limited, B.I.M., 1970.

6. Smith, A. R., *Models of Manpower Systems*, E.U.P., 1970.

7. McGregor, Douglas, *The Human Side of Enterprise*, McGraw-Hill, Maidenhead, 1960.

8. Argyris, Chris, *Integrating the Individual and the Organization*, Wiley, New York, 1964, p. 147.

9. Maslow, Abraham, *Motivation and Personality*, Harper & Row, New York, 1954.

10. Herzberg, Mausner, Snyderman, *The Motivation to Work*, Wiley, New York, 1959.

11. Herzberg, Frederick, *Work and the Nature of Man*, World Publishing Co., Cleveland, 1966.

12. Dickson, J. W., 'What's in a Job', *Personnel Management*, June 1971.

13. Tumiati, Peter, 'Changing the Assembly Line', *Financial Times*, 8 July 1971.

14. Jones, Robert, 'Liberating Woman and the Worker', *The Times*, 18 January 1971.

15. Hermann, A. H., *Self-Management at Philips*, *Financial Times*, 30 December 1970.

16. Paul, W. J., Robertson, K. B., and Herzberg, Frederick, 'Job Enrichment Pays Off', *Harvard Business Review*, March–April, 1969, p. 61.

17. Garnett, John, 'Briefing Groups Help Work Relations', *The Times*, 23 November 1970.

18. Hawtin, Guy, *Communications: The Open Door and House Journal are Just Not Enough*, 14 June 1970.

19. Blake and Mouton, *The Managerial Grid*, Gulf Publishing Co., Houston, Texas, 1964.

20. Reddin, W. J., *Managerial Effectiveness*, McGraw-Hill, Maidenhead, 1970.

21. Lee, James A., 'Behavioural Theory vs Reality', *Harvard Business Review*, March–April 1971.

22. ibid., p. 28.

23. Rush, Harold M.F., op. cit.
24. *Report of the Committee on the Civil Service*, Cmnd. 3638, Vol. II, para. 208.
25. Armstrong, Sir William, 'Whitleyism in the Civil Service', *Whitley Bulletin*, September, October 1969, p. 138.
26. ibid., p. 139.
27. ibid. (November 1969), p. 154.
28. Armstrong, Sir William, *Personnel Management in the Civil Service*, H.M.S.O., 1971, p.2.
29. ibid., p. 3.
30. Committee on the Civil Service, Vol. II, para. 210.
31. ibid., para. 240.
32. ibid., para. 249.
33. ibid., para. 229.
34. ibid., para. 235–6.
35. ibid., para. 297.
36. ibid., para. 346.
37. Committee on the Civil Service, Vol. 1, para. 252.
38. ibid., para. 235.
39. ibid., para. 76.
40. Committee on the Civil Service, Vol. II, para. 350.
41. National Board for Prices and Incomes, *Job Evaluation*, Report No. 83, Cmnd. 3772, 1968, para. 134.
42. Civil Service National Whitley Council, *Fulton: A Framework for the Future*, 1970, p. 5.
43. ibid., p. 7.
44. Williams, Leslie, *Industrial Relations Bill*, National Staff Side Circular 936/70, 4 November 1970, Civil Service Whitley Council Staff Side.
45. *Whitley Bulletin*, May 1971, p. 79.
46. Armstrong, op. cit., p. 20.
47. ibid., p. 21.
48. 'Appraising the Man in the Job', *Business Systems*, January 1970, p. 38.
49. ibid., p. 40.
50. Civil Service Department, Second Report, H.M.S.O., 1971, p. 51.
51. Bridle, J. W., and Gregersen, R. J., 'The Central Manage-

ment Staff Record', *O. & M. Bulletin*, May 1971, p. 93.
52. De Berker, P. U., 'Centre 1, East Kilbride', *O. & M. Bulletin*, May 1971, p. 79.
53. Armstrong, op. cit., p. 6.

Conclusion

1. Dearden, John, 'MIS is a Mirage', *Harvard Business Review*, January–February 1972, p. 90.

Index

Administration, 13, 15, 21–9
Fabian Society criticism, 33;
specialists excluded 20;
'starred' entry, 37

Administration Group, 54

Ansoff, Igor, 98

Archer, J. N., Under Secretary
for Management Services, Civil
Service Department, 224;
'management review', 224

Argyris, Chris, on rigid classical
organization, 62–3; 'group
laboratory', 248–9; matrix
organization, 69

Armstrong, Sir William, Head of
Civil Service Department, 54;
lesson of Whitley, 257;
Management Services Division,
224; on 'Establishments Man',
259

Arran, Lord, 49

Associated Industrial Consultants
Ltd (now Inbuson/AIC
Management Consultants
Ltd), 41

Balogh, Lord, 31, 34, 47, 52

Bamforth, K. W., and Tavistock
model, 64–5

Beer, Stafford, 154

Behavioural sciences, 247–54;
Civil Service Department
Behavioural Science Unit, 273;
Hawthorne experiment, 247;
help adjustment to change, 254;
industrial democracy and
briefing groups, 252; job
enlargement, Fiat, 250; job
enrichment, 250, 274; at ICI
and with self-managing groups
at Philips, 251; 'managerial

grid', 253; sensitivity training,
252; T-groups, 253; 3D Theory,
253; *also see* Argyris, Chris;
Blake, R. B., and Mouton, J. S.,
Herzberg, Frederick; Lee,
James E.; McGregor, Douglas;
Maslow, Abraham; Reddin, W. J.

Bishop, F. A., 48

Blake, R. B., 253

Bradbury Commission on
Organization and Staffing of
Government Offices, 254

Bray, Dr Jeremy, 34

Bridges, Sir Edward, 25

British Oxygen Co. Ltd,
Management Services
Division, 214

British Petroleum Ltd, and
consultancy subsidiary company,
216; representative in Fulton
Management Consultancy
Group, 41

Brook of Cumnor, Lord, 49

Brookings Institute Report,
comment on Civil Service, 36,
111

Brown, R. G. S., 24

Burgess, Tyrell, 142

Burns, Tom, 65

Businessmen studying problems in
Civil Service, 56

Calder, Lord Ritchie, 49

Central Policy Review Staff
(CPRS), 145, 191

Chapman, Professor Brian, 32

Chubb, Basil, on 'amateur'
Comptroller and Auditor
General, 231

Civil Service associations:
First Division Civil Servants,

Civil Service associations—*cntd*
Association of, 36, 37;
Professional Civil Servants,
Institution of, 36, 38; Society
of Civil Servants, 39

Civil Service career classes:
abolition, 50; accountants, 20;
administrative class, 13–15;
departmental classes, 15;
engineers, 20; Executive Class,
13, 15; General Clerical Class,
13, 15; origin, 12; Playfair
Committee and Higher and
Lower Divisions, 13; present
form, 12; social scientists, 20;
structure criticized by Fulton
Management Consultancy
Group, 43; Treasury classes,
14–20

Civil Service College recommended
by Fulton Committee, 46;
approved by Prime Minister,
50; opened, 55

Civil Service Department
recommended by Fulton
Committee, 47; approved by
Prime Minister, 50; Behavioural
Sciences Unit, 273; career
management, 272; improved
personnel management, 272;
investment needed in personnel
management and management
information, 276; JAR (Job
Appraisal Review), 273; 'lateral
movement' to top, 272; may
weaken staff bargaining, 272;
questions for future, 274; set
up, 54

Civil Service Pay Research Unit,
265

Civil Service political direction, 9

Civil Service positive or
interventionist tasks, 8

Civil Service regulatory
activities, 8

Civil Service total management
task, 9; efficient coping with
sudden change, 275; exemplary
efficiency in production
processes, 275; pioneered
management practices, 275

Clarke, Sir Richard, 89, 90, 183

Computers:
building data base, 181–2;
CMSR (Central Management
Staff Record), 273; faster
feedback into cybernetic control,
155; installation, 84; job ranking
order, 242; new sub-profession,
86: PRISM (Personnel Record
Information System for
Management), 273; stock
control, 153

Contingency theory and internal
differentiation, 91

Control:
appropriation and audit, 173–5;
budgetary control, 152–3;
Canadian programmes, 118–19,
173–5; category-estimating and
job-slotting not used, 178;
'charging out' not used, 177;
clerical work measurement only
experimental, 177;
information technology, aim of,
150; data-base building, 181–2;
data-base technology, 158;
definition, 150; effective system
requirements, 150;
Establishments weaknesses,
169–70; Establishments
Divisions check own
departmental costs, 167–8;
financial control and supply
procedure, 158–67; Group
Capacity Assessment: recent
experiment, 178; House of
Commons Committees, 160–67
passim; information requirement,
170–73; inter-firm
comparisons, 155; management
accounting, 152; managerial

accountability, 171; market research, 154; PPB and PAR need programme analysis and data system, 171; project costing, 178–9; responsible seniors need control systems as in U.S.A., 179; standard cost, 152; stock control, 153; time and motion study to cybernetics, 150–58; U.S. General Electric performance criteria, 156; U.S. programme analysis, 117, 119–23, 173; unsuitable management control arrangements, 166, 173; Weinstock's seven key criteria, 156; work measurement little used, 179

Corporate planning, 97–102 manpower constraints, 244; requirement for success, 101; steps in, 98–100; three main elements, 98

Cost-benefit analysis: criteria for social and economic impact, 126; examination of rough-cut costs, 125; exercising model by sensitivity analysis, 125–6; fixed-budget method, 125; fixed-utility method, 125

Crewe, I.M., 51

Crichton, Anne, 237

Crozier, Michael, 82–3

Cybernetics, 153–5

David, D. Ronald, 186

Davies Report on interview system, 51–2; criticized by Lord Balogh, 52

Departmental Agency, 194

Drucker, Peter, and management accountability, 185; management by objectives, 198–9; managers' need of comparative basis, 155; personnel management, 234

Dunnett, Sir James, 48

Efficiency measurement, with reference to U.S. Civil Service, 181

Elitism, 42

Establishments Divisions: central aim, 258; creation of, 254; 'Establishments Man' by Sir W. Armstrong, 259; role, 43, 255; view of personnel work, 258

Exchequer Audit Department, 228–33; Chubb on 'amateur' Comptroller, 231; Comptroller and Auditor General, 228, 229; Normanton's comparative study, 228, 232; organizations which 'escape', 230; Public Accounts Committee, 228; status and careers lowest in major Western countries, 231; wider powers in France, Germany and U.S.A., 228–9

Fabian Society, 33

Fairlie, Henry, 31

Fayol, Henri, 59, 61

Fulton Committee and Report, 44–7, 52–4; added increments for high performance, 207; Civil Service Department, 262; confinement of managers to economic or social streams, 264; conflicting principles, 81; confused idea of job evaluation's purpose, 265; criticized, 47–50, 114, 264–5, 270; evidence to, 36–44; fair comparison pay principle, 265; 'hiving off', 192; implementation, 54–7; management services, 222–3; Management Services Units in all departments, 223; managerial accountability, 80, 187–9; neglected junior clerical and technical staff, 270; no challenge to establishments work, 264;

Fulton Committee and Report
—*cntd*
organization, 79–81; overlap of
Treasury and Civil Service
Department, 89; planning and
research units, 113; planning
separate from control, 114;
relevant pre-service studies, 263;
responsibility delegation for
internal costs and efficiency, 195;
specialisms and sub-specialisms of
administrators, 262–3; training
grade for graduate and other
highest-ability entrants, 263;
unified grading structure, 262,
266–7
Fulton, Lord, 34, 35
Fulton Management Consultancy
Group, 40; advocated career
specialization in management
consultancy, 223; central
management consultancy unit,
223; departmental management
services units, 223; experiments
in new organizational forms, 81,
and with accountable
management, 208; job
evaluation, 262; one unified
grading structure, 261; systems
of objective setting, control and
accountability, 114, 208;
criticized Establishments
Divisions' impersonality, 261;
lack of career planning, 260;
'long-term diseconomies', 169;
parallel and joint hierarchies,
72–5; criticized promotion
arrangements, 260; relationships
of administrators and specialists,
161; staff appraisal routines,
260; described Establishments
Divisions' aims and role, 255,
258–60; evidence to Fulton
Committee, 40–44; ideas
distorted in Fulton Report, 53;
praised by Lord Shackleton, 50

Geddes Committee, 255
Gilbreth, F. B. and L. M., 151
Glassco Commission Canadian
Government study, 140, 188
Goodnow, F. J., 192
Graicunas, V. A., 59
Granick, David, 32
Grimond, J., 33
Grove, J. W., 161, 182, 222
Guardian's evidence to Fulton
Committee, 39
Guest, R. H., 62
Gulick, L., 59

Haldane Report on Machinery of
Government, 107–8, 254
Halsey, Dr A. H., 50
Harmer, L. C., Civil Service
Co-ordinator of Clerical
Work Measurement, 177
Heath, Edward, 50
Helsby, Lord, 48, 49
Herzberg, Frederick, 249–52
Hobsbawm, Eric, 48
Hooper, Sir Frederick, 212
Hoover Commission, 179
Howell, David, 90
Humble, John W., 198
Hunt, Dr Norman, 32, 47, 48

Industrial Relations Act, 271
Information for management
control, 176–82

Job evaluation:
advantages, 243; 'benchmarks',
242–3; computer ranking, 242;
defined, 240; degrees of
responsibility, 242; Direct
Consensus Method, 242;
factors, 241; pay scales, 243;
points rating method, 241;
recommended by Management
Consultancy Group and
accepted by Fulton Committee,
262

Johnson, President L. B., and PPB, 131
Joint Committee on the Organization of the Civil Service, 13
Jones, Colin, 95n.

Kahn, Herman, 27
Kahn, R. L., 65–6
Katz, D., 65–6

Labour Party, 39
Laski, H. J., 30, 90
Lawrence, P. R., 66–7
Lee, James A., 253
Leffingwell, W. H., 152
Leicester, Lord Bishop of, 49
Levinson, Professor Harry, 201
Likert, Rensis, 63
Lorsch, J. W., 67

McGregor, Douglas, 247–8
McKinsey, James O., 152
Mackenzie, W. J. M., 182, 222
Mallalieu, J. P., 30
Management accountability:
    accountable manager defined, 185; accountable unit, 187; charging out, 197; control information, 187; departmental accountability as hierarchy of blocks, 210; departmental agency, 194; developed in U.S.A., 185; effect on career structure, 196; experiments, 56; Fulton Committee definition, 187; higher levels of complexity, 208–9; 'hiving off', 192–4; information for, 206–9; management by objectives defines accountability, 198, 203; manager's staff-cost control minimal, 195; manpower controlled by line management, 196; ministerial responsibility and managerial inefficiency,

190; monitoring by macro-indicators, 210; penalties for others' mistakes, 186; public accountability, 189; quantifiable objectives, 209; U.S. experiments – 'building blocks', 210–11;
Management by Objectives (MbO), 188; at high enough level?, 205; Civil Service schemes, 203; effects, 203–5; efficacy in industry and commerce, 200–201; Management Development Adviser (MDA), 199; Manager's Plan, 199–200; problems, 201; Professor Levinson, 201; setting and reviewing objectives, 198–206
Management Improvement Programmes:
    aimed at specific results, 216; by management services group, 216; Canadian Government Bureau of Management Consulting, 220; ratios, 180; special project team, 217; U.S. Presidential Order, 180, 219
Management information system, 170; design, 157; essential to corporate planning, 102; performance indicators, 176
Management Services and Efficiency Audit:
    arguments against, 215; autonomous consultancy subsidiaries, 216; behavioural scientists, 213; British Oxygen Co. Ltd, 214; consultancy fees, 215; efficiency audits, 216; enforcing standards and procedures, 213; management services units, triple role and terms of reference, 214; O. & M. units, 213; problems, 215, 217, 218; procedure, 216; programmes, regular or cyclic, 216; qualifications, 215;

Management Services and
Efficiency Audit—*cntd*
specialists in organization and
job evaluation, 213; type of
staff, 217; U.S. and Canadian
Governments' units' tasks,
218–19; work with project
team, 216; work-study units, 213
Management Services in the Civil
Service, 220–27; changes still
needed, 227; Civil Service
Department, 221; Fulton
recommendations, 222–3;
'management reviews', 224–6;
O. & M. not administrative
rank, 222; post-Fulton
development, 223–7; pre-Fulton
limitations, 221; should report
direct to top, 233; staffs, 221;
tasks, 226; teams executive and
professional and outside
consultants, 226; Treasury
Establishments Division
Investigation Section, 220;
Treasury O. & M. Division, 220
Manpower planning, 244–6;
CMSR (Central Management
Staff Record), 273; career
planning, 246; definition, 244;
'fluid complementing', 197;
forecasting techniques, 245;
graduate staff problems, 246;
inter-departmental steering
group, 273; link with corporate
planning, 244; manpower
budgeting, 197; mathematical
models, 245; staff assessment
schemes, 246; PRISM
(Personnel Record Information
System for Management), 273
March, J. G., 64
Maslow, Abraham, 249
Mayo, Roethlisberger and
Dickson:
Hawthorne studies, 62, 247
Mooney, J. D., 59, 61

Morse, J. J., 67
Mouton, J. S., 253
Munby, D. L., 39

Nationalized industries and
Whitehall, 193
New planning systems
experiments, 56
New York Bureau of Municipal
Research, 172
Nicholson, Max, 35
Normanton, E. L., 228, 231–2
Northcote–Trevelyan Report, 12,
16, 44, 49

Opie, Roger, 47
Organization:
accountable management units,
92–3; contingency theory, 67,
91; executive–clerical pyramids,
76; giant departments, 94;
Government departments,
70–79; human relations school,
62–4; informal, 62; line
management structure, 92;
machine theory, 59; matrix, 69,
93; mechanistic, 65; new forms,
87–96; open system concept, 65;
organic, 65; parallel and joint
hierarchies, 72–4; project team
problems, 77; staff and project
groups, 67–70; structure to suit
production type, 66; systems
approach, 64; Urwick's principle,
59–60; Weber's theory, 58–9

PAR (Programme Analysis
Review), 148–9, 171, 191
PESC (Public Expenditure Survey
Committee), 106, 112, 148–9
PPBS (Planning Programming
Budgeting System), best results,
136; budgeting stage, 129–131;
classification of accounts,
115–16; developments in G.B.,
141–9, 171–2; evaluation,

131–40; experience in U.S.A. and Canada, 133; managing programme, 130; planning stage, 118–23; programming stage, 123–9; proposed new names, 140; sensitivity analysis, 125–6

Perrow, Charles, 83

Personnel function, 238–40

Personnel management, Drucker's view, 234; Establishments Divisions, 43, 254–5, 258–9, 261; future for behavioural sciences, 269, and manpower planning, 269; legislation, 235; personnel function in Civil Service, 256, 268–74; power structure, 235; technical complexity, 235; the personnel manager, 234–7, 239–40; Whitley Council, 256–8

Planning, definition, 97; departmental arrangements, 110–13; expenditure planning, 102–7; Plowden Committee, 105; Policy Research and Planning Units, 107–10; programme reviews, 111–12; steps to develop PESC/PAR, 148–9; strategic planning, 146–9; White Paper, 106

Playfair Committee, 13

Plowden, Lord, 49, 105

Policy Research and Planning Units, 107–10

Powell, Enoch, 33

Prices and Incomes Board, 265

Priestley Commission, 265

Public expenditure, 104–7

Quasi-non-governmental organizations, 194–5

Redcliffe-Maud, Lord, 48

Reddin, Professor W. J., 202, 253

Reiley, A. C., 59

Research staff, 109

Rhenman, Eric, 82

Rice, A. K., 64–5

Rickover, Vice-Admiral, 147

Rio Tinto Zinc Ltd, 216

Robbins, Lord, 49

Robinson, Webster, 59

Robson, William, 48

Roles, administrative and specialist, 19

Roskill Commission, 126–7

Rothschild, Lord, 145–6

Schon, Donald, 69

Schultze, Charles, 139

Seashore, S., 62

Seers, Dudley, 38

Sendall, Wilfred, 48

Shackleton, Lord, 50

Simon, H. A., 61, 64

Sinclair of Cleeve, Lord, 49

Sisson, C. H., 25

Sloan, Alfred P., 185

Stalker, G. M., 65

State audit, 227–33

Tavistock Institute, 64, 65

Taylor, F. W., 59, 151

Thompson, Victor A., 82

Treasury, 37, 160

Trevelyan, Lord, 49

Trist, F. L., 64

Urwick, L. F., 59–60

Von Bertalanffy, L., 64

Walker, C. R., 62

Walker, S. D., 205

Wasserman, G. J., 143

Weber, Max, 58–9

Weinstock, Sir Arnold, 156

Whitley Committee, 256–8, 266, 270

Whyte, W. F., 62

Williams, Professor Alan, 126

Wilson, Harold, 32, 34, 35, 48

Woodward, Joan, 66

Zero-base budgeting (PPBS), 124n.